HEAR
OUR
CRY

Hear Our Cry © 2024 Michael Gurn

All Rights Reserved. No part of this book may be reproduced in any form or by any electronic or mechanical means including information storage and retrieval systems, without permission in writing from the author. The only exception is by a reviewer, who may quote short excerpts in a review.

This book is a work of non-fiction. This publication is designed to provide accurate and authoritative information in regards to the subject matter covered. It is sold with the understanding that the author is not engaged in rendering legal, investment, accounting, or other professional services. These are the memories of the author, from their perspective, and they have tried to represent events as faithfully as possible.

Acknowledgment is made with thanks to the Sunday Mail Newspaper for reproduction of newspaper articles published in the Traps column written by Journalist Peter Cameron about these murders.

Acknowledgment is made with thanks to the Northern Miner Newspaper in Charters Towers and the Townsville Bulletin in Townsville for my reproductions of their stories about these murders which were published in their newspapers with special thanks for the support of Editor Trudy Brown.

Printed in Australia

Cover by Melinda Childs @studioorchard

Typeset by Book Burrow www.bookburrow.com.au

Edited by Katrina Burge

Images in this book are copyright approved for use by author.

First printing: December 2024

Paperback ISBN 978-0-646-70620-7

eBook ISBN 978-0-646-70621-4

 A catalogue record for this work is available from the National Library of Australia

HEAR OUR CRY

POLICE INACTION RESULTS IN A COVER UP OF DOUBLE MURDERS

Read why the Pentland Murders were not solved.

Was Ivan Milat one of the killers?

Follow events that happened during the working life of a Uniformed and Plain Clothes Officer in the Queensland Police Force in 1950/60s and 1970s.

AUTHOR'S NOTE

To prevent boredom for readers having to read volumes of typed correspondence, I will try to write this work piecing together the result of my investigations in a chronological order limiting as far as possible you having to read all correspondence. Anyone who wishes to read more detailed correspondence will be able to do so from the appendices to this work.

However, to my way of thinking, I believe that to get the true story out there it is for the best if the readers read some of the actual emails and letters to get a proper feel of what I am trying to achieve because the story is revealed in the letters, emails and phone calls.

Some of the cases I have been involved with in my police career will be described herein and in appendices to this work which I hope you will find interesting. The point of which is to establish in the minds of readers that I am qualified to question the correctness of police investigations into these crimes.

PROLOGUE

We can no longer cry because we have passed on. Our young lives were taken from us by a recidivist murderer together with other male cowards when we were eighteen years old, healthy and free spirited, growing up with ambitions for the future which we can never attain.

WHO are they

They are Robin Jeanne Hoinville-Bartram, born 14th April 1954, eighteen years and Anita Cunningham, eighteen years old, born 8th April, 1954.

We are two Australian girls, attending an art school in Victoria as design students. What happened to us is that we were unfortunate enough to fall into the hands of depraved young men at the Pentland Hotel in Queensland in the winter of 1972 and subsequently raped and murdered.

As author, I have decided to include into this book some of the events that occurred during my twenty-three years' service in the Queensland police force, both in uniform and in plain clothes.

It is the responsibility of police to try and obtain evidence to arrest offenders who commit crimes and in the case of these two murdered girls, everything that could be done to arrest the killers has not been done. The cause of this failure can be traced initially to inexperience and incompetence of Police who failed to properly investigate information provided to them in 2003 when a woman came forward with information that she had met these two murdered girls at the Pentland Hotel before they were murdered.

You will see as you read on how this situation developed, as I, although retired and no longer having any Police powers, investigated information given to me that was sufficient for me to believe that a miscarriage of justice has taken place.

When serving police leave home for work each day, the reality is that they may not return home after their shift of work. Thankfully, most police do return safely each day but the unlucky few do not, having run into some dangerous situation during their shift.

I served for over twenty-three years in the Queensland Police Force and although tricky situations were encountered from time to time, for the most part I only really had one situation where my life was in real danger was in the 1970s when my plain clothes team and I with other uniform police raided a house with a search warrant on 20th November, 1972, searching to arrest a man named Leslie Arthur Warburton (now deceased) for stealing property.

He was located hiding in a secret compartment behind the wood stove in the kitchen of his parents' house in Lemke Road, Zillmere, Brisbane. I had taken the precaution of obtaining a search warrant for the Warburton house because I knew from previous experience that police had with this family over many years that it would be no use asking their cooperation to enter the home to search for their son. The father, Bob Warburton (deceased), was a hot-headed individual. We knew we would have trouble going to their house looking for their son Leslie Arthur Warburton without a search warrant.

Leslie Arthur Warburton was wanted for stealing saddles and bridles. We had arrested his accomplice earlier in the day. We had seen Leslie Arthur Warburton run into the house as we approached the house in police cars. The house was set well back from the road. I showed the Warrant to William John Warburton (known as Bob) and his wife Mary Agnes Warburton (deceased) but they would not admit us, so we kicked the door open and entered the house. We located and arrested Leslie Arthur Warburton.

Inside the house, Constable Robert Atkinson (who later in his career rose to become the Commissioner of Police in Queensland) arrested Harry John Bullard for assaulting him in the execution of his duty. Bullard, along with Leslie Arthur Warburton, was escorted from the house. Leslie Warburton was placed in a police car between two uniformed police officers. Constable Atkinson was holding onto Bullard when William John (Bob) Warburton appeared at a house window above us, aiming a loaded shotgun at Constable Bob Atkinson, demanding we release his son and Bullard. It is Bob Atkinson's recollection that I stepped between him and Bullard and pushed Atkinson out of the way.

For the next few minutes, I found myself standing in the open below Bob Warburton aiming my .38 revolver at him and he is aiming his shotgun at me about twenty feet away above me. I was in my rights to shoot this man, but I did not do that. This standoff lasted a minute or two, all the while Warburton demanding we release his son and Bullard.

I told Warburton that he could consider himself under arrest.

With that, Warburton withdrew his head and shoulders and shotgun from the window space. He escaped from the other side of the house without us knowing as a high fence blocked our vision. We again entered the house, Constable Bob Atkinson found an undischarged shotgun cartridge on the floor below the window where Warburton had held us at bay with his shotgun. The shotgun cartridge bore ejection scratches from having been ejected from the loaded position in a shotgun.

Warburton was located and arrested in Church Road, Zillmere by searching uniformed police later that day. I subsequently charged him with attempting to prevent the lawful arrest of his son. He was an old hand in dealing with police and told us little except that he had pushed the shotgun down into a swamp not far from his house. He was later committed for trial in the District Court in Brisbane.

On Wednesday, 12th September 1973 Warburton went to trial which lasted five days. Warburton was represented by Barrister Col Bennett on two charges of assaulting police to prevent the arrest of his son. The trial was conducted by Judge Cormack and the Crown was represented by Mr G Forno as Prosecutor. The jury returned a verdict of guilty on two charges.

Warburton was given a good behaviour bond for two years. Warburton was found guilty of lesser charges than I had charged him with as the jury were influenced by this man's claim that he had been pointing a broom handle at us and not a shotgun. No doubt Barrister Bennett fined him a considerable sum for his services.

However, let me be very emphatic that it was a shot gun he held on us that he had successfully hidden before his later arrest. Broom handles do not have an open bore which I was looking up into. Juries can be gullible at times. You would think that the fact we found a live shotgun cartridge on the floor below the window opening later would be sufficient proof that it was a shotgun Warburton had aimed at us. I had called his bluff and got away with it. If he had fired his shotgun, I would not be here today.

Here I should say that the firearms that were issued to us were second hand revolvers and automatic pistols of varying calibres and sizes that had come into the hands of the police department over the years. We received no training at all in the use of these weapons and no target shooting practice. I bought bullets for my revolver and did my own practicing. I became reasonably accurate in shooting this revolver and was able to cut flower stems of gerbera flowers by aiming and shooting at the stems.

I have sometimes asked myself why I did not shoot Warburton when he was aiming his shotgun at me and frankly, I do not know. Perhaps because the only target I had was really his head, which would have been fatal for him. It is not an easy thing to deliberately shoot at a person. I suppose there was also the possibility that had I fired and hit him, the shotgun may have discharged. This is something I will never know.

The man's son whom we had arrested on warrant was electrocuted a few months later when trying to cut and steal copper electricity wiring from the top of a telegraph pole.

I didn't receive any recognition from the police department for facing down this man.

When I was sworn in as a constable on 15th April 1952 twenty three of us probationary constables marched in uniform from the Petrie Terrace Police Barracks down to the Treasury Building in Queen Street, Brisbane and into the office of the Commissioner of Police, Tom Harold, where he administered the oath of office to us. Then we were told to report for duty the next day to the respective police stations we had been allotted. I reported to the senior sergeant in charge of the shift at the Fortitude Valley Police Station.

That was our induction into the police force with no flamboyant parades, speeches and celebrations that occur today.

The oath of office taken by Queensland Police as under:

'I, A.B., swear by almighty God that I will well and truly serve our Sovereign Lady Queen Elizabeth the Second and Her Heirs and Successors according to law in the office of constable or in such other capacity as I may be hereafter appointed, promoted, or may be reduced, without favour or affection, malice or ill-will, from this date and until I am legally discharged; that I will cause Her Majesty's peace to be kept and preserved; that I will prevent to the best of my power all offences against the same; and that while I shall continue to be a member of the Queensland Police Service I will to the best of my skill and knowledge discharge all the duties legally imposed upon me faithfully and according to law. So help me God.'

I missed quite a lot of instruction during my probationary period in the Petrie Terrace Police Barracks as I was assigned as a driver for the Deputy Commissioner of Police, Paddy Glynn. I only had one lesson in traffic management learning the various traffic signals so when I started doing points duty directing traffic at intersections in Fortitude Valley, I was virtually self-taught. There were not many traffic control lights installed in Brisbane in 1952 and none that I can recall in the Valley, but tram traffic ran fast and often in all directions, making controlling traffic at intersections a work of art perfected by regular traffic control point police, who learned to dodge trams and cars with great skill without collisions.

FOREWORD BY DAVID CUNNINGHAM

I am grateful Mick asked me to write a foreword to this book.

I guess he asked me because I knew Anita better than anyone. As brother and sister, Anita and I grew up together and were very close. She was born less than 18 months after me. I became quite close to Robin too even though we only knew each other for a relatively brief time.

When you read this book, you're reading the story of one honourable and righteous man's struggle to achieve justice for two tragically and brutally murdered young girls.

You'll read the story of this honest and uncompromising man's struggle to bring the attention of the authorities to bear on the mountain of evidence he has uncovered and pieced together. Evidence which has revealed many new questions. Questions that only the authorities have the power to ask and demand answers. Over many years of selfless and tenacious work, Mick has single-handedly uncovered and investigated as far as the law and one man's limited financial resources will allow. Despite all the setbacks, this man has remained undaunted. Unsung heroes like Mick are too few and far-between. The authorities should honour this living national treasure and bring their sincere attention to bear on the revelations his hard work has produced.

But first, here in this foreword, you can read a little bit about my experiences, my story about the early days, the family context and the everlasting effects on my family. My father never got over it, my mother never wants to be reminded of it. That's all I'll say about that, but here below, what follows is my brief contribution to telling my experience of this Australian outback horror story. A true mystery that's now finally so tantalizingly close to being solved.

1972

It was a different world.

It was the dawning of the Age of Aquarius. Psychedelia. The Revolution of Love. Woodstock. Haight-Ashbury. Flower Power.

Teenagers were starry-eyed and carried away by the hippie counterculture.

The only similarity today is youngsters often think they know better than their parents.

In actual fact, as sheltered middle-class kids fresh out of secondary school, we knew nothing. We'd experienced nothing outside the bubble of our middle-class suburban lives.

Most of us back then had the opportunity to discover the outside world, the real world, at a manageable pace. If we wanted to walk on the wild side and see another side of life, we could always travel through India or Southeast Asia.

Anita and Robin didn't live to enjoy that comfy rate of learning. Their lives were rudely invaded, trashed and snuffed out in a grubby horror scene.

Imagine the abrupt terror, sensing you're in way too deep. That sudden panic of realisation! Inexorably trapped in a crushing grip that won't let go! Horrified and helpless as you're tossed into the mincer-chute of inevitable doom with no way out! No hope of escape. Obliterated.

We can only hope their end came quickly and the horror was mercifully brief.

Two naive but bold confident and beautiful young girls, art students in their first year, set out on their two-week holiday road-trip to visit Robin's parents in Bowen, North Queensland. Fixated on a dream, they were off on an adventure hitchhiking north, free as a bird and without a care in the world.

Everyone was concerned and had tried to talk them out of hitchhiking. Dad tried to pressure them into accepting air tickets, but their hippie fantasy was the freedom of the open road, meeting people along the way and trusting in fate to deliver rainbows and happiness along their journey to that sunny pineapple plantation, Robin's Bowen family home.

Fate was cruel.

Our parents were beginning to get worried after a week had gone by with no contact. The girls had promised they'd telephone often, and daily if they could.

After the second week of dead silence, Mum and Dad went to the police station to file a missing person's report.

The police wouldn't do it.

They told my parents the girls were over eighteen and could do as they pleased. They said most kids that age don't contact their parents for weeks at a time and suggested the girls were probably on a hippie commune somewhere out of contact range.

The police said my parents were worrying unduly and should go home and stop being so anxious, but my parents knew.

They knew their own daughter.

As headstrong as she undoubtedly was, she would never have gone weeks without family contact like that.

Besides, the girls had very little cash on them, and their bank accounts had not been touched since they left.

My parents tried again unsuccessfully to register a missing

person's report, but police just told them to relax and wait until the girls turned up.

It wasn't until Robin's decomposed body was found under a railway bridge in outback Queensland that the police decided to register Anita as a missing person. She was now elevated to a 'person of interest' in the murder of her best friend, Robin Hoinville-Bartram, and police wanted to talk to her.

Even though the girls were inseparable travelling companions, and the murder of one made the fate of the other terrible to contemplate, the police in their administrative wisdom reasonably decided the two girls were two separate cases to be handled by two separate departments, which, back then, I'm subsequently informed, had very little cross-communication or information-sharing.

Robin's case belonged to the homicide squad due to the two bullet holes in her skull, and naturally Anita now belonged to Missing Persons.

Missing Persons back then apparently was a dead-end unless some information happened to magically present itself because there were so many listed missing and there was so little information upon which to mount an investigation.

This fact, coupled with the case being split into two separate cases in two separate departments, meant that our family heard virtually nothing for many years.

Forty years of nothing.

Nothing but emptiness and a gaping hole in our family. And the only answer to the tangle of questions was a big black silent, question mark.

The homicide squad I now believe were reasonably active in pursuing an investigation into Robin's murder, but we were not to be told any of that. They were two separate cases, and that information was for Robin's family.

Mum and Robin's mother had become close friends over the

grieving, and she would pass on to us the odd snippet whenever police contacted the Bartram Family.

SUDDENLY - A SIGHTING?

We didn't know at the time, but an old family friend who was quite a distinguished airline pilot was convinced he'd sighted Anita working behind a Melbourne inner-city bar popular with airline pilots having an after-work drink.

This friend knew Anita very well. His daughter and Anita were best friends for a few years in secondary school. Our families used to occasionally have dinner together and Anita would often have sleepovers, staying at their place overnight.

Being almost certain at the time that it had been Anita he'd seen, our friend duly and keenly reported the sighting formally to the Queensland police. (Queensland Police Missing Persons had custody of the case.)

Whether this had ultimately turned out to be a case of mistaken identity, a false sighting or not, it was undoubtedly a strong lead. An airline pilot is a respected figure (and was even more so back in 1972), with well-honed powers of observation, and the recognition in this sighting was even more significant coming from someone who knew Anita with such familiarity.

I don't know what you would have done, but I'd watched a few police shows on TV and to me, it would have seemed obvious that the police ought to send an officer or two to visit the bar with a photo of Anita and ask whether she had worked there.

Many years later, the then-head of the Cold Case Squad informed me and my mother that a Queensland police officer had gone to Melbourne about another matter shortly after the sighting report was filed and could have investigated the sighting while he was there. Unfortunately, there was absolutely no note or record to indicate the reported Anita sighting was ever followed up.

Forty years later, when I heard about the sighting, I talked to our friend about the whole episode. He said that after making the report, he expected at least a phone call for further questions or clarification or to tell him the outcome of investigations or enquiries they might or might not have made, but nothing. The police never ever contacted him.

He now thinks that probably he only saw someone who resembled Anita, because if she had been still alive, she would definitely have contacted us.

I agree. I think it was mistaken identity too. The reason I am recounting this story is to show one example of how police efforts or investigations into Robin's murder and my sister's disappearance – or murder – back then appeared to have been at times either neglected or bungled. Missed opportunities.

I realise the distances, the remoteness and the limited police resources make a very difficult job even harder, and individual police members have been very kind and understanding in their manner toward my parents, but the police work behind the scenes seems to have been unenthusiastic at best.

ANITA FOUND AT LAST? POLICE INVESTIGATE

One thing did fire up police, grab their attention and spur them into enthusiastic action. In early 2008, a 'psychic detective' working in close collaboration with her team of invisible colleagues had finally solved the case of Robin's murder and discovered the whereabouts of my missing sister.

She'd been reliably informed by spiritual entities who were close confidants of Robin's ghost that Robin had been murdered by my sister Anita! Anita had then at some later date travelled back to Victoria, assumed a false identity and after seventeen years, incestuously given birth to my daughter! She must then have returned to Queensland, leaving me as a solo parent in

Victoria while she was hiding out in Queensland using the fake identity of Jody, my daughter's real mother.

It was a brilliant and cunning criminal plan!

No wonder the police took it seriously and conducted an early morning 'visit' on Jody's apartment. They took a bit of convincing but passports, family photos, driver's licenses and other forms of identification when they mount up into a comprehensive and irrefutable whole are hard to discount.

Most convincing of all was the total lack of any physical resemblance whatsoever between Jody and Anita.

A few minutes research on the internet before acting in haste might have saved a few red faces.

I couldn't understand how police, who had rejected out-of-hand without investigation what seemed on the face of them to be strong leads, nevertheless swallowed a ludicrous tale told by a hectic aggressive woman who was in league with the spirits and guided by a ghost!

It was too extraordinary and improbable to be believed.

And yet, there it was.

A total embarrassment.

I almost felt a bit sorry for the 'psychic detective' though. I think the 'spirits' were toying with her. She came all the way down from Brisbane to interview me. She didn't bother to contact me first so I could make sure I was available (the ghosts probably told her I'd be trying to avoid her). She turned up at my work looking for me, but the ghosts neglected to tell her I'd retired two months previously. Although I was retired and free to travel, I always made sure I was home on weekends, because my friends still worked so we'd have our get-togethers on weekends. It had become such a habit over such a long time that this weekend I decided to vary it and, just for a change, I went away for the weekend.

She was psychic – why didn't her ghosts tell her I was going away? Why did they let her choose the one weekend out of hundreds when I was going to be away?

Some psychic detectives team!

What's the point of being psychic if your spirit allies are leading you up the proverbial garden path? I got home on the Monday morning finding a note in my letterbox and the name of the motel she was staying at. I was eager to talk to her, so I went there straight away, but the motel told me she'd left early that morning. Didn't it dawn on her that I might respond to the note?

Some psychics!

MEDIA POWER

The next exciting episode of that information vacuum, the puzzling mystery of what happened to Anita and Robin, began with a surprise call from a popular true-crime writer from Channel 7.

Channel 7 wanted to film a segment about Anita and Robin for Sunday prime-time TV.

Channel 7 flew me and Mum up to Brisbane and Townsville. In Brisbane we met the head of the Cold Case Squad who was a gentleman and very kind to my mother. He had gone through the file extensively and found no missed clues and no further leads. He devoted a lot of time to us and to the Channel 7 story and we were very grateful for his kindness. He picked us up from our hotel and we met up with a very nice, polite and friendly couple of investigators, an ex-forensic detective and a psychic who had been at school with Robin. They patiently explained their interesting theory about exactly who the culprit was behind the girls' tragic ending and went through their chain of reasoning.

In this theory the ex-Detective reasoned that the manner Robin had been killed was like killings in the underworld by assassins who shot people in the back of the head as Robin had been shot. He reasoned that John Andrew Stuart; a known underworld character could have been responsible for the crimes as he had been at the Pentland Hotel where he was responsible for stealing from a resident. A part of the resident's property had been found near Sensible Creek where the decomposed body of Robin had been found. There was no evidence to connect him with the crimes and the time factor of Stuart's being at the Pentland hotel did not associate Stuart with the crimes.

The head of the Cold Case Squad explained that police had thoroughly investigated their story and unfortunately, was unable to substantiate it.

MISSED OPPORTUNITY?

The next revelation was the story of the note.

It had been sent from Chillagoe (a very small outback town about 450kms north of Pentland) to an old friend of Anita and written on the back of a Chillagoe store cash invoice dated the 25th of January 1973. It said, *'I do not recommend you come here for long or unaccompanied. Tis verily a dead hole, madam, and the station hands desperate.'*

I'm told police went to Chillagoe with the note in 1972, showed pictures of both girls around the town and to the store owner, but nobody recognised the girls. Police correctly concluded the likelihood of the girls going unnoticed in such a tiny, remote outback town would be very low, so without any further leads, the note was filed as unexplained.

What was also unexplained is how, during their visit to Chillagoe in 1972, the police expected the girls to have been seen in Chillagoe in the future, that is January 1973, especially when by that time Robin's body already lay buried in Cheltenham cemetery.

In the book, you'll read how Mick explains the main problem

with the investigation of the note, and what may have been a tragically lost opportunity.

ZERO INFO

The next leg of the journey took us to Townsville where the head of the Cold Case Squad took us to a private upstairs room at a police station. whiteboard and a map showed a line between the girls' departure point and the place Robin's body was found.

'Unfortunately,' he said, 'there's really only two things we know about the girls' disappearance.'

Indicating the departure point at the bottom of the map, he continued, 'The date and place of departure, and the date and place up here where Robin's body was found.'

The stark reality of knowing that it wasn't only us who knew absolutely nothing, but hearing how complete the police's lack of knowledge had struck me deep in the belly. It was a hollow feeling. The desolate vastness and remote inaccessibility of the outback setting, and the vast emptiness and silence of any knowledge or any real information from anyone, anything at all, about what happened to Anita and Robin. This good man was virtually telling us we might as well give up and go home! That's all! Nothing!

The total silence was screaming at me inside my head! It was flashing neon lights, blaring out, *THERE'S SOMETHING VERY WRONG HERE!* Two beautiful, young, educated city girls hitchhiking through the empty lawless outback of 1972 inland North Queensland, and nobody saw anything? Nothing? After all these years? Still? Nothing at all?

It was very hard to believe.

We drove out to Sensible Creek where Robin's body was discovered, and I met the officer who had undertaken an investigation into the matter back in, I think, 2003. Although polite, he was reserved and about as forthcoming as an Easter Island statue. It seemed no new knowledge could be gained so after kicking around in the creek under the road bridge for a bit, we returned to Charters Towers and back to Townsville.

An old friend of mine who knew Anita had a theory about who might have been responsible for the girls' disappearance but when I passed it on to police, it was dismissed out of hand.

Police had told us they had hardly any leads and what they had received had led nowhere; at this late stage, nothing could be learned so Mum and I should resign ourselves to the fact it was an eternal mystery with no answers.

That was the official story and remained the sad situation until I met Mick Gurn.

MICK GURN

Alone and stuck at a dead-end in this empty information desert, luck reached out and introduced me to a man who knew this desert like the back of his hand. It was no desert to him; he knew how to sniff out a faded information trail and how to track it down, how to read a person's character by the subtle signs we wouldn't even notice and how to weave scant threads together into a picture map leading to the next questions to answer and the next steps to follow.

Mick is a tall lean man, a man who grew up in the Queensland outback and spent decades in the city as a senior detective for the Queensland police.

There's no nonsense about him, but there's no pride or arrogance either. He's been able to find witnesses, quietly gain their trust and confidence and get statements where ordinary police might encounter or even generate resistance, resentment or hostility.

He's been entrusted with a true story, a deathbed confession and a promise made by a husband and a daughter to not let the tragic story be forgotten.

That is the essential message of this book. An eyewitness true story, which has been long sought and long waiting to be heard.

It's about a horrific murder that happened long ago.

It's about the circumstances that have been kept hidden for far too long.

But it's also about what happens and what doesn't happen when there's failures to investigate, botched lines of inquiry, evidence ignored, getting people offside and refusal to cooperate with those providing information or seeking answers.

It's a story that is begging to be completed, but it cannot be finished without the assistance of the authorities.

When the authorities we pay to investigate crimes and administer justice become obstacles to investigation and justice, the sick feeling in your gut feels like suspicion.

When kind and helpful police insist in a reassuring way that nothing is known and nothing will ever be known, there's an implied invitation to let the matter lie there and rest for eternity as a potentially pregnant perpetual question mark. Not everybody can comfortably do that.

Now we have eyewitnesses to the girls' whereabouts on the night of the murder, a cast of characters who need to be interviewed, a cheque cashed at the Pentland Hotel the day the girls were murdered needs to be checked, a revealing note that was gateway to a solution to this mystery, but now, forty-nine years on, without official assistance, it's threatening to become another dead-end and a tragically wasted opportunity.

Thanks to the perseverance, persistence and determination of Mr Gurn, his powerful moral compass and his sharp mind, what was once a vast unknown is now a jigsaw puzzle that's three-quarters completed. You can make out the overall picture but there are pieces missing to complete the details and tie it all together neatly.

That's where the power of a Commission of Inquiry, to investigate and to compel witnesses to testify, is the essential next step.

That's where we need your help.

We've tried but two men are not enough. We need more people to press for a Commission of Inquiry.

Mick is an old man, but his determination is strong, he needs your help.

I have had many positive experiences with police in my life and have been kindly and selflessly helped by police on many occasions. I have had good friends in the force, and I've worked alongside police.

I have also been treated extremely poorly by a few police members, but I know that's an exception. The job appeals to some of the nastier characters unfortunately, and there are bad people, disinterested people, stupid people and lazy people in every profession without exception.

I believe the good far outweighs the bad.

RIGHT TO INFORMATION?

The police I've dealt with in person in relation to my sister's disappearance and murder have without exception been polite and friendly and have treated my mother very graciously. Police on the phone have mostly been good too, but not all. There's been surly lack of cooperation at times, and even hostility.

A few years ago, I applied to Victoria Police under the Freedom of Information Act to get their file on my sister. Without any problems at all, and in due course, the file was delivered to me with the explanation that since Robin's body was found in Queensland, the case became property of Queensland Police, and so I should make application there to get the rest of the information pertaining to the case.

I did that, and put in an RTI request, all went well at first except for a small misunderstanding, which was my fault because I got confused between the Victorian procedure and the Queensland procedure.

Months went by, and excuses were made, and still I hadn't got the file. I'd received an email saying that my request would be assessed in the fullness of time., and they wouldn't respond to any further email enquiries, so I let it go again for a while with no eventual result.

So again, I called by phone. I was questioned as to why I needed the file and what parts of it I was specifically interested in. They told me they couldn't supply me the file because it was too big but if I specified a particular limited period or a particular matter I was interested in, they might be able to fulfill my request.

Disappointed, I gave them a request limited to the 2003 investigation. Nothing came, so after another long and patient wait, I called again.

I was informed the file had been sent, but they couldn't tell me if it had been sent by email or snail mail. My email client reported there was no record of having received that email, and I knew for a fact it hadn't arrived in my PO box. Besides, I would have assumed I'd need to sign for it and not only did that not happen, but neither the post office nor the RTI had any tracking record of registered mail being sent to me.

The RTI promised to resend it to me with the assurance that they would email me notification the day it was posted. I got no email, but I did subsequently receive a letter telling me my application had been refused because the case was now under investigation!

I called to ask if I would be receiving the requested documents after the conclusion of this investigation. 'No,' they said, I would just have to keep making fresh applications, but I would have no way of knowing when the current investigation would be concluded, and they wouldn't notify me when it concludes.

I have no idea why the RTI department of Queensland Police had to be hostile or why they were so adamant about withholding information, especially when the name of their department and my application is 'Right to Information'!

NEW HOPE

In January this year, I wrote to the head of homicide explaining my situation. In response to my letter, I received a personal phone call from him. I was overwhelmed with relief and couldn't suppress my emotion when he kindly told me he was going to assign a good detective to examine the file and the whole investigation from start to finish and let me know what was going on.

I subsequently received a phone call from that new detective, introducing himself and telling me he was going to start on the case in short order. It's August now and I've heard nothing. I've tried to contact him without success and my calls haven't been returned.

I suppose I'll have to send another letter. You'll read in this book how there's been a history of obstruction. In the light of that history, and the deathly silence, now it's starting to feel like I'm just being placated to buy time until everyone concerned is decrepit or dead and the whole thing gently fades away.

Until that happens, the question will always remain.
Why?
Who or what is being protected?
David Cunningham,
Campbells Creek, 15 August 2020

TABLE OF CONTENTS

Author's Note		iv
Prologue		v
Foreword by David Cunningham		xi
1	Girls hitchhike from Melbourne	1
2	Mearle comes forward to Police	4
3	Mick's Police work in 1953 and history	9
4	Attorney General denies inquest	16
5	How Mick Gurn becomes involved	20
6	Questioning police on murders	27
7	Recorded interview with Paula	34
8	Letter to CoP re White Horse Tavern	50
9	Letter requesting statement on Police inactivity	56
10	Channel Seven contact	59
11	Mick Gurn's case handled and In Service College	67
12	Contact with Anita's family	75
13	Contact with Hotel licensee's daughter	78
14	Cheque at Pentland Hotel by Madigans	81
15	Letter to CoP re. NSW Police alert	83
16	Ad in Northern Miner by David Cunningham	86
17	Letter to CoP	91
18	Various letters and Editor Courier Mail	101
19	Breakdown of Police stance with new revelations	104

20	Letter to CoP about years lost in investigations	115
21	Letter to Editor Courier Mail	123
22	Letter to CoP and following resignation	128
23	Contact with journalists	138
24	Letter to new CoP Katrina Carroll	141
25	Contact with Channel Nine	152
26	The Chillagoe letter incident	161
27	Letter to Commissioner Carroll	167
28	John Whyte's memory	185
29	Letter to Attorney General	188
30	Meeting Policy Advisor to Attorney General	211
31	The corrupted Justice system	233
Appendix List		242

CHAPTER ONE

These naïve girls Robin Jeanne Hoinville-Bartram and Anita Cunningham decided they would hitchhike to Bowen in far North Queensland to visit Robin's mother. Their parents were against the idea with Anita's father and mother offering to pay their airfare to Bowen, but the girls had this idea of an adventure of hitchhiking and declined the offer of travelling by air.

Anita's father, Gerald Cunningham, saw them off from a street in Melbourne in the first days of July 1972. Nothing further was heard of the girls who did not contact any relatives or friends, which was strange as they had assured relatives they would keep in touch.

After two weeks, their parents reported them missing to Victorian police, but little was done at that time to try and locate the girls with Victorian police telling Anita's mother that Anita was old enough to do as she wished.

Complete silence from the girls went on for over four months with no trace of their movements known until on the 15th of November 1972. The remains of Robin's decomposed body were discovered partially buried under a railway bridge over Sensible Creek, about twenty kilometres northeast of Pentland, Queensland on the Flinders Highway. The body was undressed from the waist down and had two .22 calibre bullet wounds to the back of her head.

Although I am the author of this book, I am not privy to police files on the case or what inquiries were made by the investigating police to apprehend the offenders. According to a member of the Homicide Unit in Brisbane, very little was done by that homicide unit due to the pressure of work with murders occurring and them halting inquiries on one murder to go to the next one. The author does know that a Detective Senior Sergeant Brian Hayes, who oversaw the Homicide Unit in Brisbane, went north in 1972 to assist in investigations but what he did is not available to the general public.

I know that Detective Senior Sergeant Brian Hayes returned to Brisbane with Robin Bartram's remains, which he placed in the Brisbane morgue suitably labelled for a post-mortem examination.

Detective Senior Constable John Kolence of the Brisbane Homicide Unit attended the post-mortem examination conducted by Doctor Tonge. John has told the writer that there was not a lot of the body left, principally the skull and some bones. Dr Tonge thoroughly examined the skull, retrieving fragmented pieces of the two .22 calibre bullets from inside the skull that he could detect. He even x-rayed the skull to make sure he got all the fragments.

John took these fragments of the bullets to the Firearms Section of the Queensland Police Force as it was then known and handed them over to Inspector Les Bardwell. John Kolence said that the fragments were so damaged that it would be virtually impossible to determine very much about the bullets – like make, calibre, etc – and most certainly not enough for comparison with any other bullets.

For a time, I believed that this fragmentation of the bullets when entering the skull could have been because the bullets were dumdums, which are bullets hollowed out at the front; this makes them expand on impact. I have changed my opinion now with research into the bullet that killed American President John F Kennedy in 1963 in America, where it has been determined that the firearm used to kill him was a more powerful rifle that fired copper jacketed bullets nearly two inches long with a rounded head, which is the same usual shape as long and short makes of .22 calibre bullets I have handled many times in past years.

This second bullet fired from behind Kennedy whilst he sat in his car disintegrated when hitting his skull. This copper jacketed bullet is a lead bullet covered with a copper plate and stronger than a plain lead bullet like a .22 calibre bullet. It is therefore obvious that a .22 bullet is strong enough to fragment a person's skull as happened with the killing of Robin Bartram in 1972.

CHAPTER TWO

Sadly, the murderers of the girls were not identified by the Queensland police and the case had fallen off the radar of both the police and public attention until 29th May, 2003 when a woman resident of Charters Towers in Queensland, which is 107 kilometres northeast of Pentland, gave information to Crime Stoppers that she and her mother had met the two murdered girls in the winter of 1972 at the Pentland Hotel.

This woman, Mearle Elizabeth Whyte, then fifty years of age, was spoken to by officers from Charters Towers Police, who apparently reported that they did not believe her story. Firstly, before going any further, the police stance on these murders is set out in a letter from Detective Inspector 'Peter Smith' to me dated 15th September 2014 in response to several letters to the Commissioner of Police from me, which I will deal with later.

The only interpretation the author can place on this letter from Inspector 'Smith' is that the police position is 'that the murdered girls were never at the Pentland Hotel'. This position has seen the murderers escape identification, arrest and punishment for fifty years, despite valuable and believable information given to them by me as to what had transpired before the girls were murdered and after they left the Pentland Hotel.

When we get to April 2018, I will show you how this stance of the police is destroyed and completely blown out of the water.

It might be too strong, but I say that unfortunately, these are the battle lines between the police and me. At the time of writing, it has now been over nine years of me trying to obtain justice for these girls to see the offenders punished without result.

I have certainly been up against a powerful force in my attempts to get the true story out about these murders and blocked time after time from obtaining any help from the media or press. I have suspicions about this obstruction but currently, I have no proof.

My information has been ignored and not acted on in any meaningful way despite sixteen articles supporting me appearing in the trap's column of the Sunday Mail Newspaper over four years by Journalist Peter Cameron in that paper concerning my investigations with a view to engendering interest from the press and media. Why the editor of the Sunday Mail, Peter Gleeson, did not order an investigation by his reporters is a mystery only he can answer.

Uncommonly, Peter Cameron's articles brought no such reaction from other newspaper editors or other journalists, including crime reporters to pursue my information to ascertain the credibility of what I was presenting to the police to discover the identity of the murderers.

The obvious and only reasonable explanation would seem to be that the police were contacted by the press and media for comment. The reply from police was sufficient to convince them not to act on the articles or my information.

A similar situation exists with Channel Seven who lost all interest in these cases after a detective inspector in April of 2015 went to Charters Towers to supposedly investigate the authenticity of recorded telephone interviews, I did with witnesses who have valuable information. He reported back to the representative of

Channel Seven information that led to that TV channel ending their interest. In my opinion, the representative was misled, and I leave it at that for now until that representative hopefully gives evidence in a Commission of Inquiry to relate what he was told by the inspector.

It is now 2023 and I have exhausted every possible way that I can think of to expose this blatant misuse of the power of the police to cover up this breach of public trust, aided and abetted by the media and press with some exceptions.

I am now forced into the uncomfortable position of having to write a book about the whole circumstances. I am trying to obtain justice for these murdered girls by informing the public about this scandalous position and calling on the public to support me in obtaining a Commission of Inquiry into the manner this case has been handled by Queensland Police. I have a preference for a Commission of Inquiry over an Inquest, with a strong preference for the Commission of Inquiry due to the time it takes for police to prepare statements for an Inquest as opposed to a Commission of Inquiry where the witnesses are called to the witness box and examined as we have seen many times in Commissions of Inquiry in southern states in recent years.

While writing this book, I will give examples of my treatment by the press and media to obtain justice for the murdered girls over nine years. I have decided that rather than identify those who will be offended when I describe their incompetence, inexperience or other failings – or identify them as having vital information that they have not come forward with to the police or have falsely denied involvement – then I will, when referring to them in this book, use false names and when using them place inverted commas around their names so they will not be identified to readers. In the case of police, I will at times refer to them as a police officer or just officer and in some cases do not reveal the rank of the person.

This obvious lack of professional interest by the press does not apply to the editor of the Northern Miner Newspaper in Charters Towers, namely Trudy Brown, who has conducted her own inquiries, listened to my recorded interviews and spoken with at least one of my informants to conclude that my information to the police is well grounded and true. She has written some supporting articles in her paper that have also been published in the Townsville Bulletin over these later years. Trudy's support and the support of one of her journalists, Morgan Oss, has been very encouraging and helps to keep me going despite the repeated dead ends I have run into from the press and media.

With the way my efforts have been treated, one could be forgiven for thinking that I have done something wrong in pursuing justice for these girls who cannot speak for themselves.

Everything I write or have put before the police and public in recorded telephone interviews, letters, emails and any other publishing of information from my investigations has been done in my firm belief that I am acting and have always acted in the public interest.

I wrote letters to the Commissioner of Police many, many times and it was never my intention to harass police but, in each letter, there is something new, be it information, a strategy or an angle that would help police solve these crimes. Knowing how the minds of police in administration work, I know they would have branded me a serial letter writer and a pest.

My dealing with and using recorded phone interviews is done in the belief that the following law applies to recording telephone conversations with people.

In Queensland, it is legal to use a listening/recording device to record a private conversation as long as you are a party to that conversation. However, you cannot share that recording with anyone who wasn't a party to that conversation unless it is *reasonably necessary to protect your lawful interests, or it is in the public interest to share it .***Penalty:** *Up to 2 years' imprisonment or a fine of up to 40 penalty units.*

CHAPTER THREE

My response to the letter from Inspector 'Smith' dated 15th September 2014 outlining the police position on these murders will be dealt with later but to try and keep some sort of chronological order to what can only be described as very unprofessional actions on the part of some Queensland Police, I will try to roughly follow a timeline.

It was never my intention when I began writing this book to include much about myself but a friend whose judgment I respect suggested that it would be a good idea to say something about myself, my career in the Queensland police force and some of the cases I have handled, which some members of the public might find interesting. This will also establish whether I am qualified to bring this cover-up by police of a double murder investigation to public attention.

I will try to limit those asides so as not to detract attention from the purpose of this book, which is to obtain public support for a Commission of Inquiry into the police handling of this case and/or an inquest but preferably the former, which would be quicker as not so much preparation needs to be done with police gathering statements from witnesses which seems to be the case with inquests which take months and indeed years to begin or continue after adjournments.

An example of this is the government announcing a second inquest into the 1973 Whisky Au Go Go fires in 2017 in Brisbane which killed fifteen people, and which is now scheduled for June 2021 or four years after it was announced and is continuing in 2022.

As persons involved in or have substantive knowledge of the circumstances of the rapes and murders of these two girls killed at Pentland in 1972 are now elderly, we do not have the luxury of time to bring the true facts about these crimes into the open.

At this time, I will explain by showing you my reason for preferring a Commission of Inquiry by quoting Section 17 of 'The Commissions of Inquiry Acts, 1950 to 1954':

'A Commission in the exercise of any of its functions or powers, shall not be bound by the rules or practice of any court or tribunal as to procedure or evidence, but may conduct its proceedings and inform itself on any matter in such manner as it thinks proper; and without limiting in any way the operation of this Section, the Commission may refer any technical matter to an expert and may accept his report as evidence.'

To begin, I would like to tell you something about the Gurn family. My father, John Joseph Gurn, was born in Ireland at Cloncuny, County Roscommon. He arrived in Australia on board the Orient Liner Ormuz on 29th August 1907. He was recruited into the Queensland police force on 25th September 1908 and sworn in as a constable on 29th November 1908, aged twenty-six years.

He saw service at the Police Depot Stables, Cloncurry, Mount Elliott, Boulia, Beetoota, Birdsville, Bell and Toowoomba. At Birdsville, supplies came from Adelaide by camel train. Saddle horses, pack horses and Black trackers were widely used by my father to travel around the bush in this harsh environment. Sometimes having to bury dead bodies. Conditions were very tough with an example of having to stay awake all night while on patrol using stock whips to keep rats from chewing the harness for his horses.

He was stationed at Cloncurry when he was awarded the Police Silver Medal for saving lives by stopping a runaway horse and sulky containing a man, wife and child on 28th April 1909. The breeching of the harness attaching the horse to the sulky had failed with one shaft disengaging, causing the horse to bolt uncontrollably down the street until my father rushed out, jumped on the horse's head and hung onto it until it stopped.

He was stationed at Birdsville when he was granted leave of absence from 9th June 1913 to 5th January 1914. During this time, he returned to Ireland and married Mary Ellen Hargaden. They returned to Birdsville.

One can only imagine how his wife must have felt coming from Ireland into the over one hundred degrees heat of Birdsville. He made several applications to his head station at Longreach to move from Birdsville as the heat was killing his wife. He was eventually transferred to Bell, but Mary Ellen passed away on 14th April 1931 and is buried in the Nudgee Cemetery in Brisbane.

Later, he married my mother. My younger brother, James Patrick Gurn, also served seven years in the Queensland Police Force at Birdsville in the 1960s, which may be somewhat unique for father and son to have served as the lone policeman in Birdsville. Jim is now deceased and retired as Officer in Charge of Bardon Police Station in Brisbane.

I was a member of the Queensland Police Force from 1952 to 1975 with twenty-three years of service. For eighteen of those twenty-three years, I was a detective and never wore the uniform again after 1957. I also served as a police cadet at the Brisbane C.I. branch in 1950–51.

I worked on cattle and sheep stations when a young lad and drove an International TD9 tractor with rope-operated ripper and scoop to form a tank on Canaway Downs at Quilpie. Hydraulics were not in use at that time. I was a truck driver in Brisbane with Metropolitan Carriers for eighteen months, carrying everything from bags of salt, barbed wire and everything other carriers refused to transport. This was hard heavy work that saw me strengthen and become fit for when I entered the Petrie Terrace Police Barracks as a probationary constable in 1952.

During these eighteen months of truck driving, I served my compulsory 98 days of national service in the army at Wacol and three years in the CMF attending parades at night with yearly camps at Greenbank whilst a policeman in uniform, which was sometimes uncomfortable. I served five years in uniform and eighteen years in plain clothes, resigning in 1975 as a detective sergeant in charge of Sandgate Criminal Investigation Branch, usually comprising of about five members.

During my detective years, I dealt with hundreds of investigations and dozens of criminals. Being part of the very busy Fortitude Valley C. I. branch for about ten years saw me along with many other detectives attending and giving evidence in many district and supreme court trials and sentence hearings. The investigative experience in Brisbane and Bundaberg saw me promoted to Detective Sergeant in charge of my own C. I. branch office at Sandgate, Brisbane. Detectives worked in pairs with one member being senior and in charge. After a couple of years of experience as an investigator, I hated working under anyone senior to me. I had to be the one making the decisions, such is my makeup.

A bit of a history lesson here for younger people is that when I left the police force in 1975 there were no computers or mobile phones. They just did not exist.

Brisbane police cars in 1952 were mainly old clapped-out American sedans, like Oldsmobiles, Dodges, Plymouths, Studebakers, Fords and Chevrolets. How many times they had been around the speedometers, I don't know. It was not until the late 1950s really when we were given new Holden cars for patrol etc.

In Fortitude Valley, Brisbane – more commonly known as the Valley – there were about five wine saloons, which, after sunset, usually contained mostly drunken patrons, some asleep over their tables. Police had to patrol these dens each night, arresting those who could hardly walk. Each night, the usual tally was about ten or more and police had to ride in the back of these big old cars to stop the drunks interfering with the driver.

Some drunks had wet themselves and defecated in their trousers and the stench was terrible. Drunken men urinated in the street, and I recall seeing one drunken woman urinating in the street gutter in front of the Hanwood Wine Saloon in Brunswick Street. Still, the police just got on with it and it was no good complaining anyway. The job had to be done.

Some drunks who did not have the one-pound bail money had to front the Magistrates in court the next morning. They were mostly convicted and set free. Some drunks amassed hundreds of convictions for drunkenness. One man, Eugene Ebzery, had amassed somewhere between 3000 and 4000 convictions for drunkenness. He always had a funny quip for the Magistrate and one day pleaded for leniency, saying to the Magistrate, 'Look at all the experience I am giving all the young coppers making their first arrest.'

Police walked the beat in three shifts from six a.m. to two p.m., two p.m. to ten p.m. and ten p.m. to six a.m., in the City and Valley in Brisbane. In the suburbs, police rode bicycles and if you wanted help you had to find a public telephone box. Transporting the arrests of drunks or unruly types necessitated you finding a taxi to take them to the City Watchhouse situated between George Street and North Quay, which was in Watchhouse Lane at the top of Adelaide Street. Of course, if taxi drivers spotted you before you spotted them, they turned around and got out of the way in case you signalled them. In the country, police used police horses.

When new policemen arrived in country stations, they, in lots of cases, had to take on the local bully to establish their credentials in a fist fight. Some police reputations travelled before them throughout the state and their ability in these encounters was well known from the top of Queensland to the bottom border with New South Wales, which is remarkable really because there was no wireless network but word of mouth is a great carrier from one person to another.

There were three racecourses in Brisbane, which were Eagle Farm, Doomben and Albion Park with three enclosures for patrons, which were the Paddock, St Ledger and the Flat. Admission was ten shillings in the Paddock, five shillings into the Ledger and one and sixpence into the Flat. Patrons stood three and four deep around the bars and in the Flat, the bar floors were usually wet from spilt glasses and cockroaches running around the floors was normal. Hardly a meeting went by without a fist fight in one of the bar areas. Glasses that the public drank from were hurriedly dunked in a tub of water and then stood on a tray to dry before being served to another patron. Over time, more hygienic means of washing glasses were installed.

Hundreds of bookmakers fielded in the total of the three enclosures with runners travelling between the enclosures to get the best price or to get on with the St Ledger or Flat bookmakers before news of a plunge on a horse made in the Paddock was known to these bookmakers in the other enclosures.

Another piece of Queensland history was the South African Springboks tour of Australia in 1971. The premier Joh Bjelke-Petersen declared a State of Emergency and guaranteed that no police would suffer any penalty in anything they had to do to suppress protesters.

I was, along with many other police, stationed on the football field of the Brisbane Exhibition Ground whilst the football game was played to stop protesters disrupting the game. That afternoon we formed a line in front of the Tower Mill Motel on Wickham Terrace, Brisbane in front of hundreds of protesters and suffered hours of taunts and abuse, and we were called every rotten name in the book. The Springboks were watching the action from their motel rooms high above us. When night came somebody yelled out, 'Right, go get 'em.'

With that, the police moved on the protesters, who ran down the steep slopes of Wickham Park into the dark of the park with the police in hot pursuit. A number were arrested, and some were more summarily dealt with, I think. I personally never caught anyone. In fact, most of the police agreed with the protesters' stance against Apartheid in South Africa but they had no option but to enforce the law.

Dealing with cowardly wife bashers, who were not known as domestic violence perpetrators in 1975. My approach when a wife complained was to take a signed statement from her and obtain a warrant for the husband's arrest for common assault if the complainant's injuries were not too serious.

If the complainant woman would not give a statement to have their husbands arrested or summoned, I referred them to an agency that could help them. It is not the police's job to offer advice or arbitrate between husband and wife. In more serious cases, of course, police act and prefer more serious charges. I had no time for these cowards who hit women. Some members of the legal profession were straight shooters whom I respected and got along with well.

CHAPTER FOUR

I have titled this book *Hear Our Cry* – meaning hear our cry for justice. I still believe that the offenders can be identified and arrested if investigations are sourced from the information I have provided to police in the last nine years.

Justice for the murdered girls has been denied to them till now. It is my contention that the police have been remiss in their inquiries initially caused through the inexperience and incompetence of some investigating police and that this false stance that the girls were never at the Pentland Hotel in July, 1972 is being perpetuated in an attempt to save face by other senior police due to misplaced loyalty and against the weight of evidence that I have uncovered in the last eight years.

The very sad part of all this is that an inquest has been denied by the attorney general Yvette D'Ath, who had the say in this instance. In an inquiry or inquest, those involved could be questioned on oath on the witness stand to get the truth. The attorney general's position regarding her decision to order an inquest would normally be influenced to a degree by what the police tell her, I would think.

Dealing with the decision of the attorney general Yvette D'Ath not to hold an inquest into the obvious murder of Robin Hoinville-Bartram, which I had applied for to the coroner and then using the same application to the attorney general to comply with the law as it stood at the time and because the murder had been committed prior to 2003.

I must point out in the strongest terms that the murdering and obvious rape of this girl conjures up images in my mind of where the morality lies with these people in power making these decisions in a manner where their decisions are given in an abstract manner as opposed to the decisions they would make if the victim was their own daughter or sister.

There are a few considerations that these elected representatives of the public make when ordering an inquest or a Commission of Inquiry and these are mainly centred around whether it is in the public interest to hold the Inquest or Commission of Inquiry. There are other considerations they examine also but in the case of Robin Bartram's murder, the only real situation is that she was raped and murdered by being shot in the head with two .22 calibre bullets with the offenders not known or brought to justice. These circumstances alone should be sufficient to warrant an inquest. The fact that the crime was committed in 1972 is irrelevant in my opinion.

To point out what I mean by that, I would like you to conjure up in your mind how you would feel if confronted with the almost nude body of your daughter or sister exposed to the world, probably bruised and battered lifeless on the ground with her face and head covered with blood matted hair from the bullet wounds to her head. This is the reality of what we are dealing with in these Pentland murders.

The same scenario, although equally horrifying, would probably have been the fate of Anita Cunningham whose body has not been found. In the case of Anita, as you will see later in this work, I applied to the next attorney general Shannon Fentiman in an application over forty-five pages in length for a Commission of Inquiry into the failures of police to properly investigate these crimes pointing out these failures, the unprofessional work of some Police, the bungling of a valuable opportunity for information and their unsustainable position that these girls were never at the Pentland Hotel in July, 1972 whilst hitchhiking enroute to Bowen, North Queensland. I further pointed out that the Justice system had been corrupted. This aspect is fully dealt with later in this work.

Shannon Fentiman rejected my application for this Commission of Inquiry. The decision of Ms Fentiman among other points she states as follows, 'The position remains however that there is no cogent, reliable evidence or new evidence concerning the death of Ms Hoinville-Bartram and the suspected death of Ms Cunningham which may be considered by a coronial investigation and inquest process.'

This statement about reliable evidence is also referred to in Ms D'Ath's refusal to grant an inquest into the murder of Robin Bartram. Once again, I must question whether Ms Fentiman would make the same decision if the murder referred to her daughter or sister. When I had applied to Ms Fentiman for the Commission of Inquiry, I asked her to ask the police several questions so that she would be able to know their real stance on these murders and knowing that information she would be able to make an informed decision.

After replying to Ms Fentiman asking her if she had obtained answers to my request for her to ask certain questions of police and her refusal to give a clear answer, it became obvious that she had not obtained answers to the questions from police. I pointed out to her that I could not see how she could make an informed decision to refuse the Commission of Inquiry if she did not know the answers to those questions.

Very quickly, she replied suggesting that I make a second complaint to the Crime and Corruption Commission about my suspected corruption of police work on the case. I immediately replied that I would not do as she asked because I did not know who or what was behind the circumstances I had outlined in my application to her.

I pointed out to Ms Fentiman that a Commission of Inquiry could be established by questioning the persons who I had told her need to be questioned in the witness box to get to the heart of the corruption and obtain the cogent reliable evidence she wanted. This is the very reason for the application for a Commission of Inquiry.

The correspondence concerning this application will be shown later to try and keep the chronological order in place where possible.

I would not like any reader to think that I am in any way putting down the entire Queensland police service because I am not. I think they do a remarkable job for the safety of Queensland people and property, and I respect and admire them for that. However, I do question the actions of those police involved in suppressing from public knowledge the way these two girls were raped and murdered and the actions of those few police who have prevented the solving of this case because they refuse to accept that serious mistakes have been made in the police handling of the case from the commissioner down to those involved in this cover-up.

It is accepted these days that the buck stops with the commissioner but as I point out later, the buck in this case stops with the Queensland government that employs her.

CHAPTER FIVE

After resigning from the police force, I trained racehorses for twenty-five years. This change was hardly remarkable as the thoroughbred racehorse was a passion of mine. As a teenager, I attended every yearling sale, buying the catalogue, marking down the price each yearling was sold for and studying the confirmation of each yearling to try and find that distinctive edge as to why one horse was so much faster than another horse.

After school some days, I went across the road in Brisbane to racing stables and rode racehorses bareback in afternoon exercise around a house paddock. I took long service leave from the police force to train Gun Top for his maiden win and my first win as a trainer. The horse raced under the name of a trainer. I took extended annual leave to train a horse for the Burketown Cup in the 1960s in the Gulf of Carpentaria. I bred horses under my mother's name and raced one horse in my mother's name. This horse, Kelroanin, kicked off my career as a public trainer. He won thirteen races during his career. I was the only member of the police force who was a detective sergeant and a registered stable hand at the same time. This allowed me to parade my horse in the saddling paddock before a race whilst I was still in the ranks.

In May 2000 after a marriage breakup, I started travelling

Australia, searching for gold with a metal detector. I did this in Victoria, West Australia and far north Queensland. In Victoria, I took up with Robin, a single lady, who was travelling Australia in her motor home. I taught her how to use a metal detector and we travelled Australia for the next five or six years with her in her motor home and me with a caravan and car. Sometimes, Robin would leave and return to Tasmania and South Australia but would always find me again.

In 2003/4, I spent about nine months at Pentland where some gold was found. During my stay in Pentland, I became friendly with a few of the residents of the area, which included a horse trainer named Vince Whyte. I represented him in an appeal in Townsville he made against a steward's decision to suspend his trainer's license.

Robin and I moved further north in 2004 to King Junction Station in the Laura area of far North Queensland. From there, I went down to Mistletoe Station at Georgetown and Robin went to South Australia but followed me back to Georgetown later. We parted ways in 2006 and are still friendly but thousands of kilometres apart. Eventually, I retired to a southwest town on the Darling Downs in 2008. At the time of writing this book, I am ninety years of age.

Vince Whyte kept in touch with me over the years by phone and in the early months of 2014, he began telling me that his brother John's wife, Mearle, was dying of cancer in Townsville Hospital and that she claimed she had met the two murdered girls Robin Bartram and Anita Cunningham at the Pentland Hotel in 1972 before they were murdered. I did not initially put much faith in the story really and asked Vince to find out more details from his brother. This went on for a couple of months and eventually, I began to think that perhaps there was some truth to the story.

One of my previous team members, the now retired Owen

Lindemann, who had himself risen to Officer in Charge of the Brisbane Homicide Unit, asked an officer of the Cold Case Squad to telephone me. He did this on 9th May 2014. I explained to this officer, whom I will call Detective Inspector 'Peter Smith', what I knew. He told me that all this has been gone over before. I explained to him that John Whyte's wife Mearle was dying in Townsville Hospital and wished to tell her story to police. I told him she was not expected to live very long. Smith said that he would probably get someone to interview her.

With some more information, I tried to contact Smith at his office by telephone on two more occasions, but my calls were not returned. I then wrote him a letter dated 20th May 2014 with information again saying that Mearle Whyte was dying. Mearle Whyte died in Townsville hospital on 27th June 2014 not interviewed by police who had seven weeks to interview her before she died. This was also despite one of Mearle's daughters ('Paula') pleading on the phone to Crime Stoppers for her mother to be interviewed as she wished to give the complete story of meeting the murdered girls to police.

When I first spoke to Inspector Peter Smith, I did not know at that time that some police had previously taken part in a Channel Seven TV program along with David Cunningham, brother of the missing and presumed dead Anita Cunningham with the host Alex Cullen, where these police indicated to David Cunningham and the general public where the decomposed body of Robin Bartram had been discovered under the bridge over Sensible Creek on 15th November 1972.

Draw your own conclusion on the professionalism of these police because they indicated that the body had been discovered under the road bridge over Sensible Creek but in fact, the body was discovered under the railway bridge some fifty yards further away.

I did not at that time know that there had been a $250,000

reward notice posted by the police for information offering immunity from prosecution to any person not directly involved in the murders.

Police did not interview Mearle Whyte before she died, which raised suspicions in my mind as to why this case had not been solved so I wrote to the Commissioner of Police, Ian Stewart, on 29th June 2014 about these murders. I told the commissioner that Mearle Whyte said that the two murdered girls had arrived at the Pentland Hotel from Mount Isa with a man they only knew as 'Cowboy', who had very few possessions of his own. She said that the two girls and Cowboy had left the Pentland Hotel in a band member's station wagon with four band members and named these people as I then knew the story. (Later investigations altered the information a little.)

I explained in my letter to Commissioner Stewart that Mearle Whyte, nee Madigan, then twenty-two years of age (should have been eighteen years of age) remained at the hotel with her mother after the girls had left. Mearle, who was a teetotaller, then drove their car from the Pentland Hotel when it was dark. She said they came across the car the girls had left the hotel in sideways across the Flinders Highway at Sensible Creek (about twenty kilometres away), with all doors open and headlights and interior lights on. Mearle slowed down but her mother told her not to stop so she drove slowly past this car. Someone from the area of the creek called out, 'Stop them!'

She said there was a man stomping on something in the creek and one man yelling to turn the lights of their car off. Mearle claimed that she recognised Cowboy, the only occupant of the car and he recognised her as she drove past. Mearle did not see any sign of the girls at this time.

I continued that a day or two later Cowboy attempted to get Mearle to go with him to Townsville when she was outside a hairdresser's salon in Charters Towers but she declined. She noticed that Cowboy had a noticeable scratch down the side of his face. (Later information revealed this happened the next morning.)

Other parts of my letter dealt with Mearle speaking to police officers from Charters Towers. I explained to the commissioner that the information I was giving him was the result of conversations Vince was having with his brother John (Mearle's husband).

Later in my letter, I said that I could not understand why inquiries were not made at the Pentland Hotel. I asked why the band members weren't interviewed. I said that from outside looking in, it seemed to me that the investigating officer had discredited Mearle's story and has apparently claimed she changed her story to fit in with newspaper reports but even if some information was in the newspapers, it was unbelievable that we had two girls under extremely suspicious circumstances involved in an incident at night on the same lonely highway as described by Mearle in roughly the same location in the same time frame. I said that this was far too much of a coincidence for there not to be some truth in it.

In a letter to then Commissioner of Police Ian Stewart dated 29th June 2014, I elaborated on the band members as far as I knew at the time and I said that when Mearle Whyte was interviewed by a police officer at Charters Towers, he allegedly asked her why she wished to be involved and what she was aiming to get out of it.

At that time, the information was that when she was interviewed by a police officer, who we will call 'Bob Black' for the purposes of this work. He was accompanied by a clairvoyant woman who turned out to be Ann. Every time Mearle said anything, this Ann chided Mearle that she was wrong. In the end, Mearle told Black that he could do the other thing (meaning please himself. Later information seemed to show that when Black interviewed Mearle, she was on her own and not accompanied by 'Black.')

In a letter to the commissioner dated 4th July 2014, I identified a band member living in Charters Towers. I also told him that a 'Ted West' or similar name had been interviewed but denied all knowledge of the matter.

This Ted West is said to have arranged the lift for the girls with the band member and was even seen putting the girl's luggage on the roof rack of his car before they all left the Pentland Hotel together.

The police stance is contained in a letter to me dated 15th September 2014, from Inspector Peter Smith who wrote to me as follows.

Dear Mr Gurn,

On 29th May 2003, Mearle Whyte contacted Crime Stoppers in response to a television program appealing for information. This initial call was approximately thirty years after the discovery of Robin's remains. In her initial contact with police, Mearle could not name the person(s) she suspected of murdering the missing girls or whom she had seen in the blue Valiant or at the river.

In August 2005, Mearle claimed she had seen and named four members of the Milat family and two others with the girls she identified as Robin and Anita. There are claims one of the Milat brothers was working at the meat works at the time. I wish to advise I am in possession of the full list of employees at the meat works in Pentland, prior to and during 1972. This information was obtained by investigators in 1972. No Milats are listed as employees during that time.

Mearle initially stated she had seen the suspicious activity at Cape River but later changed this to Sensible Creek.

On 8th May 2004, Mearle spoke to 'Police Officer Bob Black'. Mearle advised 'Officer Black' she had met the two missing at the

Pentland Hotel on a Friday night in November 1971, three weeks after the White Horse Tavern had been pulled down. Mearle confirmed November 1971 from a history book her daughter located in the library showing the tavern being pulled down in late 1971.

The missing girls did not leave Melbourne until July 1972. Even if you accept Mearle, after thirty years, meant November 1972 when Robin's remains were located, Robin had been deceased at least three months before being located and therefore the alleged sighting by Mearle Whyte cannot be associated with this case.

Whilst I appreciate you, Mearle Whyte and her family have the best intentions to assist in solving this case for the sake of the families and community, I hope these few clarifications (not all) clearly demonstrate whilst Mearle may have believed she had seen these girls and their killers, this was a mistaken belief or at least her memory after thirty years may not have been a credible account of her observations.

I trust this information will finalise your interest in this matter; however, you are invited to contact me at [redacted] *if you wish to discuss this matter further.*

With respect to this letter from Inspector Smith, he is quoting what Officer Black said Mearle Whyte told him, but we have to remember that his conversations with Mearle are subject to suspicion in view of remarks contained in recorded interviews with family members.

Remember there are no known signed statements from Mearle Whyte as to what she was telling Black.

Nonetheless, would any reader recalling events thirty years later be confident that they would know whether the events occurred in the autumn, summer, winter or spring or their recall was exact?

CHAPTER SIX

On 5th October 2014, I wrote to Commissioner Ian Stewart. I enclosed my email reply to Inspector Smith dated 15th September 2014, which read as follows:

Dear Inspector

Thank you for your correspondence on the information I have supplied concerning the murder of the two girls named.

Your reply and estimation of the investigation is totally acceptable and reasonable if you accept Officer 'Black's' versions of what Mearle Whyte conveyed to him. However, the tremendous difference in the information must raise serious concerns about the information.

I do not understand how it is possible that people have been named as being involved in some way as opposed to the information from Officer 'Black.' Obviously with such a discrepancy, someone is lying, delusional or worse.

It seems to me that unless the persons named in my information have been interviewed and exonerated, the lingering doubts will always remain. I can understand why this seemingly tenuous information is being disregarded. I feel that the family of Mearle Whyte or at least her husband and Vince Whyte will never be satisfied that all that could be done has been done.

I will be speaking with Vince Whyte shortly and will advise him of the police stance on the matter.
Sincerely
Mick Gurn

I continued to the commissioner that Vince and John Whyte were not impressed with Smith's reply. Inspector Smith said that he hopes my interest has been finalised but in fact; after speaking with Mearle's daughter and husband, I am totally convinced as to the truth of Mearle Whyte's story.

The full list of employees of the Cape River Meatworks and the uselessness of this list is explained in that employees seldom used their correct names to dodge tax as they were paid at the end of their shifts each day. Inspector Smith never commented on this matter.

I told the commissioner I was forwarding him the recorded telephone interviews I did with John and Paula Whyte on a USB flash drive. I complained that Smith could have interviewed Mearle before she died. I informed him that Mearle's mother, Betty Madigan, had cashed a cheque for cash in the Pentland Hotel, which could be traced to prove that they were at the Pentland Hotel and the date this occurred.

Regarding information in the recorded phone interviews, I told Commissioner Stewart that Dennis Madigan, brother of Mearle, could corroborate Mearle about the man hiding in the grass at the Twelve Mile Outstation at night. I also mentioned that Mearle had been shot at whilst on the veranda of a house in Charters Towers sometime later as recalled by Paula (her daughter) in her interview with me.

Further to that, Mearle's father had told her not to get involved when the body was discovered.

I pointed out that when Mearle Whyte went to Pam List's house (Pam was then known as Pam Barry) about her making her bridesmaid dresses a person named Wally Barry who I later established as a suspect was at her place, whom she recognised as one of the killers.

The informant Mearle Whyte was just nineteen years of age when she met John Whyte. John described Mearle to me in conversations years later as just under six feet tall (183 centimetres) and a strikingly beautiful natural blonde woman being just under medium build. He said she was a good dressmaker, efficient around cattle yards and a good horsewoman. She had her own horses on which she contested ladies' programs at rodeos, roping cattle and barrel racing along with other events.

John said that the Madigan family came from Goondiwindi, Queensland about 1970 after working on a cattle station there. Mearle's father, Brian Madigan, had obtained a position of being in charge of the bullock camps at the Twelve Mile Outstation on Wondo Vale Station outside Charters Towers.

John met Mearle in 1973. They both followed the rodeos competing in events. Mearle was usually accompanied by her brother Mick Madigan to whom she was close.

It is very interesting and very poignant I believe that Officer Bob Black never at any time interviewed John Whyte to ask him what he knew of Mearle's claims of meeting the murdered girls. I ask, 'Why?'

Wouldn't you think Black would want to know if Mearle had ever told him that she met the murdered girls? Also, he never interviewed any children of John and Mearle to see if they corroborated Mearle in that she had mentioned meeting the murdered girls to them.

Also, the family have no knowledge of Black ever interviewing Mearle's mother Betty Madigan, her father Brian Madigan or any of her brothers.

FIRST RECORDED INTERVIEW WITH JOHN WHYTE

The interview John Whyte had with me lasted fifty minutes on Thursday 2nd October 2014. John said that he was sixty years of age and that he married Mearle Elizabeth Madigan in 1975. Mearle was born on 27th October 1953. He said that they had six children.

All these children, I am told, have some knowledge of their mother meeting the murdered girls in varying degrees after hearing the story from their mother over many years.

He said that in the 1980s one night when they were living at Aland Street, Charters Towers, a program came on television about the disappearance and murders of the two girls. Mearle became very upset on seeing the girls she recognised as having met at the Pentland Hotel in 1972, which brought it all back to her. He said she was very frightened because at least two or three of the offenders were living in Charters Towers.

Mearle and her mother lived at the Twelve Mile Outstation on Wando Vale Cattle Station in 1972, where her father oversaw the bullock camp. Mearle and her mother travelled via Pentland on their way to Charters Towers to buy supplies. (This is a three-hour trip.) They called into the Pentland Hotel and sat down in the lounge. Robin and Anita were already there. They became friendly with the girls who told them that they had hitchhiked from Mount Isa in a truck accompanied by a young man who they knew as 'Cowboy' and that they were going to Charters Towers. In the hotel, she said that a Kevin or 'Ted West' had arranged a lift for the girls to Charters Towers with members of a band that had played earlier that day at the hotel for the customers. He believed it was a Sunday.

She told her husband that this Ted West helped the girls to the band members' car and placed the girl's luggage on the roof rack of a blue Ford Falcon Station Wagon, about a 1967–68 model with the colour stained by the sun. She could see all this through the door of the lounge. She said the band was four young fellows and a girl. One of them had long blondish hair to the shoulders with tinges of blond through it.

She believed that Cowboy could have been Ivan Milat who was apparently named in the TV program.

John said it was wintertime when this happened and that Mearle's father Brian was doing a full muster, which he did in the first months of winter. About a half-hour after the girls and the band members left the hotel when it was then dark, Mearle and her mother left the hotel in their Holden sedan. When they came to Sensible Creek, the band members' car was sideways across both lanes of the highway with all lights on and headlights shining towards the railway line. The lights included interior lights. All doors were open including the back of the station wagon.

Mearle said that she saw one man near the railway line jumping up and down on something and that others were coming out of the creek. Her mother told Mearle not to stop. They drove to the Mexican Caravan Park in Charters Towers where they had accommodation booked.

The next morning, Mearle went to a hairdressers Shop in Charters Towers and that three of the men who had left the hotel with the girls were walking up and down outside the hairdressers' shop. When Mearle came outside, she was approached by 'Cowboy' who wanted her to drive them to Townsville, which she refused to do. She said that Cowboy had a scratch down the left side of his face from the left eye down. She believed it was caused by a fingernail.

When Mearle told Cowboy that she had to return to the cattle station, he asked her which station. She said she had told him that the previous day. Mearle asked Cowboy how he got the scratch on his face, and he said there had been a misunderstanding.

She walked to the White Horse Tavern, walking past the police station, which was closed. Mearle and her mother did their shopping and returned to the Twelve Mile Outstation via the Lynne Highway.

John thought Mearle said it was two weeks later that her fifteen-year-old brother Dennis was outside at night trying to shoot wild pigs when he nearly trod on a man on the ground. Dennis came inside and said, 'There's a bastard hiding in the grass out there.'

Next day, a mechanic from the home station came down with fruit and other supplies and said that someone had spent a lot of time at the second gate as there were a lot of cigarette butts on the ground there.

John asked Mearle to describe Cowboy, and she said he was about John's height or 175 centimeters but heavier than John and about 110 kilos. At that time, Mearle said she could not understand how the girls did not speak to her at the caravan park but after the body of Robin was found, she realised the truth of what had happened to the girls. From then on, she was frightened that the murderers would try to harm her. She did not report what she knew to the police.

Later, there was another TV program where Ann (the psychic) and former Police Officer Black appeared. After this program, John rang Crime Stoppers to complain that what Black and Ann were saying on TV was lies. John said his daughter Paula also rang Crime Stoppers to complain. Crime Stoppers seemed to take it all as a joke.

John said Black spoke to Mearle on two occasions that he knew of, and that Mearle was very disappointed in what he said to her, even asking her if she was involved in all this. As a result, Mearle just shut up not telling much to Black.

John said that everybody who worked at the Cape River Meat works in those days gave false names to dodge income tax. He said words to the effect that every Tom, Dick and Harry did it. Consequently, any list of employee's names at the abattoir would be useless in identifying them. The meat works paid everybody at the end of their shift each day.

He said that Mearle pointed out Pam List (Pam List was known in Charters Towers at the time as Pam Barry) as being part of the band this fateful day and another resident of Charters Towers whose identity for the time being I will leave undisclosed.

John supplied other information about band members which for the moment I will leave until and hopefully when there is an inquiry or inquest. He had heard that West had been spoken to by Black who denied involvement.

Because I am telling what John said in his interview, it is unfortunate that I must repeat information which has already been provided previously.

CHAPTER SEVEN

RECORDED INTERVIEW WITH 'PAULA' WHYTE

On Saturday, 4th October 2014, I conducted a similar recorded interview with one of John's daughters who I will call 'Paula' for the purposes of this book as she has been threatened and is frightened for her life.

(I have tried to keep what Paula said as near as I can to the way she spoke when talking to me.)

She began by giving me her name, address and her age, telling me that her mother was Mearle Elizabeth Whyte nee Madigan who had been dying in Townsville of bowel cancer. She said that her mother in hospital wanted her to ring the police to listen to her story, but no one ever did listen to her.

She said she wrote down some of her mother's stories. when her mother was nineteen years of age, she travelled from the Twelve Mile Outstation on Wando Vale Station by back roads to Pentland and there cashed a cheque at the hotel. This was around September 1972. Her mother and grandmother first sat at the bar and then at a table where the two girls were sitting. Robin and Anita's baggage was pushed up against the wall of the lounge. Then this guy came along, John or Richard (Cowboy). She said, 'I can't really remember.'

She told me it was a bit weird her telling the story because no one wanted to listen.

Mum sat down. The dark-haired girl was sitting near her. She was quiet and reserved. The other girl who would be Anita was playing with bangles on her arms, jingling them and laughing with my grandmother. My grandmother bought them drinks and this fellow John came and sat on the other side of her. He was sweet-talking my mum, but she was a bit stuck-up and half-ignored him.

The girls said they had just come that afternoon from Hughenden and they had come on a truck. That was about five o'clock in the afternoon. Mum wanted to know why they were hitchhiking because nearly everyone had a car, and they did not believe in hitchhiking. That's what my mum said anyway.

I said to Paula, 'Are you saying that this chap was travelling with these two girls or not?'

She replied, 'Yes, even the dark-haired girl said to Mum that he was with them.' She continued that they got on the truck with him at Mount Isa and they travelled to Hughenden because that was as far as that truck was going. They had to wait to find a truck that would take them to Charters Towers.

The dark-haired girl said, 'Don't listen to him. He's an idiot.' (Meaning Cowboy). I don't know why she said that. I never asked my mum. He just laughed and looked away. The other girl kept talking to my grandmother and she was jingling the bangles on her arms.

This young fellow wanted to get a ride with my grandmother and her. Because they were travelling by themselves, my mum said no. She did not like him because he was onto her straight away; he wanted to know her ins and outs and what she was doing, so she said she felt a bit uncomfortable.

Mum got up and went for a drink and then went back to the table. She got up again and told my grandmother she was going to the toilet. That fellow who was sitting at the table had left before she got this drink, and she went out the back to where the toilets were. It is all enclosed today. I have even been out there myself because Mum took me out there and showed me. She was going to the toilet, and they were sitting on the back steps. There was about five or six of them all laughing. Cowboy said to her, 'Where are you going?' Mum said, 'None of your business."

She went to the toilet and when she came out, this other fellow called Walter that she met later in the evening whistled at her. She stuck her nose up and went inside and talked to the girls. One of the girls said they were going home to Bowen and that is no lie. They said this and Mum said the exact same story for years and I don't think my mum would lie. They said they were going to family in Bowen.

My mum asked them if they needed a lift because she was going to Charters Towers with my grandmother.

The girls were going to come and then a fellow who worked at the bar – his name was Ted West – came up to them and said, 'I've got that lift for you now,' to the girls. They said, 'Ok.'

Apparently, one of the band members had his own car. He was taking some people in and said he knew some fellows who were travelling in and they would take the girls, no problem.

The dark-haired girl said, 'No, a man has already got us a lift.'

The blonde-haired girl said, 'Don't worry about it. We'll go with them.'

Mum said quickly, 'Are you sure that you don't want us to take you into town?'

And the blonde one said, 'No, we'll go with him.'

These other fellows were over near the bar; Mum said they were looking at their table and they were ready to go. The fellow from the bar who had cashed their cheque, and the girls were already gone so Mum and Grandma took off in their car. As they went down the road, they had the headlights on. They saw a car parked half on the road and half off the road, but the high beams were shooting across the road, across into the paddock towards the railway track. Mum slowed down and she wound the window down as she got close to the car.

This John (Cowboy) fellow was sitting in the car in the driver's seat and Mum said there were fellows across the paddock. As they went over this bridge prior to coming up to that, there was a light under the bridge as if someone was having a campfire. My grandmother at that time said, 'Just a mob of fellows having a party.'

Mum sort of half-slowed down getting to the car and she noticed all these people across the paddock yelling out and carrying on. As she got to the car, someone across the paddock yelled out, 'Stop them.'

Grandma said, 'Wind your window up and keep going. Keep fucking going.'

I think it is quite funny because that is what she used to say.

Anyway, they got to Charters Towers. It would have been Friday night, that was. The next day, Mum was getting her hair done at old Betty Noonan's shop in Gill Street. What was the scariest part was that when Mum was finished getting her hair done, she walked out of the hairdressers, and they were parked right outside. This John or Richard (Cowboy) – they even called him Dick – stepped out of the car and said, 'Where are you going?'

Mum said, 'I have just got my hair done and I am going to do some shopping.'

And he went on, 'Do you want to come to Townsville with us?'

One of the fellows in the passenger seat said, 'It will only be an hour over there and back.'

Mum felt strange and she thought to herself it was more than hour. They were singing out, 'Aw, come on. Come in the car, come with us and we'll go and have a party or something.' This Richard or John or whatever his name was said, 'Come with us.' (Referring to Cowboy.)

Mum looked at him and he had a scratch down the right-hand side of his face and on his cheek.

Mum goes, 'What happened to you?' and he goes, 'Aw, we had a bit of a problem back at the creek, but it is alright now. Never you mind, it's all good.'

Mum felt a bit weird, and she asked him where the girls were and he said, 'They are with their family.'

She said, 'Okay.'

Apparently, the dark-haired girl(had) said (the previous day) she would have a drink with Mum that day Saturday in Charters Towers and all they were doing was going to Charters Towers and Mum said she wasn't even there with them. Mum collected herself and said, 'No, thank you'. As she started walking down past the police station to the tavern where my grandmother was, Mum said they got out of the car and followed her down Gill Street, and she felt nervous. (Mearle was referring to conversation the previous day.)

She quickly walked into the tavern where my grandmother was and told her what had happened. She said, 'I think they have done something to the girls.'

My grandmother said, 'Shut up, it is nothing to do with us.'

Later, that evening, they left to go back to Wando Vale but strangely when they got to the turn off at Pentland, this car flicked its lights on because it was off the road a bit. It started to follow them. Mum said, 'I think it's them.'

My grandmother, who was a good driver, put her foot down and left them for dead.

A couple of nights later, my grandfather was out mustering cattle from the Twelve Mile and apparently, they had visitors in a car. My uncle, who was fifteen or something, was going across *the paddock as he was coming back from shooting pigs and came across a man in the grass. He screamed because he pointed the gun at him, thinking he was a pig. He ran back to the house and said what he had seen.*

They turned all the lights out and up the paddock, they could see a car near the gate. They were there all night and scared shitless, Mum said, waiting for my grandfather to come home. The next day at breakfast, they told my grandfather what had happened, so he went for a walk. Mum and that went with him and up near the gate there was beer cans, and everything squashed up. My grandfather did not believe my mum. He said they were probably just going pig shooting or something, so my grandmother said to my mother not to talk about it anymore and that was it.

Mum said she remembered their faces like it was yesterday, how they looked and what they were wearing. It is a bit sad.

I said to Paula, 'Is that anywhere written down? Did she write any of those descriptions down?'

She replied, 'No I just wrote them down on a piece of paper when she was in palliative care. I wrote them down myself because Mum was too sick, and no one wanted to listen.'

We had a lady come and visit us years ago and she said she was a psychic or something. She was a simple case, and she didn't want to listen to anything my mother said. Bob Black came and seen my mother but all he wanted to know about (I deleted her next words of her saying Black asked something about her mother's private life). Because they all know each other, it was just a shit show, and no one wanted to listen to her. I can't understand why a woman would say the same thing over and over for years, God knows how many years. She was nineteen or twenty back then. It is a bit sad but anyway.

I said, 'There was something about Crime Stoppers came on. Do you know anything about that?'

She said, 'Yeah, Crime Stoppers.'

I said, 'Did she contact Crime Stoppers?'

Yes, many times, but what Bob Black and that other woman had said – they just did not listen to her, and I didn't think anyone would ever ring me. I rang Crime Stoppers not long ago before my mother passed away and no one rang me back. I was near crying to them this woman is dying from cancer, and she had this story, and no one wanted to bloody listen.

It just baffles me. She even took Bob Black to the spot where the car was parked on the road. He just made fun of her, and he goes to her, 'Are you sure you never killed them?'

WHAT? And I'm thinking I could say a lot more, but I am pissed off that no one wanted to hear my mother's story and now she is dead.

I said, 'I want you to say it if you can please whatever you know because this is going to be very important.'

Yeah, well, Mum said it was a blue Valiant that they had on the road that they took the girls with, and it was a four door. I got some paperwork here. She said the time they got into Charters Towers; it was about September or October because she said there was Christmas decorations in the shops, and no one wanted to listen to it.

They said Mum said something about the tavern or something, some shit, and I don't know but Mum said the tavern was built or renovated in '72, but my grandfather wouldn't let them come to town every six months or four months if you were lucky.

The fellow at the Pentland that night, one of them or a couple of them were singing in a band, a live band was there. You could probably trace it back – I don't know if you can't trace it back, but my grandmother cashed the cheque at that bar that night and I wrote down here what she said. They travelled with this. I tell you this: Mum said there was a fellow called Richard (Cowboy), a Walter. Cowboy was driving the car that night parked on the road.

This John that was with them – this John or Richard or whatever this name was(Cowboy) – he travelled with them on the truck to Pentland with these two girls and he had a scratch on his face the next day. Mum went to the Hairdressers in Charters Towers, and it was Mrs Noonan. Everyone knows Mrs Noonan.'

I said, 'Did your mother contact Crime Stoppers herself at any time?'

She replied, *'No, she used to get me to contact them, and I think they rang back once. Mum spoke to them, but it was years ago, and they sent this woman around to 13 Miner Street – that's where we were living at the time. Her husband was in her car, and he sat in the car all the time and she took down these notes. She told my mother she was an author, but I had seen her in the Woman's Weekly magazine as a psychic reader or something. She did not want to listen to what my mum said. My mum got cranky with her. One part, she said you are just putting words in my mouth. The psychic got the shits and said my mother would not know but that this other girl was still alive, and Mum said, 'She is not alive.'*

So, Mum got up, walked inside, had a cry and said, 'No one wants to listen.'

I said to my mum, 'Just forget about it.'

I said, 'Do you know if this Bob Black was accompanied by this woman whenever he interviewed your mother?'

'No, but he sent her around to our place.'

I said, 'Aw, did he? If I told you the name of this woman, would you know it? Do you think you would know it?'

She replied, 'Yes.'

I said, 'Ann.'

She replied, 'Yes, that's her.'

I said, 'And she was in Charters Towers investigating this matter, saying she was writing a book or something. Is that it?'

She replied, 'Yeah, writing a book. She said she was an author.'

I said, 'Did it happen in Charters Towers or Townsville?'

She said, 'Charters Towers. Yes, 13 Miner Street. She pulled up in this white little car with her husband or partner sitting in the driver's seat because I can remember it as plain as yesterday.'

I remember the shit they threw at my mother and made her seem like she was a simple case. I'm a bit angry to think no one would listen, you know, and my mother's gone.

She cried. I said, 'That's okay.' She continued.

It would be even better now; my mum could tell you word for word what happened. I am just going on what I wrote down when she was in hospital. I'm pissed off at that 'Bob Black'. All he thought about was my mother's (deleted as does not refer to this case) and stuff like that. Because one of my brothers had been in trouble with the police, he looked upon my mother as if she was a liar or something. But how could a woman say this over and over for decades, you know? I just don't understand. And even on her deathbed, she still had her brain. She was still there, and she could tell you word for word. She cried and said she would take it to her grave. I rang Crime Stoppers because I seen it on T V not long ago and I told them they need to get someone down here to talk to her before she passes away. No one ever listened. No one gave a shit.

My mum took me to the spot she seen the car on the road and where they buried the girl. My mum reckons they buried that girl not at Sensible Creek but up the road where the car was parked across the road.

I said, 'The body was found under Sensible Creek Bridge.'
She said, 'Yes, one body was, and the other girl is up the road.'
I said, 'Would you be able to point out that particular part of the road?'
She said, 'Yep, I sure can. I sure can. I'd be able to take you straight there.'
I said, 'Well, it won't be me because I am not in the police force any longer. I retired many years ago and I am involved in this through your uncle Vince. When did your mother first become aware that a body had been discovered? Do you know?'

My mum was married to my dad when they found the body – or she was with my dad, I think. I can't remember. My dad came home and said they found it. He was working at the meatworks – at Pentland Meatworks. That's another thing; my dad said he worked with some of the fellows who were at the pub that night. My mum described it to him, but he said he knew that fellow, but my dad got head injuries because this is a shit situation because my grandmother is dead. She died in March.

My dad got head injuries so there are only certain things he can remember and the woman that knew everything about everything is dead.

I said, 'What I am getting at... this body, one of the girls, was found in November 1972. What I am trying to get at is when did your mother first become aware that a body had been found? How long after that?'
She replied, 'Probably a couple of months or something or a month.'

I said, 'What did your mum do then about it, or did she do anything?'

She replied, 'No, my grandparents told her to shut up because apparently you don't get involved in that stuff. My mother said that years later when she had us kids and they went to the rodeo, the Charters Towers Rodeo, I think I was born but she said she had my brother Daniel and my brother Colin and she said she ran face to face into one of them and his name was Walter, yes, at the rodeo in Charters Towers.'

I said, 'Well, your story varies a little bit from what your father said but he got bashed over the head or something, didn't he?'

She said, 'No.'

I said, 'Didn't your father have some head injuries at some stage?'

She replied, 'Yes, my dad got hit over the head with something just before my mum had my brother Colin in '78, I think it was.'

I said, 'Are there other members of the family who have heard this story?'

She replied, 'Yes, all my mother's brothers are still alive.'

I said, 'And you said your uncle discovered this bloke in the bushes at Wando Vale. What was your uncle's name?'

She replied, 'Dennis Madigan.'

I said, 'Is he the one they call Mad Dog?'

She said, 'Yes, that's him.'

'Funny thing that.'

'He was only a kid back then.'

I said, are you saying that where this car was parked was not at Sensible Creek?'

She said, 'Not at Sensible Creek. Mum's been telling them for years it wasn't at Sensible Creek. It was down the road a couple of kilometers.'

'Before or after Sensible Creek?'

'After, going to Charters Towers, just one bend it was, just coming off the bend, you come around the bend and on a straight stretch and she seen the car. I can take you to the spot today where she took that stupid Bob Black, and they made fun of her.' (Next few words deleted as not related to the case.)

I said, 'Who was with Bob Black then?'

'Some other fellows are now. I can't remember – Igmon or something. I can't remember.'

I said, 'Was he in uniform or plain clothes?'

After her answer, I said, 'Have you ever spoken to Inspector Smith?'

'Not that I know of.'

'What I am doing, I am putting this together and I am writing again. I have sent some letters to the Commissioner of Police and this Inspector Smith. We have got a reply, and I have given your father a copy. I have also given a copy of the reply to Vince and what I must do now is put this together and send it again to the Commissioner of Police and try to see if they will reverse their thinking. They are convinced that all that has been done is all that could be done has been done but I am not. Now I will have to get back to you, Paula.'

She said, 'That's alright.'

'If you think of anything, you have got my mobile number. If you think of anything you could have told me, write it down and send me a letter or something. It would be better if you rang, I suppose.'

Paula said, 'Mum said the fellows in the car… there was one that had long hair, and he didn't look at her. He looked straight ahead.'

I said, 'When was that?'

She replied, 'When she came out of the hairdressers on the Saturday.'

I said, 'Were they the same fellows who were at the Pentland Hotel?'

'Yes.'

I said, 'Were any of those chaps in the band, Was there a band playing there, did she say?'

She said, 'Yes, she said something about a band playing and that they were in a band. I don't know if one was singing in a band, or they were all singing in a band.'

I said, 'Have you heard of a chap called John Fox at Charters Towers being involved?'

'Aw no, not that I know of.'

'But you do know about this Ted West?'

'Yes.'

'Do you know where he is now?'

'He's in Charters Towers.'

'What does he do there?'

'I don't know. I think he's in the mines.'

'Do you know of any girl who was singing in the band?'

She said, 'Pam List.'

I said, 'Pam West.'

'Pam List.'

'Pam List?'

She said, 'Yes.'

I said, 'The name Pam Rogers has been mentioned. Do you know anything about that?'

She said, 'My mum said that when she got married, like not long after this incident, this Pam List, or Pammy Rogers or whatever her name was, was making Mums bridesmaid dresses. She had to go around to see this Pam List with my dad's sister Irene Roth. Pam List had one of these fellows in the house with her that was on the creek that was at Pentland, I mean, and his name was Walter. But this Pam denied this to Bob Black and Mum said he was fucking with her. She said she could identify the bloke if someone showed her photos. She could identify the whole lot of them but Bob Black never did it.'

She continued, 'He reckons, aw Mel, blah blah, you've had all these kids, and you wouldn't remember. He was saying all this crap to her – making out she was a mental case, in other words.' (There was further discussion which is not included now as it may identify Bob Black to the public.)

I said, 'Do you know of an ex-policeman there called [redacted]?'

She said, 'Yes. I don't know him, but I have seen him and heard of him.'

I said, 'You don't know if he is involved in this in any way?'

She said, 'Not that I know of. No one ever mentioned him.'

I said, 'Right, I think we better leave it there because there is quite a difference between what your father said and what you have said. Basically, it is all the same but little things are different, you know. Your father is saying that they were members of the band – they went in the band's car, they left Pentland in the band's car. You're not so sure about that.'

She said, 'Actually, I think my mum said that they were loading the car up with the band's stuff. That's it – you're right'— she got excited— 'because Ted West came up to the table and said that their ride will be ready. They were just loading all the gear in the car – that's it. Mum said they were in a band. I didn't know – I hadn't remembered that that is what she said. I'm sure she said they were in a band and that Ted West worked at the Pentland Pub and he said your ride will be ready soon and they were members of the band.'

I said, 'Ok, we'll just leave it at that, Paula.'

She said, 'And if my mum was here, she would tell you the whole story. I think it's just too late, you know.'

I said, 'They say it's never too late.'

'And I can take you to the exact spot on the road where my mother said she seen that car. I will never forget that spot because it was eerie to me.'

I said, 'I hope somebody will follow this up. I'm doing what I can. I am trying hard and I'm making a fool of myself with the police, but I don't think it can be let go.'

She said, 'Anyway, I am going to stick to my word because I remember what my mum said and I believed her.'

I said, 'Did she see a picture of the two girls?'

She said, 'Oh, yes, definitely.'

I said, 'Did your mother see these two girls on TV?'

'She saw them years ago when the story came on the TV and before she went to the police. It was me that convinced her to go and talk to someone because it even made her crazy like she was frightened. She thought they were coming after her. I'll tell you the funniest thing that happened.'

I said, 'Yes.'

She said, 'We were at 5 Aland Street, and I was on the veranda with my mother. This car – like an old Ford, you know the one with the seats straight across in the front? – drove slowly past our house and went down to the end of the street and turned around, which is only a house away. It turned around into the gutter and came back up the street on our side and fired two shots into our house. I reckon you would find that bullet in the wood today.'

I said, 'Who do you think they were?'

She said, 'Fired two shots at my mother.'

I said, 'Did they see your mother at the house?'

She said, 'Yes, they seen where my mother was, and they fired at her. It hit the window and went through the old louvre; you know those windows where you pull out and put them back in?'

I said, 'And when was that – when did this happen?'

She said, 'Must have been in the eighties. Eighty-seven, eighty-six.'

I said, 'Did she report the shots being fired to the police?'

'She reported. You know what my dad said? It was probably

a rock or something. The cops just laughed and walked away. My mum and dad got into a big fight, and she called him all the so-and-sos, mental case bastard and everything. I was there that night, and I remember it like yesterday. The fellow who was in the passenger seat, he had blond hair, short blond hair.'

I said, 'Did she know who he was?'

She said, 'She reckons it was a Milat. She said that he was the Milats out at Pentland and it was Milat that killed the girls.'

I said, 'How did she establish that, Is she saying this John or Richard was Milat?'

She said, 'Looking back, she did not know them. She said Richard or John was Milat and she said there was a good-looking fellow in the car, and he was looking at her and he kept smiling at her.'

I said, 'When was this?'

She said, 'When she came out of the hairdressers.'

I said, 'Did she ever see a photo of Ivan Milat?'

She replied, 'No, she saw an old photo of him on the TV when he murdered all of them people, but she said she would like to see a photo of him when he was younger. He's still got the same face shape, but he has got a beard or mustache or whatever.'

I said, 'Alright, Paula. I think you will be hearing some more later.'

She said, 'Okay then.'

I said, 'Thanks very much.'

Although some of what Pala said is repetitious to this work, they are her words and need repeating for authenticity.

CHAPTER EIGHT

Following my letter of 5th October 2014, I wrote again to Commissioner Stewart on 20th October 2014. In this letter, as I said in chapter six, I went more deeply into the letter from Inspector 'Peter Smith'.

I began by saying that I felt very uncomfortable having to write to him again on these crimes, but I do not see that I have much alternative as I seemed to be at odds with the Homicide Cold Case Squad. I told him that on 16th October 2014, I had forwarded the underneath email to Inspector Smith to which there had been no response.

Dear Inspector,

I have established that the White Horse Tavern in Charters Towers was never pulled down completely, but work was done in sections from late 1971 and the licensee never lost a day's trading. The tavern was reopened on 17th May 1972 officially by the Local Member of Parliament Mr Lonergon on 17th May 1972. This is consistent with what Paula Whyte has said – that her mother went to the White Horse Tavern after leaving the hairdressers where her mother, Mrs Madigan, was at the time. I purposely did not question Paula Whyte about Black's report of Mearle being there three weeks after the tavern was pulled down, which, on the face of it, is a bit strange now.

I continued to Stewart that Inspector Smith and his men seem to be relying on Officer Black's reporting that Mearle Whyte said the event at Pentland happened three weeks after the White Horse Tavern was pulled down, which begun in November 1971. He then went on to say that the missing girls did not leave the south until July 1972 and consequently, these girls met by Mearle Whyte could not be the same girls.

When I interviewed Paula Whyte and John Whyte over the telephone and recorded their words, I let them speak almost uninterrupted and with little input from me so that I could not be accused of influencing their stories.

In the recordings I sent you recently – and you have to be quick to catch it – but both Paula and John Whyte say that the event at Pentland occurred in the WINTERTIME. This is consistent with August 1972, which is the most likely month in which the girls were slain. Most certainly not in the summer months of November and December relied on by the Homicide Squad. This, to me, is a very telling part of the interviews with me.

In Paula's interview with me, she said that her mother went to Pam List's place with her soon-to-be sister-in-law Irene ROSS (should be Roth) who now lives in Darwin and that one of the suspects, Walter, was there with her, whom she denied knowledge to Officer Black. Perhaps this Irene Ross could corroborate Mearle on this point.

There is also the placing of the dead bush turkeys near the decaying body of the girl Bartram to allay any interest from anybody smelling her body. This points further to a local, or locals being involved.

I do not want my police force with whom I spent nearly twenty-

five years of my life including Cadet service embarrassed about this investigation, but any reasonable person must realise that this is an unenviable position for the force and sooner or later, the story will leak out. Realistically, how many pairs of girls would you have hitch-hiking on the Flinders Highway in 1972?

Yours faithfully,
M. J. Gurn

As I write in 2022, I have concluded that the girls were probably murdered on Friday 7th July 1972. This date would therefore be about seven weeks after the White Horse Tavern reopened on 17th May 1972, which is very consistent with Mearle Whyte guessing that she met the girls at the Pentland Hotel about three weeks after the tavern reopened when you consider she was recalling events thirty years later.

This date of the girls being at the Pentland Hotel would be established if police had helped me to establish the date Betty Madigan cashed the cheque at the bar in the Pentland Hotel with this Ted West by assisting me with inquiries from Westpac Bank. This reluctance to pursue anything that would prove or disprove my investigations shows a complete disinterest in accepting that their stance that the girls were never at the Pentland Hotel is wrong.

In 2014, I spoke to another of my old team of detectives, the former Commissioner of Police Bob Atkinson, who had a private conversation with Deputy Commissioner Ross Barnett. I received word that the matter would be investigated after the G20 meetings in Brisbane in 2015. I had previously written to Deputy Commissioner Barnett myself.

Deputy Commissioner Ross Barnett wrote to me on 18th November 2014 saying that my correspondence had been forwarded to Assistant Commissioner Gayle Hogan of Queensland Police Service, State Crime Command for evaluation by the Homicide Group, Cold Case Investigation Unit.

In a letter dated 8th January 2015, Assistant Commissioner Hogan wrote to me as follows:

Dear Mr Gurn,

I acknowledge receipt of your letter to Deputy Commissioner Barnett dated 6th January 2015 regarding the cold case investigation of the murders of Robin Bartram and Anita Cunningham. I also confirm receipt of your letters dated 20 May 2014 and 26 June 2014, which have recently been responded to by Inspector Smith of the Homicide Cold Case Unit.

The original investigation was reviewed by Police Officer Black and is now being reviewed by the Homicide Cold Case Unit.

The Homicide Cold Case Unit has investigated information provided by Mearle Whyte, prior to her passing in June 2014. The outcomes of these investigations have been provided to you in the response by Inspector Smith.

As part of this investigation and review into this matter, investigators intend to speak with the persons you nominated in Charters Towers and Pentland. It is anticipated this should be completed within six (6) months. ***If this review fails to identify further lines of inquiry, the investigation will remain an open Cold Case.***

If you have any further questions about this matter, please contact Inspector Smith on [redacted].

Yours sincerely,
Gayle Hogan
Assistant Commissioner
State Crime Command

On 5th February 2015, I wrote to Assistant Commissioner Gayle Hogan as follows:

In response to your letter of 8th January, this year and received by me on 12th January 2015, instead of taking your advice to telephone Inspector Smith I sent him the underneath email.

In response to Assistant Commissioner Hogan's letter to me of 8th instant and received 12th in which she suggested I ring you with any further questions, I found it quite staggering that she indicates it may take six further months, and this is in addition to the eight months from when I first raised the Bartram-Cunningham crimes with you. To wrap this information up, I have chosen to email you instead.

As someone who had been associated with 1219 arrests from 1957 to 1965 – I kept no totals after that for the next ten years – as a detective, I have a pretty good idea of how investigations progress and what time is involved.

The obtaining of photos of Richard and Walter Milat from when they were in their twenties, if available from NSW or Victoria and showing John Whyte and Irene Ross is straight forward, as is obtaining the notes made by Paula Whyte at the death bed of her mother.

Establishing whether Ann Villiers had entered an arrangement with Officer Black as to reward money offered should not be a problem.

Comparison of bullets from the head of Robin Bartram and from the house veranda in Charters Towers, if found, with bullets from firearms of the Milat family and from victims – especially Caroline Clarke in NSW, who was shot in the head – is also straight forward.

Establishing if Anita Cunningham wore bangles should be easy.

Who had a blue Valiant in the Charters Towers area in 1972 should be simple. Verifying the cheque cashed at the Pentland Hotel would be helpful but not essential.

Questioning and putting together data to put to suspects should wait until after these matters are resolved.

Having said all that and not wishing to jeopardise the prospect of an arrest, I will go along with the Department for now.

Even if some of Mearle Whyte's story falls in some area, there is one thing that is hard to deny and of which I believe is a 99% certainty and that is that she did meet the murdered girls at the Pentland Hotel in the winter of 1972. This is supported by telling her brothers who are still alive what she knew.

And that basically is what REALLY counts here. After forty-two years, there are bound to be inconsistencies somewhere.

I am forwarding this letter to you so that it is on the official record. It is pretty obvious that the investigators are having trouble believing my information otherwise there would been some developments.

Getting back to Mearle Whyte's information to Officer Black, it is curious that nowhere have I heard that he interviewed Betty Madigan, Mearle's mother, as to what she had to say about the events at Pentland in the winter of 1972. Wouldn't the first thing most police would do is interview Betty Madigan for her version to see if she corroborated Mearle's? Black may have interviewed her, but the family do not know that this happened as far as I know. Betty Madigan died in March 2014.

I feel that eventually the whole scenario may have to come out of a Coronial inquiry or a Star Chamber hearing of the CMC, but as I said, I will not jeopardise a possible arrest at this stage before taking the matter further.

Yours sincerely,
M. J. Gurn.

CHAPTER NINE

On 18th January 2015, I telephoned Irene Roth who is a sister of John Whyte who lives in Darwin. She confirmed that she had gone with Mearle Whyte to Pam List's house in Charters Towers when Mearle made inquiries about her bridesmaid dresses being made by Pam (then known as Pam Barry). She confirmed that Walter (Wally) Barry was there at List's place and that not long after this, Pam had broken up with Wally Barry. (This phone call led to me finding out Wally's surname as Barry.) Irene Roth has now in 2023 returned to Queensland to live.

And so, it goes on with me trying to get action from the police and receiving no word of any such action, so I wrote to the commissioner on 21st March 2015. I told him that once again I was forced to write to him and to be further regarded, I suspected, as a pest, but I wished to assure him that if his Inspector Smith had worked with me on this matter, it would not have been necessary to write additional letters to the Department.

I told the commissioner that because my phone call to Inspector Smith on 17th February was not returned and despite being told he would be emailed to call me back, I would not have had to contact Channel Seven to try to be put in touch with David Cunningham and other family members who are relatives of the deceased girls with a view to ascertaining if Anita Cunningham was in the habit of playing with bangles on her arms and to advise them of my investigations with a view to making an application to the state coroner for a Coronial Inquiry into these crimes.

I told the commissioner that I had interviewed Irene Roth, previously named Ross by me.

I said that every aspect of this man's life needed examining with a view to identifying possible accomplices.

I told the commissioner that Mearle Whyte had told her daughter that this Walter or Wally was one of the men who accosted her outside the hairdresser's shop in Charters Towers. She also said this man was one of the murderers and most probably the Walter who she ran into at the rodeo in Charters Towers in later years. Roth, however, believed that List would not have concealed information on the murders all these years knowing the type of woman she is but in view of this development one could be forgiven for thinking otherwise. I said that there was also the distinct possibility that she and other lives were threatened should they ever go to the police.

This information is confirmation of that part of Mearle's story.

I understood that Inspector Smith wanted HARD EVIDENCE to act on.

I said that in my experience, hard evidence is obtained by digging into an investigation and creating the hard evidence. It does not happen by waiting for it to fall into your lap. In this case the solving these murders is being handed to the detectives on a plate (to use a very old C.I.B saying), so to speak.

I felt that a positive result could be achieved if handled by Detectives experienced in investigating serious crime, particularly with the immunity from prosecution being available to be offered to some persons. The first step was believing that Mearle Whyte met these girls at the Pentland Hotel in the winter of 1972 and of that I was fully convinced.

(My frustration with the inactivity of police boiled over I am afraid here and I later apologised for those remarks about experienced detectives etc.)

I said that I had email advice from the Office of the State Coroner and the State Archives that there was no record of an inquest ever having been conducted into these crimes.

I said I had reliable information that no person using the name Milat was ever known in Pentland.

I told the commissioner that I had been working on these murders for almost twelve months and a lot of the hard work had been done for the Department. I could only hope that arrests were imminent. I said that if this matter had been handled differently in 2003 with basic investigative procedures adopted when Mearle is said to have first contacted police with a detailed statement obtained from her and her mother when interviewed to corroborate Mearle, these offenders would most likely have been arrested twelve months ago.

CHAPTER TEN

On 10th March 2015, I telephoned a man I knew at Channel Seven in Brisbane who arranged with his Sydney office to contact me.

On the same day – 10th March 2015 – Alex Cullen contacted me from Channel Seven in Sydney about these murders.

On 16th March 2015, I had a long-recorded phone call with Thea Dikeos, a producer of Channel Seven, Sydney. She said that she and a crew would interview me on 23rd March 2015 at my home in Queensland. During this interview, she told me that one of Ivan Milat's nicknames was 'Cowboy'.

Alex Cullen arrived at my home on 21st March 2015 and spent most of the day with me talking about the murders and listening to the recorded conversations with John and Paula Whyte. Cullen said that Inspector Smith had requested a month's grace from Channel Seven before they did anything on the story. He said this was why Thea Dikeos and crew were not with him.

On 24th April 2015, I received an email from Inspector Smith from Charters Towers; he had gone from Brisbane to investigate the information obtained from John and Paula Whyte in my recorded telephone conversations with these people, and presumably to interview the persons I had been told by Assistant Commissioner Hogan would be interviewed.

The email from Smith reads as follows and was sent at

8.22 p.m. – the highlighting of some words are my doing. This email from Smith becomes very important in highlighting the fact that he was not interested at all in establishing the truth of the recorded conversations I had had with John Whyte or his daughter Paula, which you have read. He makes no mention of interviewing the persons he was supposed to interview.

Dear Mr Gurn,

As previously advised, the Homicide Cold Case Investigation Unit has conducted a review of the matters raised by you in your numerous letters to the Commissioner of Police and emails to me since last year. This review includes me personally attending Charters Towers this week with members of the Cold Case Team and the local CIB and the interviewing of Mearle Whyte's former husband John Whyte and her daughter Paula Whyte.

I can advise that your primary contact Vince Whyte did not wish to be interviewed on advice to us from John Whyte. This was because 'Vince has no direct knowledge of the matter' and only knows what John has told him, which, in turn, is what Mearle has told John since 1984.

You can expect me to formally reply to your correspondence in the near future; *however, two matters have arisen during our visit to Charters Towers, and I have been personally requested to provide you with immediate advice that **I urge you to heed**. These are as follows:*

Paula Whyte wishes to have no further contact with you, does not want you to call her again on her telephone and requests you delete all contact details you have for her.

*Retired Officer Bob Black has requested I advise you **to immediately cease your derogatory and unfounded written comments** about his professionalism during his investigations into this matter as **he is considering legal advice regarding defamation**. This is especially pertinent when you consider neither* you nor any person you have interviewed have any direct or even reasonably inferred knowledge of the extent of the investigations undertaken by Black and his colleagues since the discovery of Robin Hoinville-Bartram's remains in 1972. I do have personal knowledge of the extent of investigations, and I can advise your criticisms of Black, and the other highly noted investigators are totally unfounded.

I would also appreciate you delete my email address as I will no longer communicate with you expect in formal response to your previous correspondence.

I have personally advised Alex Cullen of Channel 7 of the outcome of our further review. I can also advise that both John and Paula Whyte have never believed any assertion that Ivan Milat was at Pentland or that Mearle had ever met or seen him.

Regards,
Inspector Smith

I replied as follows:
Fri 24/04/2015 10:23 AM

Thank you for your email, Inspector.

Strangely, John Whyte told me yesterday he has had no contact from the police.

It looks like Paula and John have left me high and dry but luckily, I have the recorded interviews with them to back up my letters. As for Bob Black, nothing I have written has been on the public record and I find it disturbing that he has apparently had access to my correspondence to the police or has been informed in some detail of it despite him being no longer a member of the police force.

Anything I have said or done has been in the public interest based on the information given to me and my sense of trying to see a possible injustice corrected. As for Vince Whyte, I always told *you that anything he has said to me was second-hand from his brother John.*

It is my hope that a full Coronial Inquiry will be held where everybody involved will get their chance to support their actions and views.

Your email address is being deleted from my records and I will not be contacting Paula Whyte again.

Everything she has said in the interview was from her own mouth and not prompted by me so she will have great difficulty retreating from her interview and her frustration of receiving no help from the police despite repeated pleas to Crime Stoppers and her disparaging remarks about the way Bob Black carried out his duties and her disturbing allegations about his interest in Mearle Whyte's sex life.

In all investigations, things are ruled out and others ruled in as you go along and my suggesting Ivan Milat could be involved is just another line of inquiry that should be explored, having in mind his modus operandi and the fact that Paula Whyte specifically mentioned the Milats in her interview with me and that one of the men had a similar face shape of Ivan Milat as told to her by her mother. I do not think this is an unreasonable suggestion.

Regards,
Mick Gurn

I must admit that this email from Inspector Smith sat me back on my heels a bit. I thought the police seemed pretty sure of themselves here to be sending me an email like that. He was ordering me not to contact Paula again and lecturing me about my criticism of Black. After giving this more thought, I considered what could the police stance be to be so sure of themselves. I could not come up with anything other than the reports of former Police Officer Bob Black to superiors in which he had apparently dismissed Mearle Whyte's information as false, but the manner of Black's questioning was such as stated by John and Paula to be very distasteful to say the least.

I could not see how the police had any evidence other than Black's reports to discredit Mearle Whyte's story. Nowhere did John Whyte say that Black ever obtained any information from him about Mearle's story and he did **not** interview him at all. Black most probably had interviewed some persons Mearle had mentioned to him and they had or must have denied any involvement. They had absolutely no one to discredit Mearle's story or to say she was lying and making the story up.

The persons interviewed by Black and the questions he asked of them would have to be gone into at an inquiry or inquest to see if their positions had changed with available new evidence that could be presented to them following the work I had done.

Not having access to the police reports by Black, I concluded that he had interviewed Mearle Whyte but had not taken a detailed written and signed statement from her or her mother Betty Madigan, which is the most basic standard police practice in these circumstances.

Black must have interviewed some other people, possibly Pam Barry (List), Wally Barry and Ted West, who had all denied involvement. Now we must remember that Black refused to believe the information from Mearle Whyte in 2003 and reported as such. When she came forward again in 2005 as stated by Peter Smith, he had to interview her again and report his findings, which, if he then reported he believed her then his previous reports of disbelieving her, would look bad for his investigating ability.

The family know nothing of Black interviewing Brian Patrick Madigan (Mearle's father) who could have verified that he had given his wife a cheque to cover the purchase of groceries and other items in Charters Towers. Brian was Betty's husband. He did not interview Mearle's three brothers, Mick, Pat and Dennis who all have some knowledge in varying degrees of Mearle and Betty meeting the girls at the Pentland Hotel.

Not interviewing Mearle's brother Mick Madigan or having him interviewed by other police is especially pertinent as Mearle used to attend rodeos and other horse sports with him, whom she was especially close with. Dennis Madigan assures me that she and his mother did meet these murdered girls at the Pentland Hotel and knows more about the whole circumstances.

With John and Mearle's six children and her three brothers, this makes ten adults who can in some way support Mearle's story of meeting the murdered girls plus the cheque cashed at the Pentland Hotel. This transaction was more provable in 2003 than it is today, on more than one occasion, I asked the police to ascertain the truth about this transaction and assist me to get this information from the banks involved without success which indicates a complete lack of desire to gain any information that would support Mearle's story of meeting the murdered girls and solving these cases.

In my experience, it is easy to get the answers you want from persons who do not want to be involved by asking questions in such a way that you will get these answers. An example of this strategy is cleverly portrayed in the great British comedy television series *Yes Minister* by Humphrey Appleby on several occasions.

Of course, it later became obvious that Mearle was so upset and humiliated by Black's questioning of her about her story that she gave him and any police accompanying him some false information in an attempt, unwisely, to make fools out of them, such as saying the events had taken place at the Cape River Crossing and changing it to Sensible Creek and probably other information to try to fool them, which was very foolish of her and has caused this unholy mess that is this case today.

I can also understand why she wanted to tell the truth of

meeting the murdered girls to clear her conscience before she died, which she knew was going to happen to her. People releasing their minds shortly before death of which they are fully aware is known in legal circles as a Dying Declaration – when the person realises, they have no chance of avoiding death, but it mostly refers to some other event and not their own death. So, the circumstances are not all that removed one from the other.

I had concluded that the email from Smith was no more than a gigantic bluff. But I had to wait three years until April 2018 for proof of this bluff. The truth of Smith's visit to Charters Towers in April 2015 came out; his behaviour there did not involve investigating. The only purpose he was supposed to be going to Charters Towers for was to investigate the truth of my recorded telephone interviews with John and Paula Whyte and to interview the persons I had been told would be interviewed in the letter from Assistant Commissioner Gayle Hogan dated 8th January 2015.

After this email from Smith, there was a certain coldness from Cullen of Channel Seven towards me and he did not respond to further emails from me after he told me he was going to interview Paula, presumably to see what she had to say. Channel Seven lost all interest in the case because of what Smith told Cullen and what Cullen must have reported to his superiors in Channel Seven in Sydney.

Here was a missed opportunity for Channel Seven to get in on the ground floor of the most mishandled and bungled double murder investigation in the history of the state, in my opinion. You can draw your own conclusions about a police force cover up but, in my opinion, it would have been the easiest case to solve if properly investigated when Mearle first came forward in 2003.

In my reply to Inspector Smith, I cleared up where I mentioned John Whyte said he had not heard from the police.

The explanation for this is that John misunderstood what I had asked him.

On Saturday night, 25th April 2015, Vince Whyte rang me with further information he had received from his brother John to say that the car the girls had left the Pentland Hotel in had come into the Mexican Caravan Park about 1.30 in the morning, but the girls were not with the men.

The next night, Sunday, 26th April 2015, Vince rang me to say he had further questioned his brother John and was informed that the girls had arranged to stay with Mearle and Betty at the Mexican Caravan Park but when the car arrived, the girls were not with them. He said Mearle had arranged with the girls that she would drive them to Townsville the next day, but they were nowhere to be seen.

John also told Vince that the car the girls had left the Pentland Hotel in was without doubt a Falcon and not a Valiant and that the car was owned by Wally Barry. He said he had seen the car parked at Pam List's place when he, Mearle and Irene (his sister) went there about her making Mearle's bridal gown and bridesmaid dresses and that Wally Barry was living in the house then with Pam.

John said to Vince that he did not tell Inspector Smith any of this when Smith interviewed him because he did not seem to want to listen to anything he had to say. I asked Vince why John had not told me all this when I interviewed him. He said if I had questioned John, all this would have come out.

You will remember that I said when I took the recorded interviews with John on 2nd October 2014 and Paula on 4th October 2014, I just let them talk without me contributing much to the conversations because I did not want it said that I was putting words in their mouths.

CHAPTER ELEVEN

At 11.20 a.m. on Tuesday, 26th May 2015, I phoned Matt Condon at the *Courier Mail Brisbane,* who is a crime reporter and journalist. He said he was interested and would come to my home on the Darling Downs and interview me about my Pentland murder investigations.

On 1st June 2015, Matt Condon texted me that he was still keen to do a story on the murders, but he had been given an assignment.

A couple of days later, I rang Condon. He said he would ring me back, but he never did. He had obviously been in touch with police and had no further interest in hearing from me.

I was not getting anywhere with the press in getting any help with getting the truth out about the murders, so I decided to apply to the coroner for an inquest as a means of getting those involved into the witness stand being questioned on oath as to their knowledge of the murders. On the 29$^{th\,of}$ June 2015, I posted my application to the coroner for an inquest.

My application to the coroner for an inquest under Section 30 of the Coroner's Act, dated 29th June 2015, can be read as Appendix Number One.

In a letter dated 3rd June 2016, David Cunningham, brother of Anita Cunningham, wrote to the attorney general supporting my application to her for an inquest.

This letter can be read as Appendix Number Two.

Four months after applying to the coroner for an inquest, I received a reply from him on 30th October 2015, to the effect that he had no power to order an inquest as the murders had been committed prior to 1st December 2003. He said that only the attorney general had the power to order an inquest.

I immediately applied to the attorney general, Yvette D'Ath for an inquest using the same application I made to the coroner, which he forwarded under the Attorney General's reference number 5711194/1,3064609.

Before going on with the result of my application to the Attorney General I will take the opportunity to mention some matters concerning my Police career which help to establish my credentials to question Police handling of these cases

I said earlier in this book that I would include some of the cases I have been involved with during my service in the Queensland police force as it was then known. These cases will form part of the appendix section of this book.

However, I will make short mention next of one case of robbery, followed by my time at an in-service school for police followed by the swearing in of the first policewomen in the Queensland police force as it was known followed by the difficulties police in my time had with presenting evidence in court cases. Portions of these mentions support my claims that I have the necessary experience to claim that these murders have not been handled correctly by police up to now.

I arrested a couple of men for attempted robbery of a paymaster when he arrived from his bank in front of his employer's building with a sum of money to make up the weekly pay packet for employees.

Nearly every person in Australia was paid weekly with cash in a small pay packet in the 1960s. One of the offenders I arrested was the brother of one of my fellow detectives at the Valley C.I.

Branch. These offenders pleaded guilty in the Magistrates Court and were committed for sentence to a higher court. When they appeared for sentence before the judge, they also pleaded guilty to a few breaking and entering offences, which were preferred by a high-flying detective whose photograph and some story about him appeared regularly in the press. He cultivated crime reporters and received good newspaper coverage with a view, no doubt, to further his ambitions in the force. The offenders were sentenced to about seven years jail from memory on the charge I preferred against them.

When the papers reported the case, the story read as though this other detective was responsible for the arrest on the robbery charge and my name was never mentioned. This caused quite a lot of hilarity and jokes in my office. One wag typed up a false memo to me allegedly from Inspector Norm Bauer who oversaw the C.I. Branch, calling on me to report as to whether I had anything to do with the arrests. In those days, we called this sort of thing 'going in off someone'. This other detective was successful in his career and rose to be Commissioner of Police but unfortunately, it all ended very badly for him.

When I was a detective sergeant at Sandgate C.I. Branch in 1971, I was drafted to attend the In-Service Training College for Police at Chelmer in Brisbane. This was a live-in course for eighteen days. The intake was the 23rd in the series. The class I was in had about twenty-odd police, mostly uniform, from around the state. I don't think I knew any of them personally before then, so I was stunned and surprised on the first day to find that in my absence I was voted President of the Intake.

I had to give lectures along with other police and visiting lecturers to the college. I recall two of the subjects I gave a lecture on. One was the need for sworn in women in the police force. I stressed the need for these women instead of the few women we had attached to the C.I. Branch who we asked for their services when typing long reports and to accompany us when talking to complainant women and children, mostly about sexual cases. There were none of these ladies stationed outside Brisbane. In the country, you just made do as best you could.

On 31st March 1965, eight serving ladies took the Oath of Office and became fully sworn officers.

They were Elizabeth Boyle, Laura Frisch, Ailsa Warnick, Pat Ryan, Clair Conaty, Yvonne Weier, Judith Barrett and Olwen Doolan. The photograph by courtesy of Queensland Police Museum shows the women from the C.I. Branch being officially sworn in.

Another lecture I gave was how to make records of interview with suspects so they would be admissible in court. A trend had crept into the force of taking these records and putting questions to the offender at the end of the interview, which we were required to put to offenders in confessional statements from them such as 'Did you make this confession of your own free will?'

We were not allowed to ask questions of an offender in his written admission.

I argued that I would not do this as the typed interview might then be pleaded by a clever defence barrister that the interview was in the mind of the detective a confessional statement because these questions had been asked at the end of the document and therefore, this made the document inadmissible. It is ironic that this question of the admissibility of a record of interview I made was a talking point in the rape case of the sleeping woman I handled, which is outlined in the Appendix to this work.

As President, I had the right to invite a guest lecturer and so I invited a professor to the college to lecture the class on a subject that escapes me now but was the basis of a public dispute in newspapers between this professor and the then Commissioner of Police Ray Whitrod. Whitrod was pretty upset with me about inviting this man to lecture this class.

I disagreed with Whitrod on some of his changes to the police force, which were, to my mind, the type of changes that would come from someone who was more about the theory of police work rather than the practical application of doing it. In saying that, I believe Whitrod genuinely thought he was doing the best for the force.

Whitrod was a fair man and held no grudges on me; he even supported my application for the Police Act to be amended to allow police to own and race racehorses. This application was killed off by the then Premier Joh Bjelke-Petersen who was a known wowser with anything to do with gambling. I understand that the Act has been amended and police are now allowed to own and race gallopers, greyhounds and pacers, which include trotters.

Police Commissioner Terry Lewis was in power when I oversaw my own C.I. office in Brisbane in the early 1970s. He introduced the Police Arts and Science Course, which you had to pass to be eligible for commissioned rank. I was sworn in as a constable when I was nineteen years of age. Natural attrition of police due to retirements and death would leave me as the most senior man in the force and therefore a likely Commissioner of Police in my early fifties.

I bought the required books to do the course and attended at night at the technical college at Kangaroo Point for a few weeks. In my mind, I began to question the benefit to police of the course from the point of view that it had nothing to do with actual police work but seemed to be all about some form of lifting your educational standard. I asked a lecturer how the course helped me catch criminals or break down a safe blower and he could not answer me.

I never went back to the college and when I resigned in 1975, I told Commissioner Terry Lewis what I thought of his Police Arts and Science Course.

As a further history lesson for young police, I should tell you that in the 1950s and 60s police when giving evidence in trials in the Supreme and District Courts and committal hearings in the Magistrates Court about their arrest of an offender and supplying evidence on which to prove the charge they had made against the person accused gave their evidence solely on memory.

We prepared statements for the prosecutors, but we could not refer to those statements when giving evidence. We had to memorise five, ten or more pages of our statements, which was no mean feat when sometimes you might have a trial in the Supreme Court and a trial in the District Court to give evidence in, at the same sittings of these courts, plus a committal hearing in the Magistrates Court.

So, it was a case of who had the best memory really. If you were halfway through your evidence and you had a mental blank, it was very embarrassing, which is why when memorising statements you tried to fix on a date or something in your statement thar could jog your memory.

Of course, defence barristers sometimes gained an advantage

here when an officer forgot something in his evidence that would have helped to prove the guilt of a person. Sometimes prosecutors got around this hiccup by other means.

Quite a lot of accused persons have long criminal histories, and these cannot be disclosed by the prosecution to the jury, judge or magistrate. They appear for trial squeaky clean to all intents and purposes. When convicted, their criminal history is revealed by the prosecutor to the Judges who are tasked with sentencing the offenders.

Sometimes, jurors are startled when they hear the accused criminal history if they remain around the court to see what sentence the accused receives. You can guess my opinion of the value of this non-disclosure in our legal system.

As time went on over the years, we were then allowed to refer to notes taken at the time from our police notebooks. Then we were allowed to refer to our statements, then read our statements and then Records of Interviews came in, which made the whole evidence-giving task much easier. From memory, a senior detective named Don Braithwaite was mainly responsible for thinking up the concept of using Records of Interview of suspects.

Some police – especially uniform police who were not accustomed to giving evidence – shied off giving evidence in courts and were only too happy to hand over to detectives persons they caught for some offence. They then only had to give basic evidence in lots of cases and did not have to prepare the brief, which in some cases was quite involved and meant obtaining numerous statements for the brief for the prosecutors and took weeks to prepare.

A way some detectives acted when giving evidence was you gave an answer that you knew would ensure the questioning barrister would have to ask you the next question and then a similar reply that the barrister would then have to ask another question of you and this would then place you in the position of, if you gave the answer the jury would know the accused had a criminal history. So, the procedure was to tell the judge that if you answered Mr So-and-so's question, the accused case would be damaged. The judge would then warn the defence barrister that if he really wanted the answer, it could be detrimental to his client.

Sometimes the defence dropped the question and sometimes they took the risk. On other occasions, the judge ordered the jury to retire, and the trial proceeded in the absence of the jury. When the matter was cleaned up, the jury was brought back into the courtroom. The jury was always left to ponder what this was all about, but some brighter ones would catch on.

Another somewhat mischievous tactic adopted by one detective, not me, was to answer questions in cross examination of some barristers that he knew would inflame them and throw them off their attack.

There was one Brisbane barrister who was renowned for his tantrums in court when he got an answer he did not like. He would throw his arms up in the air and virtually scream out his indignation very loudly and go very red in the face to the amusement of all in court and in the precincts of the court. By the time he had settled down, he had often forgotten the question he had asked of the witness.

There was another incident in a court trial where the accused's barrister was giving the detective a very hard time, accusing the detective of assaulting his client to obtain a confession from him. He put various accusations to the detective who replied, 'No, I treated your client exactly the way I would treat you.' With that, the court erupted in laughter.

It is only with lengthy experience that you learn how to handle yourself in the witness box. There is no book of rules to follow. There will be mistakes made and learned from over the years. The golden rule, however, is to always tell the truth and you will come out of it okay.

CHAPTER TWELVE

Vince Whyte rang me and told me that he had killed time in a building in Charters Towers on 6th July 2015 and met a woman there who told him the building was the town's art centre. He said the woman's name was Barry, but he thought her name was spelt differently to Wally Barry. She said she knew Pam Barry (List) and that she thought Wally Barry had died in Mount Isa of cancer. (I later learnt from Pam List that Wally Barry had died of cancer in a Brisbane hospital.)

Time went on and I was unable to obtain information from Channel Seven on how to contact the relatives of the murdered girls, but I learned from Peter Cameron that Anita Cunningham's father Gerald Cunningham was a board member of the Victoria Racing Club. I contacted that body on 18th August 2015 and spoke to Judith Fitzmaurice who contacted David Cunningham and Anita's mother Eileen Cunningham. As a result of my contacting the VRC, David Cunningham contacted me by phone.

On 20th August 2015, I had a long talk with David Cunningham and his mother Eileen on the telephone and on speaker mode I played the recorded interviews I had had with John and Paula Whyte. I informed Anita Cunningham's brother and mother the results of all my investigations and months later, I asked David to write and send a letter to the attorney general supporting my application for an inquest. Unfortunately, neither David or his mother could recall if Anita wore bangles on her arms or not.

On 9th November 2015, I wrote to the Crime and Corruption Commission and lodged a complaint about the mishandling of the case by police.

On 18th November 2015, I received a phone call from a senior complaints officer that the CCC wanted a Statutory Declaration from me to support my complaint, which I immediately forwarded to them.

On 30th December 2015, I received a letter from the CCC that they were taking no action on my complaint of the mishandling of the case by police and that they were forwarding my complaint to the ethical standards branch of the Queensland police service.

On 5th January 2016, I received a reply from the attorney general that she would reply with an answer to my application.

On 13th January 2016, I posted a letter to the ethical standards command of the police service supporting my application to the Crime and Corruption Commission.

On the 16th of February 2016, I received a letter by post from Detective Inspector CS Herpich of the Ethical Standards Command which basically said they were taking no action on my complaint to the Crime and Corruption Commission, which had been referred to them by that commission.

A letter dated 10th May 2016 was received from the attorney general Yvette D'Ath as under.

Dear Mr Gurn,

Thank you for your letter dated 30 October 2015 requesting an inquest into the death of Ms Robin Jeanne Hoinville-Bartram and the suspected death of Ms Anita Cunningham. I apologise for the delay in responding.

I note your letter included a letter of support from Ms

Cunningham's brother, Mr David Cunningham. I have given careful consideration to your request.

In reaching my decision, I have considered the Coroner's Act 1958, which is the relevant legislation in Ms Hoinville-Bartram's case and the Coroner's Act 2003, which is relevant to Ms Cunningham's suspected death. I have considered whether it is in the public interest to hold an inquest into the death of Ms Hoinville-Bartram and the suspected death of Ms Cunningham.

In making my decision, I have noted that Ms Hoinville-Bartram's death is still the subject of an investigation by the Queensland Police Service (QPS).

I have also noted that your request relies on the recollections of a now-deceased person that have been provided second hand. The existence of cogent, reliable evidence or new evidence is a relevant factor in determining whether to direct the holding of an inquest. However, the information and evidence you have provided is not sufficiently cogent or reliable to persuade me to consider holding an inquest.

Therefore, after careful consideration of all of these issues, I have decided not to direct the State Coroner to hold an inquest into the death of Ms Hoinville-Bartram or the suspected death of Ms Cunningham at this time.

It is clear from your letter that you have spent a great deal of time and effort investigating the death of Ms Hoinville-Bartram and the disappearance of Ms Cunningham, and in raising these matters with the State Coroner and myself.

I thank you for bringing this matter to my attention and for your concern about the circumstances surrounding the fate of these two women.

Yours sincerely,
Yvette D'Ath MP
Attorney-General and Minister for Justice
Minister for Training and Skill

CHAPTER THIRTEEN

To see if any information could be obtained about the cheque transaction at the Pentland Hotel by Betty Madigan, I sent an email to Kareen Forster who is the daughter of the then Licensees of the Pentland Hotel in 1972 as follows:
Sent: Tuesday, May 24, 2016, 7:55 AM
To: Kareen Forster
Subject: Re: Pentland Murders

Dear Karenne and Geoff,
I think you will remember me from Pentland in 2003/4 when I was in the caravan park.
As you have probably read in the Sunday Mail from time to time, I have been investigating the murders of Robin Jeanne Hoinville-Bartram and Anita Cunningham at Pentland in 1972. The body of Robin was discovered under Sensible Creek Bridge in November 1972.
I will insert into this email the article that was shown in last Sunday's paper.
I understand that your parents, Mr and Mrs Pugh, operated the Pentland Hotel in July/August, 1972 and my inquiries reveal that the two girl hitchhikers travelled from Mount Isa with a man who they knew as Cowboy, which is one of the nicknames

of the notorious killer Ivan Milat, in a truck from Mount Isa to Hughenden and then in another truck to Pentland, which was as far as that truck was going.

Inside the hotel, they teamed up with Betty and Mearle Madigan (later married to John Whyte). Betty (the mother) cashed a cheque at the bar, which her husband Brian Patrick Madigan had given her to buy supplies for the family where they lived on Wando Vale Station.

Establishing particulars of this cheque is vital in establishing the date which the girls arrived at the hotel and because I believe your parents, Karenne, operated the hotel, I ask you if there is some way you could still have access to the old deposit banking books from your parents. Are they stored somewhere in an old shed or the like?

What bank did your parents deal with in 1972?

How did they deposit receipts from hotel takings? Did they wait to go to Charters Towers or was it possible to bank them at the Pentland Post Office?

When Robin's body was discovered, it must have generated an enormous amount of talk in Pentland and although I know you had left the hotel and married Geoff before 1972, you must have heard the talk and people must have connected the body to the girls who had landed at the Pentland Hotel and left with men, some of whom were from a band playing at the hotel for the entertainment of patrons.

What were the names of the band members who I believe came from Charters Towers?

I realise no one wants to get involved in court proceedings but eventually people must give evidence even if they don't have direct involvement. In your case, it will be about how the hotel operated and the bands etc. I will pursue inquiries up until an inquest is held or the murderers are charged.

I would very much appreciate your help in this matter and

anything however insignificant in your eyes may be something I can piece together with something else.

We must think of this in terms of 'What if the girls had been part of our family?'

Regards,
Mick Gurn

Karenne Forster's reply is as under:

Hi Mick,
Re: your letter about the murders of the 2 girls back in 1972. Both my parents are deceased, and they left no banking details etc. from the hotel. Mum went on to have several businesses from then and I have kept no records from any of them. It has nothing to do with not wanting to become involved but in 1972 I had a toddler and was having a new baby. I did not go out much and I can't remember anything at that time re the band, etc.

Sorry I couldn't be more helpful, but I hope you have success with your inquiries.

Regards,
Karenne Forster (nee Peut)

CHAPTER FOURTEEN

A case of attempted murder that I handled in Bundaberg can be read as Appendix Number 13.

On 3rd June 2016, I rang a hairdresser's shop in Charters Towers to learn that Betty Noonan, who had the shop when Mearle Whyte was there in July 1972, was in Eventide.

On 20th June 2016, I wrote a letter to the manager of Commonwealth Bank in Charters Towers asking that a search of records be made for the cheque transaction made at the Pentland Hotel by Betty Madigan drawn on her husband Brian Madigan's cheque account. (At that time, I was under the impression that the cheque was drawn on the Commonwealth Bank, but later information established that it was drawn on the Bank of New South Wales taken over by Westpac.)

On 3rd July 2016, I received a phone call from Dennis Madigan, who heard I was looking for him when I wrote to the manager of Wando Vale Cattle Station seeking information about employees there in 1972.

Dennis clearly remembered nearly tripping over the man hiding in grass outside the Twelve Mile Outstation on Wando Vale station in 1972. This is further confirmation of Mearle's story.

On 5th July 2016 I had a conversation with Dennis Madigan

who supported his sister Mearle's story of her and her mother meeting the murdered girls at the Pentland Hotel in 1972 when he was much younger, about 15 years of age, when it happened, and he did not pay much attention to the story. After talking with Dennis Madigan, I then wrote to Westpac Bank in Charters Towers seeking information on the cheque transaction I refer to in my letter to the Commonwealth Bank.

Later, I made phone calls to Westpac Bank in Charters Towers to learn that the manager could not conduct the search unless the request came from the police.

I also rang Eventide Home, Charters Towers about Betty Noonan's health and was informed that she would be okay to talk to, but I decided not to interview her as it may distress her with her dementia.

I also rang the Mexican Caravan Park in Charters Towers or at least rang the number there to learn the Mexican Caravan Park had closed years ago and no records from 1972 would be available.

On 5th July 2016, I wrote to the general manager of Westpac Bank in Brisbane requesting him to authorise the search at Charters Towers for the cheque transaction. He never replied to my letter.

On 20th July 2016, I again wrote to the attorney general.

This lengthy letter can be read as Appendix Number Twelve in the Appendix pages.

In this letter, I told the attorney general that following on from my letter to her of 8th May 2016, I had obtained corroboration of Mearle's meeting the murdered girls at the Pentland Hotel through her younger brother Dennis Vincent Madigan.

This letter is basically asking her to reconsider her decision to deny a Commission of Inquiry.

CHAPTER FIFTEEN

On 22nd September 2016, I posted a letter to Commissioner Stewart as under. This letter is relatively short so I will leave it in the main body of this work.

> *Commissioner of Police*
> *Brisbane*
> *Dear Sir,*
> *In respect to my ongoing pursuit of justice for the murdered girls Anita Cunningham and Robin Jeanne Hoinville-Bartram at Pentland, Queensland in 1972 and in response to the urging of the attorney general Yvette D'Ath, I formally enclose a copy of my latest letter to the attorney general dated 20th July, 2016.*
>
> *In this letter I provide information that corroborates the story of Mearle Whyte, which I have received from her brother Dennis Madigan. Further corroboration of her story can be obtained by acquiring detailed written and signed statements from Dennis Madigan of Maxwelton, Michael Madigan, a windmill expert of Winton and from Patrick Madigan of Charters Towers, who are brothers of the deceased Mearle Whyte.*
>
> *In respect to the finding of the body of Robin Bartram under Sensible Creek Bridge at Pentland in 1972, which I state may be just too much of a coincidence.*

I advise that the finder of the body, is said to be a railway worker by Dennis Madigan and to be a brother-in-law of John Fox of Charters Towers. Fox is believed to be a member of the band that was playing at the Pentland Hotel when the murdered girls arrived. The man who had accompanied them hitch-hiking from Mount Isa was one of the men who murdered these girls.

On another note, I wish to sincerely apologise to Inspector Smith and other members of the Cold Case Squad for my commenting that the investigation should be handled by detectives experienced in investigating serious crime. My explanation is that my frustration with the lack of police action got to me and I regret making that comment.

There seems to me to be a complete imbalance of justice when the police were stumped with the investigation of the much-publicised murder of Tiahleigh Palmer by asking the Crime and Corruption Commission to hold a star chamber hearing and did not make the same request of that body in respect of the two murdered girls at Pentland, which it can be argued is twice as vicious, as two girls were violated and killed after having placed their trust in the men who murdered them to give them a lift to Charters Towers from Pentland. There is little doubt Anita Cunningham met the same fate as the girl Bartram in my mind.

One cannot truly imagine the humiliation, degradation, fear and terror these girls must have suffered before being shot in the back of the head like the girl Bartram. One girl viciously fighting for her life, clawing the face of one of her attackers with her fingernails, leaving scratches that Mearle Whyte saw when she emerged from Betty Noonan's hairdressing salon the next day in Charters Towers on Cowboy's face.

Then these men, not satisfied with killing these two girls, hunted down the witnesses Betty and Mearle Madigan to the outstation on Wando Vale Station at night. They were not there for a social visit but obviously there to silence these women.

M.J. Gurn
Copy to Lawrence Springborg, M.P.
Copy to Ian Walker, Shadow Attorney General.

In a letter from Inspector Damien Hansen dated 27th September 2016, and received 4th October 2016, he says,

Thank you for your letter to the Commissioner of Police dated 22nd September 2016 re these murders.

He continued that the information I have provided will be forwarded to investigators for relevant action.

At this time, the suspected murder of Anita Cunningham and Robin Hoinville-Bartram remains an open investigation and therefore, we are unable to provide you with any information. **Unless you have any new information, all future letters received from you in relation to this matter will be filed.**
Signed,
Damien Hansen
Detective Inspector
Homicide Investigation Unit
STATE CRIME COMMAND

On 2nd March 2017, I forwarded a letter to the Commissioner of Police, New South Wales about the possible involvement in these murders of the infamous murderer Ivan Milat.

This letter can be read as Appendix Number Seven.

The reply email from the Office of the Commissioner of Police, New South Wales can be read as Appendix Number Eight.

CHAPTER SIXTEEN

I had a conversation with David Cunningham, brother of Anita Cunningham and asked him to pay for to put an advertisement in the Northern Miner newspaper to which he agreed. We both had talks with a journalist at this paper in Charters Towers, namely Morgan Oss, and in March 2017, the following advertisement appeared as a quarter-page article in that paper.

Information sought
In November 1972, the decomposed body of Robin Jeanne Hoinville-Bartram, nineteen years of age, was discovered under Sensible Creek Bridge at Pentland with two bullet wounds to the head and undressed from the waist down. Her companion, Anita Cunningham, eighteen years of age, has been missing since then and presumed dead.
These girls left Melbourne in early July 1972, hitchhiking to Bowen to see Robin's mother. They are believed to have travelled to Mount Isa and then on a truck to Hughenden with a male companion they only knew as 'Cowboy' then in another truck to Pentland, which is as far as that truck was going.
These girls entered the Pentland Hotel on a Friday or Sunday afternoon and sat at a table in the lounge. Their luggage was pushed up against a wall. Later a woman and

her daughter entered the hotel and became friendly with the girls and sat at their table. The man who came with them from Mount Isa introduced himself to locals as Richard and he became friendly with young men, drinking at the bar and at the back of the hotel who could have been meatworkers or station hands.

The girls and Richard accepted a lift to Charters Towers from a member of a band that had played at the hotel that afternoon. Another one or more men also left in this car. The girls were never seen alive again.

Next day, the man, Richard, was seen in Charters Towers with a deep fingernail scratch to his face.

Anita Cunningham was the apple of her parents' eye. Her father died not knowing what happened to his daughter. Robin's mother has also passed away.

If you know who the men were in the Pentland Hotel this afternoon in July 1972 or the identity of the band members or have any information, no matter how trivial, you are asked to contact

'Searchers' at Post Office Box 4, Campbells Creek, Victoria 3451 with your name, address and phone number. Or by email @ [redacted].

It is important to know that police have offered immunity from prosecution to anyone who comes forward who is not the actual murderer(s).

Signed

David Cunningham (Brother of Anita Cunningham)

The responses to that advertisement will not be disclosed at this time; however, one person supplied information that he had uncovered some buried tent material, a Kambrook food warmer and an enamel mug that travellers may be expected to have. David Cunningham established that this make of food warmer was not manufactured until after 1972, so the information was discounted.

On 13th March 2017, I telephoned Pam List (deceased) mentioned throughout this work and had a conversation of sorts with her.

Recorded interview with Pam List (aka Pam Barry or Rogers)

I said, 'Is this the number for Pam List?'

Answer, 'Yes.'

I said, 'Is this Pam?'

'Yes.'

I said, 'My name is Mick Gurn. You might have seen from time to time in the Sunday Mail newspaper that I have been investigating the murders at Sensible Creek in 1972.'

She said, 'Aw, yeah, I might have. I don't know.'

I said, 'I was wondering if you could tell me what you know about it.'

She said, 'I know absolutely nothing, darll. I wasn't even in the country at that time.'

I said, 'I understand that you with a man named Wally Barry at the time.'

She said, 'Not then. Later on, I was, but not then.'

I said, 'What happened to Wally Barry? Do you know?'

She said, 'Yeah, he died.'

I said, 'Whereabouts did he die?'

She said, 'In Brisbane.'

I said, 'Cancer, was it?'

She said, 'Yeah.'

I said, 'Did you receive some notification or letter or something from him that he was involved in this?'

She said, 'No way, because before that he was in New Zealand.'

I said, 'Do you know if he is involved in these murders at all?'

She said, 'Absolutely not.'

I said, 'Did he have a blue Falcon station wagon?'

She said, 'No.'

I said, 'Were you with him at Wando Vale Station?'

She said, 'He never worked at Wando Vale Station.'

I said, 'We must be talking about two different Wally Barrys I think because Wally Barry did work at Wando Vale Station.'

She said, 'Not the Wally Barry I know. He wouldn't know which end of a horse was what.'

I said, 'I think we must be talking about the wrong person.'

She said, 'Absolutely.'

I said, 'Are you a friend of Roth up at the Northern Territory?'

She said, 'Who?'

I said, 'I forget her first name. Roth.'

She said, 'Irene. Yes, I know Irene.'

I said, 'Well, you can't help us at all?'

She said, 'No, I'm sorry. I can't.'

I said, 'Were you a member of a band? Weren't you a pretty good singer of country and western music?'

She said, 'Yes.'

I said, 'Well, this band… there was a band used to go around playing at different hotels, I suppose, and one was at Pentland Hotel. Did you go there at all?'

She said, 'Never in a band, no.'

I said, 'Did you ever sing there at the Pentland Hotel?'

She said, 'Only with the club.'

I said, 'What club would that be?'

She said, 'The country music club.'

I said, 'Alright.'

She said, 'I don't know what information you have got or where you got it from, but it sounds pretty queer to me. I wasn't even in the country when those girls were killed, and neither was Wally Barry because he was in New Zealand at the time too.'

I said, 'I see. Okay then, thank you very much.'

I did not take the information from Pam List any further with the police. It was hopeless trying to get any positive action from them. The reason I interviewed Pam List was because I received information that she seemed to be in ill health and slipping. As the police were making no effort to interview her, I decided I had to take the risk and talk to her. Despite her ill health, I came away from the phone talk convinced she was lying and had some part in these murders.

A further explanation or result of my talk with List is gone into the letter written to Inspector Hansen on 14th March 2017, which is dealt with shortly.

Not long after interviewing Pam List and not really pursuing the matter too much with her as I did not wish to give her any information of what I really knew and for her then to have a ready answer to questions if the police did question her, I received a phone call from John Whyte to the effect that he had been in Woolworths in Charters Towers and that Pam List had confronted him about my telephone call to her and she was very, very upset. John said, 'I don't know what you said to her, but it sure upset her.'

In fact, my talk with Pam List was very mild indeed and her reaction was way out of proportion to what you would normally expect.

John said you could see guilt written all over her. She told John that she was going to see Bob Black about me ringing her.

On 4th October 2017, John Whyte rang me to say that Pam List had died.

CHAPTER SEVENTEEN

I wrote to Detective Inspector Damien Hansen of the Homicide Investigation Unit on 14th March 2017 advising that I had been in touch with the New South Wales police about the possible involvement of Ivan Milat in these crimes and other work I had done on these crimes.

The letter is quite long and can be read as Appendix Number Fourteen.

Throughout the year 2017, other relevant events occurred such as talks with Morgan Oss of the Northern Miner who wrote some stories about my work.

Peter Cameron continued writing articles about my work in his traps column in the Sunday Mail. He even approached the editor of the Sunday Mail, Peter Gleeson, to try and have him detail a reporter to investigate my work. Gleeson told him that he had delegated a reporter to do this work in July 2017, but I never heard from any reporter on behalf of the Sunday Mail.

Peter Cameron wrote sixteen articles over four years supporting my investigations but no matter how hard we tried; I was never contacted by the police in any way to explain their stance and no journalist from any paper took any interest in pursuing these cases.

On 12th December 2017, I wrote to a detective sergeant at a

North Queensland C.I. Branch office who I believed had been with Bob Black when he interviewed Mearle Whyte. I informed him that I knew he knew the true story of how Black had conducted his talks with Mearle Whyte and asked him if he had any useful information, he should contact the Commissioner of Police.

I never had a reply from him, and I do not know if that officer contacted the commissioner or not.

Later information indicated that an officer with a name like Burn or Byrne was with Black during at least one interview Black conducted with Mearle.

On 18th December 2017, I wrote to Commissioner Stewart about these murders, and I did not hold back. This letter is an important part of telling the real story about police not being interested in pursuing my information. My frustration with police inactivity boiled over, I am afraid. I wrote in very strong language.

I told the commissioner that this letter would expose the hypocrisy, false loyalty and blinkered tunnel vision of some police that have reviewed the cold case of the murders of Robin Jeanne Hoinville-Bartram and Anita Cunningham, resulting in their not appreciating that there could be a different take on what has been revealed in the investigations of ex-officer Bob Black. I said that police refuse to accept an alternative view that I put forward where I have asked them to rule a line under everything reported by Bob Black and begin their investigations, starting with the recorded interviews I did with John Whyte and Paula Whyte on 2nd and 4th October 2014.

I told the commissioner that I had for some time been baffled as to how there could be so much difference in the available information that has been unearthed in my recorded telephone conversations with John Whyte and Paula Whyte on 2nd and 4th October, 2014 to what ex-officer Black had apparently reported on his dealings with Mearle Elizabeth Whyte who passed away in Townsville Hospital on 16th June 2014.(should have been 27th June 2014).

I said that what Mearle told Black was largely false information and rubbish that she gave him in what she contrived as payback for his humiliating treatment of her when she came forward to the police. He gave an example of her saying the events happened at Cape River Bridge and later changing to Sensible Creek Bridge. John said that Mearle knew the area like the back of her hand as she was reared in the area. He says there is no possible way that she could mistake Cape River Bridge for Sensible Creek Bridge and that if she said this, it was deliberate on her part. She fed Black some truths and some untruths. (John later corrected this and said Mearle came from Goondiwindi, in fact).

I pointed out her disgust with Black and that this was born out in the recorded interviews I did and in the interview with John Whyte where he said that Mearle said, 'FUCK THE POLICE. I WILL TELL THEM NOTHING.' In Paula's interview, she went a lot further, describing Black's treatment of her mother in no uncertain terms to the extent that she was disgusted with him.

I said that the police are perpetuating a HOAX played on the police service and that many times since May 2014, I had told the police to disregard everything Black reported on his dealings with Mearle Whyte and begin their investigations with the recorded interviews I made with John Whyte and Paula Whyte. I said that much of what Mearle told Black was rubbish.

I said the police could prove or disprove my claims by simply requesting the manager of the Westpac bank in Charters Towers to scour the bank records to find particulars of the cheque Mearle's mother Betty Madigan cashed at the Pentland Hotel with this Ted West.

West was apparently working part-time in the hotel on this day in July 1972 when Robin Bartram and Anita Cunningham entered the hotel when accompanied by the man (Cowboy) who had travelled with them from Mount Isa, hitch-hiking, and who later was one of their killers.

I pointed out that the bank has refused to undertake this search for me and that I had even gone to the extent of asking the general manager of Westpac in Queensland for assistance, which fell on deaf ears. I said I believed that the cheque was probably drawn on Brian Patrick Madigan's bank account with the Bank of New South Wales, later taken over by Westpac.

I said I had previously told the police to interview Mearle's three brothers who know the story because the family was living together at the Twelve Mile Outstation on Wando Vale Station in July 1972 when all this happened and that these brothers would confirm at least in part some of Mearle's story depending on their memories after forty-five years.

I suggested that investigations into this cheque should be taken further by trying to establish how the cheque was deposited and into which bank by the licensees of the Pentland Hotel, Mr and Mrs Peut. I said I had contacted Kareene Forster who lives on a cattle station just outside Pentland with her husband Geoff. She is the daughter of the licensees but says she was not actively involved with the hotel at the time because she was pregnant with children during those years. She may be able to at least confirm which bank her parents dealt with if she was pressed a bit further by police.

I pointed out that the purpose of getting particulars of this cheque was that we will know an on or about date that Mearle and her mother entered the Pentland Hotel, which we would find was in early in July 1972 and most probably either Friday the 7th or Friday the 14th. I said that although it is not significant now but that it may be useful later that there was a full moon on Tuesday the 11$^{th\ of}$ July 1972, which may have relevance to the man hiding in grass at night outside the Twelve Mile Outstation.

I reasoned that Mearle may not have been too good with recalling seasons past in 1972, some thirty to forty-two years later, or months of the year in 1972 that all this happened or types of motor vehicles in 1972 but that she was very accurate in telling her daughter what she personally saw and heard with her own faculties, describing the killers and giving their Christian names.

I informed the commissioner that notes were taken by Paula of a lot of this and that those notes should now be in the possession of police. I asked if these notes have been disregarded in determining the truth of Mearle's dying statements. I said Mearle was dying and knew it. She also knew then that the killers could not hurt her now. I pointed out that she was very unlikely to be lying in those final days wanting to get this terrible guilt off her conscience before she died.

I reminded the commissioner that one had to remember here that Mearle had lived her life in fear of these killers who knew where she was and where she lived. She had said she ran into one of them at the Charters Towers Rodeo one year. I asked him not to forget that shots had been fired at her when she was on the veranda of the house at 5 Aland Street, Charters Towers. I informed him that this incident was dismissed by the police in a cursory manner when John Whyte suggested it was probably a rock that led to a very heated exchange between Mearle and John with her calling him all sorts of brainless names. Was it any wonder she was reticent to pursue information to the police?

I pointed out further that Paula said that her mother had been in fear of these men all her life and was frightened they were going to come after her.

I told the commissioner that I had named the following persons as involved in these crimes. A John Fox, a Walter Barry, (deceased and died in a Brisbane Hospital of cancer), and the family members who were avid band members at the time. I named Pam List, Barry's de facto at the time.

I reminded the commissioner that these people were supposed to be interviewed by the police when Inspector Smith went to Charters Towers in April 2015 as reported in a letter to me from Assistant Commissioner Hogan who said in her letter that it may take a further six months to interview these people, which drove me to contact Channel Seven for assistance. I said that these named people were not interviewed by Smith in keeping with the police advice to me that they would be interviewed.

I informed the commissioner that I had not tried to interview these people myself except for John Fox until recently after I interviewed Pam List and whilst Fox claimed he knew nothing, he was very active with bands at the time, and he needed further scrutiny. I said that I did not want to detract from whatever investigations the police were making, which seemed to be none. However, some months ago I had received information that Pam List was not well and there was a possibility she could die. I could see I could not afford to wait any longer in case she died.

I said I had rung this woman and came away convinced she was a liar and that she knew a lot more than she was telling me. She had denied that she was with Barry at the time and said that they were not in Australia at the time; they were both in New Zealand but not together. She denied that Barry had a Falcon station wagon, which was common knowledge. She denied that Wally Barry ever worked on Wando Vale Station and yet Dennis Madigan recalled Barry working on Wando Vale Station.

I said I had reported all this by letter to Inspector Hansen about my interview with List, who passed away since I talked to her. I said I had hidden nothing from the police but all I had got was to be ridiculed which had come back to me from Charters Towers after Smith's visit there in April 2015.

I said that it was a most amazing feature of this whole

debacle that this Ted West is named as cashing the cheque in the Pentland Hotel for Betty Madigan, that he is named as securing the lift with the men in the hotel for the murdered girls, Anita and Robin, to Charters Towers. He is named as having put the girl's luggage on the roof rack of Barry's car and he is still free as a bird.

I said that John Whyte when interviewed by Inspector Smith in April 2015, told him that he could not understand why he was wasting time when he should be pursuing West, who knew the whole story. How far West was involved after he put the girl's luggage onto Barry's car was not known. West was a boner at the Cape River Meatworks in 1972.

I told the commissioner that when Inspector Smith was at Charters Towers in April 2015, he sent me a very strange email which virtually threatened me not to contact Paula Whyte again. For this to happen and for Paula to have had any change of heart, there would have had to have been some pressure applied to her in some manner and there would have to be a very real possibility of a criminal offence being committed for that to happen. I said that the interview with Paula will stand on its own two feet anyway.

I pointed out that Smith in his email to me said both John and Paula had never believed any assertion that Ivan Milat was at Pentland or that Mearle had ever met or seen him. This statement of Smith is completely at odds with what Paula said in her recorded interview with me where Mearle believed one of the killers could be Ivan Milat, but she would have liked to see a photograph of him clean shaven as she had apparently only seen Milat with whiskers or a moustache.

I said Inspector Smith in this email took me to task for criticising Black's investigations and that it does not matter two hoots how thorough Black was in his work because he was reporting on rubbish, which was a mixture of lies and truths to him from Mearle Whyte as some sort of payback against him. Smith said in his email I would get his review shortly. No such review has been received despite several requests for this review. I said the reason was because they knew full well that I could tear it to shreds.

I said I have been in this lonely place before relying on my own instincts and judgment in believing a situation against the opinions of other police.

I pointed out I did not have a diploma from universities, but I had an A in detective smarts and an A in common sense.

I gave an example that this is very similar to an occasion where I believed a complainant woman that she was raped while asleep in her own bed, in her own house, in the middle of the night, in the dark, by a stranger while her husband was downstairs in his office talking business to overseas clients. Other police did not believe her and one senior officer said to me, 'If you think this is fair dinkum, get out and catch the bastard.'

I said I did catch him and that he was convicted on trial in the Supreme Court where his appeals to the Court of Criminal Appeal and the High Court of Australia were rejected.

I said that this present farce must end. Christmas joy was around the corner for most people but not for the murdered girls deprived of their lives in the most dreadful, horrific and terrifying manner.

I pointed out that I could go on and on pointing out holes in police investigations and once again repeating asking them to make certain inquiries. The uselessness of the list of employees of the Cape River Meatworks used to tell me that no relative of Milat was employed there at the time was interesting. The list is useless because employees were paid daily and seldom gave their correct names to avoid taxation responsibilities.

I remarked that this list was compiled by the original investigators, which makes one wonder how thorough those initial investigations really were and how the police came to miss that the girls had been at the Pentland Hotel in July 1972 with the discovery of the body of Robin Bartram the talk of Pentland at the time. There was a police station at Pentland at the time, which, in normal circumstances, one would wonder why some useful information did not come from there. There may be a dozen valid reasons for this, but it raised a question with me.

I said that none of this fiasco would have happened if the most basic of investigative procedures had been followed by Black when Mearle Whyte first came forward. Any experienced police officer would immediately take a detailed written and signed statement from the informant and then they are tied down. I asked if this happened with Mearle and her mother Betty Madigan. It could not have, or all this confusion could not have happened.

I asked about Mearle showing Black where she said Anita Cunningham's body was buried. Was a proper search conducted with metal detectors, etc? I had heard nothing about this happening. It seems to have been dismissed as a figment of Mearle's imagination, which Paula leaves no doubt in anyone's mind what she thought of all that because her mother took her to the spot.

I told the commissioner that when I spoke to Paula, she was quite prepared to show me where this was on the Flinders Highway, which was not at Sensible Creek at all but further towards Charters Towers. There may well be a simple explanation for this with one girl held at Sensible Creek where the campfire was burning under the bridge when Mearle and her mother passed and with Anita escaping towards Charters Towers until again captured and killed by others in the group.

I concluded that I was hopeful that police would honour their Oath of Office, acting WITHOUT FEAR OR FAVOUR and act to end this farce, disregarding the damage it will do to the reputation of the service, which is unfortunate but unavoidable.

CHAPTER EIGHTEEN

So as not to detract anyone's attention from gaining your support for a Commission of Inquiry, I will mention here that I handled two very interesting but utterly opposed cases of a genuine rape of a woman and the other case of a false complaint of rape if a reader is so interested.

These two cases may be read in the Appendix Pages as Appendix Numbers Fifteen and Sixteen.

In January 2018, I sent letters to the Premier Annastacia Palaszczuk, Deb Frecklington, the Leader of LNP and further advice to the Attorney General Yvette D'Ath requesting assistance basically.

Deb Frecklington replied that as the LNP was not in government, she could not assist at that time.

A shorter letter dated 14th January 2018 to the Commissioner of Police is worthy of including in this work and can be read as Appendix Number Three.

In this letter, I made special reference to the disturbing interference with the informant witness Paula Whyte, which was obvious by her change of heart after being spoken to by Inspector Smith in April 2015 as opposed to the frank and detailed information she had provided in her recorded telephone interview with me.

On 3rd February 2018, I wrote to the officer in charge of Townsville Police District asking for a search of an area of the Flinders Highway to try and locate the body of Anita Cunningham.

No reply was received.

On 20th February 2018 in response to an article in the Courier Mail newspaper in Brisbane I sent the enclosed email to Mr Sam Weir, editor of that paper to gain some support.

Dear Mr Weir,

Your second page in today's paper about boldly pursuing truth regardless of consequences prompts me to forward you a number of copies of correspondence between me and the Queensland police service, which are of themselves, self-explanatory.

I have been fighting a losing battle for nearly four years with the police to get justice for the murdered girls Robin Jeanne Hoinville-Bartram and Anita Cunningham who were slain at Pentland outside Charters Towers in 1972. The body of Robin was recovered but the body of Anita has never been discovered. She is for the record reported as missing but undoubtedly suffered a similar fate to Robin Bartram.

I am not prepared to deal with your Matthew Condon as he had his chance to have the story years ago but must have decided against it and probably after consulting some member of the police service as he failed to keep an appointment to come to my home and view what I have uncovered and listen to the recorded telephone interviews I did with witnesses.

The attachments I am sending you are but a small parcel of the numerous letters I have sent regarding this matter. The attachments I am sending you plus other information have been forwarded to the premier, the attorney general and the leader of the Opposition, Deb Frecklington.

It is with quite some reluctance that I am contacting you as I did not want to become exposed in the press and TV, but it seems that I have no alternative if the truth of all this is to come out into the open.

My mobile phone number as disclosed in the correspondence is [redacted].

Yours faithfully

M.J. Gurn (Mick)

No reply or any contact from Mr Weir was received.

On 24th February 2018, I had a conversation with Morgan Oss of the Northern Miner newspaper about an article she had published in that paper about my work. This article was forwarded to Deb Frecklington for her information.

On 26th February 2018, Denise Spinks, Deputy Chief of Staff to the Premier replied on behalf of the premier and attorney general. She said that coronial matters, including the holding of inquests, fall within the portfolio of the attorney general.

She said that in my letter I requested that the premier seek to influence the attorney general's decision as to whether to hold an inquest and it was not appropriate for the premier to seek to influence the attorney general in her decision.

She said that my letter raised concerns about submissions I had made to the police service and my dissatisfaction with my interactions with police and the Crime and Corruption Commission. She said she had forwarded a copy of my letter to the police commissioner. She gave me particulars of how to complain about the Crime and Corruption Commission.

CHAPTER NINETEEN

This chapter is really about the complete destruction of the police stance in this case, the reason why my information is not being followed up and why murderers have not been arrested.

About 28th April 2018, I asked David Cunningham if he would contact Paula Whyte and ask her to measure the distance from Sensible Creek Road bridge to the position on the Flinders Highway where the car was sideways across the road. I had an idea of going up north to further inquiries and wished to have a look at the area.

On 29th April 2018, I received the following email from David Cunningham, which exposed and blew up completely the police stance on these murders. The email revealed for all to see that the investigations by Detective Inspector Smith at Charters Towers in April 2015 were not intended to delve into the truth of the recorded interviews I had done with Paula and John Whyte in October 2014 at all, but a foolish attempt to cover up the inexperience and incompetence of a police officer in his dealings with Mearle Whyte and what he had reported to his superiors. This resulted in a botched police investigation of mammoth proportions.

From: David Cunningham
Sent: Sunday, 29 April 2018 1:19 PM

To: Michael Gurn
Subject: Spoke to Paula

Hi Mick,

Here's my recollection of this morning's phone call with Paula Whyte.

I phoned Paula Whyte this morning. She was a passenger travelling in a car driven by her husband, and the reception was a bit unreliable, but we managed to have a decent conversation.

I asked her if she would mind doing me a favour, and she said she would go next weekend to measure the distance between the Charters side of the Sensible Creek Bridge to the spot where her mother said the body of Anita was left or buried.

Paula reinforced to me several times that she was afraid of being identified in relation to giving evidence in investigations into Anita and Robin's disappearance and murder as she had been threatened and warned off on several occasions.

I asked her what happened when she was interviewed by Peter Smith at Charters Towers Police Station in April 2015.

She said Peter told her that her mother must have a mental problem, that the family's story was 'fiddlesticks', to 'give it up' and 'don't even try' to go there as the young men implicated are now, 'good people' with friends in the police force. The young men implicated have now become magistrates, lawyers and bailiffs. They are people of influence who don't want this sordid story to come to light.

Paula said her mother had been warned by her grandfather saying don't get involved.

She also said her mother was treated badly by interviewing police years ago and it seemed obvious they were not interested in receiving information but instead were just trying to discredit the witness as a way to discount their testimonial evidence.

She said her father was also a witness when the young men

were threatening and trying to intimidate the family by stalking, by 'coming through the house' and firing at the house, narrowly missing the five-year-old Paula and her parents. She said Bob Black was a new junior cop in the town at that stage and he was one of the three or four police who attended after the shooting incident. She said when Black was shown the bullet hole(s?), he dismissed it saying it was probably just a slingshot. She said some other things about Black (which I will not repeat here).

Paula then reiterated strongly her desire to remain anonymous for her safety and that of her family.

I hope that helps.

Best regards,

David

THEN from Paula to David:
From: Paula Whyte
Date: Thu., 31 May 2018, 9:04 pm
Subject: Re: David here
To: David Cunningham

Hello David,

I think I've read your email quite a few times in the past week. I'm not very trusting when it comes to this case cause they belittled my mother that much and made her sound crazy even though I believe her and my grandmother. Peter Smith and Bob Black, I will never trust again in this life time.

I haven't measured the kilometres yet. I think I might just wait until you are hear cause ppl talk, and Mr Gurn put in the papers clear as day so everyone knows I'm Mearle Madigan's daughter... and also there is no coverage in that spot on the highway. To tell you the truth, it make me six in the guts whenever I'm near that old town...

You look like your sister. Also, if you would like, I'm on fb if you ever want to look me up etc and so is my mother's profile. I think she would cry if she was alive today to know that Mick has finally got her story out there...

I'll keep in touch,

Paula

Ps. Tell Mick I said hello and can he send me a copy of everything?

Then, me to David Cunningham on Friday 1st June.

No, David, I have no objection to you giving Paula my email address, but I think she probably already has it as it has been published in the Northern Miner on at least two occasions.

What I intend to do is send her a copy of Peter Smith's email to me when he was in Charters Towers in April 2015 and see if she did say the things he told me she wanted. That will be a start, and I will judge what to convey to her from there.

You could point out to Paula that she is only person who knows the spot on the highway and that she can measure the distance without even getting out of her car; she could do it by the trip meter on her car. Even if it is 100 yards out, it will be close enough for us.

I have already put her email address into my contacts from the forwarded email from you.

From: Michael Gurn
Sent: Saturday, 2 June 2018 7:56 AM
To: Paula Whyte
Cc: David Cunningham; Peter Cameron
Subject: Pentland

Good morning, Paula,

It is nice to hear from David that you are willing to discuss this whole thing with me as I was told by Peter Smith that you wanted no further contact with me at all.

I will forward you the email I received from Peter Smith after he spoke to you in Charters Towers in April 2015 and I would like you tell me if what he wrote was correct or not. Do not be bluffed by what he wrote. I have drawn everyone's attention to the flaws in his reply.

I am quite prepared to let you read many of the letters etc I have written in this four-year battle to get justice for the murdered girls and to try and find the location of Anita's body for the peace of mind of her family.

This has never been about money for me as I did not even know that any reward was offered for information when I started this investigation. I got involved because I thought there had been a miscarriage of justice and at the time I did not know that your father had been asked by your mother on her deathbed to find someone to get justice for the girls as the police would not listen to her. He did find me through Vince, but Vince never told me about that when he first started mentioning the murders to me.

Further, there is little or no chance that anyone would be entitled to any reward money because a conviction would be required and as far as I can tell, most of the killers are dead. I will enlarge on that down the track with you but first, let's clear up this business with what happened when you met Smith and if Black contacted you first and threatened you in any way to stop you going ahead with your story.

You can be absolutely assured that I will be straight with you. If everyone just tells the absolute TRUTH in all this, we will WIN.

Regards,
Mick

And an email from Paula to me:

Hmmm, I read though what Mr Smith wrote. Yes, I did say that I didn't want to be involved with you or the case anymore. But that what because he made it clear even before I was sighted, that my mother didn't know what she was talking about and the men that were involved that night are upholding citizens and that they could never do a thing like that and that my mother's accusations could get good ppl in trouble.

He also went on to say that Bob Black is a great man and raised his voice and overpowered me at the time. So, I did nothing as I was pregnant at the time of the interview all the while his partner didn't say a thing until later that day when I was leaving. But back to him!! He then told me to show him where my mother had seen this all go down – driving, mind you, at 140 along the highway is not something I'm used to. But when we got to the spot it seemed like he already knew from what my mother had described to Bob Black years earlier 😠😠😠

He then said, which I haven't the proof, that I could get myself hurt in a way of speaking and that I should let this story go and be buried with my mother. If lie detector was needed, I'd pass it with flying colours but he made sure that all that was said was out of the room... My sister was with me when we went to Pentland and she was there when he said those things. Also, the lady gave me her card and said call me if Mick troubles you. That's all she said other than mumbling, which Mr Smith would overpower her as if to say shut up, I've got this. And he, like Bob Black, belittled my mother as if she and her mother made this shit up and that they were mad, but I know they are not and maybe one day something will come of it. I've even been tempted to search the area that mum showed with metal detectors.

My reply to Paula:

Ok, Paula. I accept what you have written, and I have believed the story from you and your father who also made a fifty-minute interview with me over the phone, which largely corroborates what you told me in your interview.

The best way to keep you up to date is to attach a number of letters etc I have written. I remember telling you to make photocopies of the notes you made when your mother was in hospital, and I hope you still have them.

Has anyone threatened you to keep quiet? Apart from what Smith said to you and if so, who?

Best see attached and you will realise that I have devoted four years in trying to get an inquest into these murders where everyone involved will get their chance to tell their story including the band members. This is the way the truth will come out.

Please read the attached carefully and make any comment you wish to make.

Regards
Mick
Might have to send others separately or it will be too big to send

From: Paula Whyte
Sent: Saturday, 2 June 2018 6:30 PM
To: Michael Gurn

Subject: Re: Murders

Mr Michael Gurn

If okay with you, can you please forward me your number as I have decided from reading all the information that I'm not going to back down from Mr Smith and his stand over threats and if that puts me in danger in anyway helping you help solve this case, so be it. At the end of the day, I know that my mother was telling the truth, and I will not let these murderous bastards intimidate me and threaten me.

I'm here if you need talk to me.

But I would also advise you to meet me in person and make sure that if something was to happen to me that my family is safe cause I get the feeling that they don't want this case solved for some reason.

From: Michael Gurn
Sent: Sunday, 3 June 2018 10:07 AM
To: Paula Whyte
Subject: Re: Murders

Dear Paula,

Thank you for your reply, which is very heartening for me. No one is trying to harm anyone here; we just want the truth to come out and get some measure of justice for the murdered girls and find whatever remains of Anita's body. I am not able to offer safety to you or for your family. Having said that, I do not believe you or your family are in any real danger from anyone.

The so-called exalted citizens of the band are not people who would go that far in my experience. They are probably just as frightened as you and are probably shameful that they have not come forward and done what a responsible citizen should have done in 1972. If there are any of the real killers still alive... well,

Ivan Milat is spending his life in jail in NSW. The other unidentified one is an Arthur, according to what you told me in your interview. He was probably a meat worker or a ringer from a cattle station and is more likely to be deceased now anyway.

I know that the band member with the Falcon station wagon was Wally Barry, and he is deceased of cancer in a Brisbane hospital. Pam List died after I interviewed her on the phone, which really rattled her as she accosted your father about me ringing her and said she was going to see Bob Black. She was very upset by me ringing her and that probably hastened her death. Just how far she was involved, I will never know but chances are that she was present during the rapes and murders but too scared to do anything about it.

With your assistance, we will convince the world that your mother was telling the truth and was not mental and the reasons why she did what she did.

It would be helpful if you would undertake not to have anything to do or say with Peter Smith or his Cold Case Squad. I will again approach the hierarchy of the police with what you have told me, and you will be required to tell other detectives what happened when Peter Smith and his Cold Case Squad who spoke to you in April 2015. If these detectives do not give you a firm guarantee that they are taking your story seriously and that the case will be investigated based on what you and your father have revealed in the recorded telephone interviews with me, then decline to talk to them.

I have enough, I believe, to again approach the attorney general for an inquest where everyone will be required to tell their story.

You have absolutely nothing to fear from giving your story at an inquest. In fact, it will be a relief for you I am sure that you will be clearing your mother's name and carrying out her dying wishes.

My phone number is mentioned many times in the correspondence I have forwarded you, but it is attached here again.

I would like you to answer the questions I have asked you by email as there will be a typed record then of your answers.

1. Did Bob Black contact you before Peter Smith interviewed you in 2015?

2. If so, what did he say?

3. Have you been threatened by anyone to keep quiet about what your mother told you?

4. If so, by who and what was said?

5. What were the standover threats made to you by Peter Smith?

I would like to meet you in person too but that is not possible at the moment. I am a pensioner now and do not have the financial resources to travel. I live in the Darling Downs, which is southwest of Toowoomba.

You will see that what I have forwarded to you is but a fraction of the work I have done on this case. My only assistance has been from David Cunningham and from Peter Cameron, author of the traps column in the widely circulated Sunday Mail. Peter believes your story. He has written about fourteen articles in the Sunday Mail assisting me with stories about what I am doing. He has also approached and told prominent citizens about the case like ex Commissioner of Police Jim O'Sullivan and has contacted members of parliament in the corridors of Parliament House.

Regards,
Mick

Email from me to David Cunningham:

Morning David,

I have just had a very interesting conversation with Paula who is now right onside.

I tried to ring you, in fact, just now and they said the number was not connected. I rang [redacted]. Is that correct?

She said she has not yet looked at my latest email and will do so and answer my questions.

She said she now has a gun license and is not frightened now. She said she will measure the distance from Sensible Creek Bridge next weekend.

Unfortunately, although I told her to make photocopies of the notes she took while her mother was in hospital, she did not do that, and Smith took all those notes with him. They included actual writing on paper by her mother.

She described how Smith stood over her. However, she told Smith she was not going to the spot on the highway unless her sister was allowed to accompany her, which she did, and she will be a witness to that part of what happened with Smith. She said he was driving at 140 to 160 kms an hour like a maniac. He apparently already knew the spot. He drove past it and she told him to slow down so she could get her bearings and told him to go back a bit. Smith was accompanied by a policewoman detective, a big woman with brown hair.

She agrees with me that Anita probably escaped from under Sensible Creek Bridge and was recaptured at the spot where the car was sideways across the road.

There is just so much I could learn if I could talk to her directly and she wants to talk to me, which is very encouraging.

Regards,
Mick

CHAPTER TWENTY

I consider this letter to Commissioner Stewart to be very important and warrants repeating in the main body of this work.

Commissioner of Police
Brisbane
Dated 6th June 2018.
Relative to the murder of Robin Jeanne Hoinville-Bartram and the missing and presumed murder of Anita Cunningham at Pentland in 1972.
Dear Sir,
I refer you to my letters to you and members of the Queensland Government on 18th December 2017, wherein I began my letter with explaining that the letter will expose the hypocrisy, false loyalty and blinkered tunnel vision of some police that have reviewed the cold case into the above-mentioned murders.

I pointed out to you that when Inspector Smith went to Charters Towers in April 2015, he was supposed to interview persons I had named who may be connected to these investigations in an attempt to solve these crimes. I pointed out that all he did was cause the person, Paula Whyte – who had provided me with an interview which I recorded on the phone with her on 4th October 2014 – to say that she wanted no further involvement in the case.

Inspector Smith emailed me from Charters Towers of this development among other comments that I have dealt with in prior correspondence. I pointed out how his statements about Ivan Milat were wrong and that he had been mentioned by Mearle Whyte and Paula Whyte.

I pointed out to you that this change of heart by Paula Whyte could not have occurred without pressure being applied to her by someone and that this pressure would have involved the perpetrator in committing a criminal offence. I say this interference with this witness would constitute the offence of attempting to pervert the course of justice.

The actions of Inspector Smith have stymied a proper investigation of these murders by three years with one involved person, Pam List, dying recently and who knows what other potential evidence has been lost.

Inspector Smith's lack of purpose when interviewing Paula is highlighted by the fact that he never took her through her recorded interview with me and asked her if it was true or if she wished to alter anything or add anything. He just blindly told her, 'What is all this rubbish?' or words to that effect. His bombastic manner frightened this woman into saying nothing, she told me. She said he 'just would not listen'. She said that all he seemed to want to do was protect Bob Black.

Earlier, Smith tried the same tactic when he interviewed John Whyte with whom I conducted a similar recorded phone interview on 2nd October 2014, but John stood up to Smith and they had some sort of a clash with John telling Smith that he did not know why he was wasting time with the Whytes and Mick Gurn and that he should be going after Ted West who holds the whole key to this matter. John also said that Smith 'just would not listen'.

Paula Whyte has contacted me at HER instigation and has informed me how she was treated by Inspector Smith. I will paste here segments of emails from this woman that highlight the conduct of this officer, which are evidence of this perverting the course of justice in this investigation. He then has the temerity to lecture me in his email to me in April 2015.

I would urge you to put a stop to this tactic of not responding to my letters and take my four-year investigation seriously as I firmly believe that everything, I have uncovered is a true version of how these women met their deaths, however distasteful you find them.

I have pieced all this together bit by bit over four years with no assistance from the police. Some facts in my initial letters were slightly off the mark but as I uncovered more, I informed you correctly as I went along.

This lack of a proper investigation into these murders based on the recorded telephone interviews I conducted with John Whyte and Paula Whyte on 2nd and 4th October 2014 is, to say the least, absolutely appalling. The whole circumstances of the lack of police investigations and the mishandling of these matters will undoubtedly become the topic of national television in the not-too-distant future.

David Cunningham, brother of Anita Cunningham, contacted Paula Whyte to get her to measure the distance from Sensible Creek Bridge to the spot where her mother said Anita's body was buried as he intends to search the area.

[EXTRACTS FROM THOSE EMAILS WERE INCLUDED IN THIS LETTER BUT TO AVOID REPETITION HAVE NOT BEEN SHOWN IN THIS PART OF THIS WORK.]

Paula Whyte has telephoned me and discussed her treatment at Charters Towers by Inspector Smith and others of the police service.

My requests for an inquest have been denied by the attorney general to date but this is the only way that the truth about this matter will be revealed. Why didn't the Integrity Unit act instead of apparently just blindly accepting what Smith told them? I am afraid that there are many questions to be answered on the police conduct in this case. I never thought I would be forced into this position of criticising a police force that I have so much respect for but I have no alternative if justice is to be served.

I believe the remaining band members who played at the Pentland Hotel this fateful day are members of the [redacted] family and are known to Inspector Smith. They are now or have been prominent members of the Northern community with one being a magistrate, another a solicitor and another a court official. How far they are involved remains to be seen when questioned on oath in the witness box at an inquest. I have dealt with who I believe the other killers were. I have declared that I believe Ivan Milat, the infamous serial killer, was involved. Paula told me yesterday that her mother named him as the man who had travelled with the murdered girls from Mount Isa and later was one of the killers who confronted her in front of the hairdresser's shop in Charters Towers the next day.

I have elaborated on all this in my letter to Inspector Hansen on 14th March 2017 wherein I stated my reasons for naming Milat and the timeframe where this was possible. I also told him how I had contacted New South Wales Police.

The disgraceful failure of the police to take action to find the cheque cashed by Betty Madigan this fateful day which would establish an or about day of the murders is unbelievable to me an experienced investigator in my own right.

That this Ted West is walking free as a bird when he was the one who obtained the lift for the murdered girls and put their luggage on the roof rack of the band member's car is astonishing. It could well be that West and other band members have been interviewed but have denied involvement, but I believe you have a stronger position now to get the truth out of them coupled with the exemption from prosecution offered for persons not actually guilty of the crimes. Plus, the fact that two brothers of Mearle Whyte corroborate her that their mother and sister did meet these girls at the Pentland Hotel. The other brother is said to have been out of the country at the time but that is not confirmed yet.

As a matter of urgency but belatedly, you should search the area indicated by Paula Whyte where her mother said Anita Cunningham's body was buried. I have months ago contacted the Officer in Charge of Townsville District asking him to search this area, but you can bet it has not been done. Whatever remains of Anita's body may be uncovered to give some measure of comfort to her family.

I have pointed out many other avenues that need investigation in my letter to Inspector Hansen and there is no need to repeat those measures here.

I have advised Paula not to have anything further to do with Inspector Smith or the Cold Case Squad and that she will be interviewed by other detectives. If they refuse to give her a firm commitment to investigate these crimes based on the recorded telephone interviews with me, she should decline to be interviewed. I doubt that in the history of crime in Queensland there has ever been a double murder investigation so mishandled and botched as this one.

A copy of this letter will be forwarded to the attorney general, Yvette D'Ath and others where it will do the most good.

Yours faithfully,
M.J. Gurn

David Cunningham received this email from Paula.
From: Paula Whyte
Date: Wednesday, 20 June 2018 1:54 PM
Subject: Re: just keeping you up to date
To: David Cunningham

Sorry, David. I do have a lot happening at the moment with school travel etc but I'll be happy to meet you when you do arrive and hopefully Mick as well ☺

Thank you, Mick.

I'm a little busy at the moment but I'll keep in touch.

From: Michael Gurn
Date: Thursday, 21 June 2018 9:54 AM
Subject: Re: just keeping you up to date
To: Paula Whyte

Hello Paula,

In case you did not get last Sunday's Sunday Mail I will paste hereunder what Peter Cameron said.

Regards,

Mick

Below is what Peter Cameron wrote in his traps column in the Sunday Mail on Sunday 17th June 2018.

'MURDER PROBE SOUGHT'

'New INFO ON THE 1972 Pentland murders, including suspects, was sent to Attorney General Yvette D'Ath and Police Commissioner Ian Stewart this month.

Former Detective Mick Gurn told Traps he would continue to push for an Inquest into the murder of Robin Hoinville-Bartram and likely murder of Anita Cunningham. 'Most of the killers are dead,' says Gurn, who admits witnesses remain cautious.

Gurn wants police to search for Cunningham's remains at a spot near the Flinders Highway to Charters Towers.'
I forwarded the following email to the attorney general.

Dear Ms D'Ath (Attorney General)

Your reference 571194/1,4166993

Further to my applications to you asking you to order an inquest into the murders of Robin Jeanne Hoinville-Bartram and the missing and suspected murder of Anita Cunningham at Pentland in 1972.

I can now confirm that I have had a phone conversation with another of the brothers of Mearle Whyte (nee Madigan) in the person of Patrick Madigan. Mr Madigan confirms having heard the story from his mother, Betty and his sister Mearle about them meeting the two murdered girls at the Pentland Hotel in 1972.

He says he had discussions with his mother and sister about this meeting but never took the matter any further.

In all, we now have five people who are alive today who confirm in varying degrees having been told by Mearle Whyte (nee Madigan) and Betty Madigan of them meeting the murdered girls at the Pentland Hotel in 1972. They are Mearle's three brothers, her husband and her daughter.

I will pass on this email to the Commissioner of Police with further comments about the lack of police action in investigating this case properly. I have already, as you know, had the very distasteful duty of accusing Inspector Peter Smith of perverting the course of justice regarding his visit to Charters Towers in April 2015 and his lack of purpose in dealing with the daughter of Mearle White in the person of Paula Whyte who now wishes to continue to assist me in solving these crimes.

I have held off taking this matter into the public arena of making further approaches to have the cases featured on national TV because I do not want to really be exposed on that media. I did originally agree in 2015 to going on TV with Channel Seven but changed my mind, which was probably another reason they dropped the story.

I can only ask you in the interests of justice to order this inquest. Without the whole of the circumstances being brought out into the *open, there is little hope for the integrity of the justice system. Just because these murders occurred forty-six years ago, there is no need to act as Inspector Smith suggests and told Paula Whyte to let the matters die with her mother.*

Compounding the mistakes made in investigating these murders by hiding the perpetrators does not augur well for our system of justice with many citizens already sceptical and losing faith.

Yours faithfully,
M.J. Gurn

On 26th August 2018, I wrote to crime reporters Kate Kyriacou and Peter Hill of the Brisbane Courier Mail newspaper enclosing some correspondence, seeking assistance with getting the real facts out into the public arena.

No response and no reply was received.

On 13th September 2018, I wrote to Sam Weir, editor of the Courier Mail, Brisbane seeking assistance.

No response and no reply was received.

David Cunningham wrote to Sam Weir, editor of Brisbane Courier Mail on 18th September 2018.

David received no response from Weir.

His letter to this editor of the Courier Mail can be read as Appendix Number Nine.

On 24th September 2018, I sent emails to Rachel Hancock of the Courier Mail Brisbane re this matter which she was passing on to her superior and crime staff.

No further response or reply from Rachel Hancock was received.

CHAPTER TWENTY-ONE

If the publication and circulation of this book is to achieve the desired result for a Commission of Inquiry or an inquest into these murders, then I really have no alternative but to show you some of the contents of the writings I have done. These have been placed in the appendices at the end of the book, which can be read there in more detail.

On reading this work, you will see what I have done and why I make the findings I make. Showing some letters etc., is essential for you to understand my reasoning.

The death of Frederick Whyte, who was a brother of Vince and John Whyte, is not fully explained and is somewhat suspicious. I included this in my letter to the Commissioner of Police, which deals with the abilities of Officer Black who also investigated this man's death in circumstances that leave unanswered questions as to whether another person could have been involved in his supposed accidental death with no mention of the missing five hundred dollars.

This letter can be read as Appendix Number Four.

On 16th October 2018, I emailed David Cunningham as follows:

From: Michael Gurn
Sent: Tuesday, 16 October 2018 12:25 PM

To: David Cunningham
Subject: Update

David, I emailed Paula for her postal address so I could post her my latest letter to COP, which I also sent to you. She has not replied.

I am tipping she has once again been threatened in some way and after I suggested Smith was guilty of perverting the course of justice.

When you get back, I would like you to again phone her and see if you can get any sense of this from her. I also said in my letter to the COP that Paula's sister could corroborate some of what Smith said so I wonder if they have threatened her as well.

Another ex-detective told me at the outset that they will protect Smith at any cost.

I think this is getting nasty, the closer and more pressure I am applying. I will email her the letter like I did to you and see what happens.

Also, the Northern Miner is going to run the story Morgan Oss put together on Frederick Whyte's death, might be Friday possibly.

Regards,
Mick

From: Michael Gurn
Sent: Tuesday, 16 October 2018 12:37 PM
To: Paula Whyte
Subject: Latest letter

Paula,

You have not replied to my request for your latest postal address so I could post you my latest letter to the COP for your information. So, I will attach the letter to this email.

I am wondering if more threats have been made to you since I accused Smith of perverting the course of justice. If so, make notes of everything and hang in there.

The Northern Miner is going to publish a story on Frederick's death shortly, which exposes Black's abilities to some degree or at least question his abilities.

I am here to help you at any time or offer any advice. Always make sure you have a friendly witness with you if anyone interviews you or being interviewed in the presence of a solicitor would be even better.

Regards,
Mick

Paula did not reply.

On 9th December 2018, I sent emails and correspondence to Peter Gleeson, previous editor of the Sunday Mail, now working for Sky News, hoping he would take some interest in getting the case into the public arena.

No response was received.

31st January 2019

Trudy Brown, editor of the Northern Miner in Charters Towers, said she had forwarded Sam Weir, editor of the Courier Mail, a copy of an article that appeared in her paper on December 13th, 2018, about David Cunningham search for his sister's body and my investigations into these murders written by me.

The article that appeared is shown underneath:

Families deserve to know the truth concerning the murders of Robin Hoinville-Bartram and Anita Cunningham at Pentland in the winter of 1972. I have been informed that when the woman who met the girls at the Pentland Hotel with her mother was on her deathbed in hospital, she begged her husband to try and find someone to get justice for these murdered girls as the police would not listen to her. This was despite pleas from her daughter to Crime Stoppers to interview her mother before she died and my own advice to the police that the woman was dying.

It is only for the courage and tenacity of her husband and a daughter who has withstood threats and intimidation to keep her mouth shut about these murders that I, a retired detective sergeant, have been able to piece together what really happened to these girls after four and a half years of delving into the circumstances.

All my information has been reported by me to the Commissioner of Police in detail.

Queensland police refuse to admit that their investigations in 2003 and 2005 were seriously flawed. They are relying on a police officer's reports into the deceased woman's story, which lacks credibility because basic investigative procedures could not have been followed for this serious situation to develop in the first place.

The press in Brisbane, in contrast to your local Northern Miner newspaper, which has particulars of the detailed investigations I have made, refuse to give me any assistance or traction to get the story out into the public arena with a view to having the attorney general order an inquest into the murder of Robin Bartram, which would also involve Anita Cunningham.

The attorney general has, to date, denied this inquest to me where those involved would be subjected to cross examination of their testimony, which would likely unveil the true story. There are persons who are involved directly and indirectly, still living, who could provide vital information, but they do not have the courage or decency to come forward. Their actions are only half a step away from being accessories after the fact or even perverting the course of justice and I would urge them to contact me through the Northern Miner.

Immunity from prosecution has been offered to persons who

did not commit the actual crimes, so there is no reasonable excuse for their silence other than trying to save their reputations.

One must wonder just who is really behind keeping the truth from the public and obtaining justice for these naive, trusting and innocent girls who were murdered in the most degrading and terrifying manner with complete lack of any compassion for the gratification of persons who could only be described as animals.

MICK GURN.

There was no contact with me by Weir. I do not know if he replied to Trudy Brown or not.

CHAPTER TWENTY-TWO

I wrote to Commissioner Stewart on 13th February 2019, which caused the VERY SURPRISING RESULT of Stewart announcing his early retirement as Commissioner of Police in Queensland twelve days later. I ask, did my blunt accusation to him cause him to announce his early retirement?

13.2.19

To: Commissioner Stewart
Queensland Police
Brisbane
Re. Perverting the Course of Justice
Dear Sir,
I cannot understand why you have not directly ordered an investigation into my information to you, that one of your most senior detective inspector's actions cannot be described as other than the actions of a person who has perverted the course of justice.

99% of my letters concerning the murders of Robin Jeanne Hoinville-Bartram and Anita Cunningham at Pentland in 1972 have been directly addressed to the Commissioner of Police.

I refer you to my previous advice to you regarding Inspector Peter Smith.

Channel 7 had screened a TV program featuring the

disappearance and murder of these two girls. Subsequent to that, I contacted Channel 7 with the information I had, and as a result, Channel 7 contacted Inspector Smith.

I did not know at the time I contacted Channel 7 that officer [redacted] and former officer [redacted] had taken part in this program, pointing out where the remains of the body of Robin Bartram had been discovered under Sensible Creek Bridge in a decomposed state, undressed from the waist down with two .22 bullet wounds to head.

However, these police indicated to the public that the body had been discovered under the road bridge over Sensible Creek whereas in fact, the body had been discovered under the railway bridge over Sensible Creek.

Inspector Smith asked them to hold off for a month before doing any research on the way police have dealt with information from Mearle Whyte over the years. Smith then went to Charters Towers in April 2015. He acted in a most extraordinary manner which I will enlarge on shortly.

The information from Mearle Whyte in 2003 and 2005 was apparently discarded as the rantings of a deranged woman, when, in fact, her information was perfectly factual.

It is conceded that she gave some information to the then investigating officer, in the person of former officer Bob Black of Charters Towers Police, which was not correct, but that she did this unwise tactic as payback for the humiliating treatment she received.

But the point I am dealing with here is that Inspector Smith emailed me in April 2015, a most peculiar email, which I considered threatening but more concerning. His statement was that Paula Whyte, daughter of Mearle Whyte who died on 19th June 2014 (should have been 27th June 2014) wanted no further contact with me, which was quite a turnaround from the detailed and specific information she gave me in a recorded telephone interview on 4th October 2014. This set me on the right trail to identify the murderers as I have previously told you. This surprising situation was not in keeping with her recorded interview.

I previously advised you that Paula Whyte asking Inspector Smith to tell me that she wished no contact with me could not have occurred without someone applying pressure to her causing this about-face.

In view of the serious crimes investigated, I expected that you would cause Paula Whyte to be interviewed about this matter immediately, but no such investigation has apparently taken place.

The cause of this apparent turn around in attitude on the part of Paula Whyte was not explained until April 2018, when David Cunningham, brother of the missing and presumed dead Anita Cunningham, spoke on the phone with her.

She revealed that when Inspector Smith interviewed her at the Charters Towers police station in April 2015, he did not take her through her recorded interview with me asking her if she wished to add or delete anything in the interview. He did not ask her if what she said in the interview was true or not.

His words to this woman who was pregnant at the time and accompanied by her sister were quite blunt and have been the subject of information to you in letters from me in the past.

As a result of a letter from Assistant Commissioner Hogan, Smith should have interviewed persons I had named as persons possibly involved in these murders when he was in Charters Towers, but I have no advice that these named persons were interviewed in accordance with the Assistant Commissioner Hogan's advice to me.

This is but another example of the lack of purpose of Inspector Smith in pursuing this matter.

The crux of what Smith said to Paula in a conversation with David Cunningham was that her mother (Mearle Whyte) must have a mental problem; that the family's story was 'fiddlesticks'; to give it up; don't even try to go there as the young men implicated are now 'good people' with friends in the police force; the young men implicated have now become magistrates, lawyers and bailiffs; they are people of influence who don't want this sordid story to come to light.

There were other matters said by Smith and the full content has already been forwarded to you in other correspondence. In a letter to you on 6th June 2018, I fully informed you what Paula Whyte said in an email to me about the way Smith treated her and what he said.

Paula wrote that she had said that she didn't want to be involved with me or the case anymore, but that was because Smith made it clear that Paula's mother did not know what she was talking about and that the men that were involved that night are upstanding citizens and that they could never do a thing like that and that her mother's accusations could get good people in trouble.

He also said Bob Black was a great man; he raised his voice and overpowered Paula at the time.

Paula and her sister took Smith with a policewoman in a police car to a position on the Flinders Highway where her mother had indicated the body of Anita Cunningham (in Paula's mothers' opinion) was left or buried. She said that Smith seemed to already know the location.

Smith also said, as Paula put it, 'I could get myself hurt in a way of speaking and that I should let the story go and be buried with my mother.'

There was quite a lot more, but you already have that information.

Paula has said that all Smith seemed to want to do was protect Black.

Now to any reasonable investigating detective, the actions of Inspector Smith in this instance cannot be described as anything other than perverting the course of justice, and no amount of soft-soaping it will change that. I would have thought that you would have immediately caused an investigation into my information to you on this matter, but I have no advice from any source that this has happened.

I have no advice from you that you are making inquiries.

I have pointed out to you that shutting Paula up from April 2015 to April 2018 put any investigations into the murders of the two girls Bartram and Cunningham back three years, during which time one of the prime suspects in the person of Pam List (also known as Pam Rogers, and also as Pam Barry) died after I conducted a very soft interview with her over the phone, but which caused her so much anxiety that she confronted John Whyte in a shop in Charters Towers about my phoning her.

John said she was most distressed and that in his opinion she had realised that I knew she and her then de-facto Wally Barry were prime offenders in these murders. This Pam List had told me that she and Wally Barry were in New Zealand at the time of the murders in 1972 but although they were both in New Zealand, they were not together.

I am told that it is possible to place her in Charters Towers in 1972 as she was an active person in the country and western music genre. I pointed out to you the remarkable coincidence of this, as New Zealand was where Ivan Milat had supposedly returned to Australia from in 1974, having been 'on the run' from police since 1971.

I previously explained to you and Inspector Hansen in a letter dated 14th March 2017 how I connected Ivan Milat to these murders. I also explained to you how it was possible that Mearle Whyte had said that the events at the Pentland Hotel had occurred in a period after the White Horse Tavern had closed down, and how it was winter time when this happened, and that it actually coincided with several weeks after the re-opening of the White Horse Tavern in Charters Towers on 17th May, 1972, which brought the date into the range of the first week of July, 1972 and most likely Friday, the 7th July, 1972.

I will attach to this letter, for your information, a page from the Northern Miner Newspaper edited and published in Charters Towers in January this year, which contains a letter to the editor from me.

Paula Whyte has been the subject of threats and intimidation to keep her mouth shut since my interview with her on 4th October 2014. She is a frightened woman. It does not take much imagination to guess who is behind those threats but she will not elaborate at this time, although she has previously, in emails, indicated her support for me despite these threats, and the content of those supporting emails has been given to you.

Of course, Channel 7 retreated from involvement in delving into the murders of the two girls as a result of what Inspector Smith told them, which is just another poor result of his visit to Charters Towers in April 2015. I wish to mention that it is with sincere regret that I speak of Inspector Smith in this manner and wish that I had not been forced into this most uncomfortable position but what else can I do?

I am advising Paula Whyte that I am asking you to instruct your detectives to make arrangements with her to be interviewed at a time and place where she may be represented by a solicitor or at least have an independent adult present.

I am advising you that as my correspondence has been forwarded to you since 2014, **I hold you personally responsible for the manner these murders have been investigated** and advise you that an experienced person is formulating a social media campaign in Victoria with a view to having the attorney general order an inquest into the murder of Robin Bartram, which will encompass the murder of Anita Cunningham who is at present posted as missing.

Yours faithfully

M. J. Gurn

(The person did not pursue the social media campaign due to financial difficulties.)

A short time after I posted this letter to Commissioner Stewart, he announced his early retirement. However, a few months later, he accepted another position with the Queensland government.

On 20th February 2019, I emailed Sam Weir, editor of the Courier Mail.

Dear Mr Weir,

You or your staff have not given David Cunningham or me the courtesy of a reply in our endeavours for assistance in solving the unsolved Pentland Murders from 1972.

It is quite apparent that the police have until now successfully managed to brand me as a nutter or something similar to hide the mistakes in their investigations into these murders and shut me down from receiving any publicity apart from the astute Peter Cameron and also the astute Trudy Brown of the Northern Miner newspaper. This will shortly change. Channel Seven was conned into believing there was no credibility in my investigations and now stands to be embarrassed on two fronts.

I have bought and read the Courier Mail since I was a young man, but I have some trouble understanding the two-page self-emulating promotion of the good deeds of your paper this morning, especially the words, 'We're committed to accuracy, integrity and fairness. You deserve to be given the facts versus the fake.'

I am attaching a letter to Ian Stewart, Commissioner of Police, Queensland, which is self-explanatory and gives lie to the stance taken by the police and should, to any reasonable person, dispel the unwarranted tag that has obviously been placed on me and my work in this matter.

I am open to discussions with your staff in the interests of bringing justice to the murdered girls and hold no grudges.

As I said in my letter to the commissioner, it is with sincere regret that I speak of a detective inspector in this manner but of which I have no alternative.

Yours faithfully,
M.J. (Mick) Gurn

No response from Weir.
I emailed Paula Whyte as follows on 14th February 2019.

Dear Paula,
I hope the floods in Townsville did not affect you too much.

Today I am posting by Express Post a letter to Ian Stewart, Commissioner of Police concerning the perverting of justice by Inspector 'Peter Smith'. I am attaching a copy of that letter for your information.

I am advising you that you should be interviewed in the presence of a solicitor or an independent adult person. I want you to truthfully tell these investigators all you know about the threats and intimidation to you and anything else about what your mother told you about the murders that they ask.

You should print out all the emails between you and David Cunningham and me around April 2018 and have that information ready for the interview to refresh your memory.

If you do as I advise you, you will come out of this confident and relieved and untouchable as I do not think that anyone will be game enough to make your life uncomfortable now that I have directly contacted the commissioner in this way.

I advise you to purchase the Olympus digital voice recorder to record any phone calls you wish to. This device is small, light and easily concealed on your person. You may even record the interview with detectives.

David is organising a social media campaign to try and get an inquest into these murders. I will be advising any of my friends or relatives who have been following my efforts over these last five years not to mention you or your father's name anywhere if they contribute to the Facebook campaign.
Regards,
Mick

The underneath email from Paula was received just after my letter to the commissioner saying that I hold him personally responsible for this situation.

Thu 21/02/2019 11:54 AM
I would like to advise to you not to further contact me as I'm over this case and this story I can now understand way my mother gave up and said she's moving on; they did what they set out to do and make it know that my mother was crazy. I will not fall into the same category and proceed with this bullshit, and I advise you not to do so. As for media, if they come to my door, I'll tell them to fuck off. I'm putting an end to it from my side and my mother has been gone now and the story is buried and that what they wanted and if you want someone for the story look somewhere else cause I'm done.

My reply to Paula was:

Thu 21/02/2019 12:50 PM
Your email is very disappointing, Paula. I did not start this quest for justice for the murdered girls. You and your father started it to comply with your mother's wishes. Contrary to what you say, it was your mother's wishes to your father to find someone to try and get justice for the murdered girls and that has been my only objective right from the start. It has been a very hard road for me

too. Your father has repeatedly thanked me for the many hours I have devoted complying with your mother's wishes. Your stance now is very hard to understand especially now just after my last letter to the commissioner which begs a question. WHY? What a coincidence?

    Regards,
    Mick

CHAPTER TWENTY-THREE

On Tuesday 28th May 2019, I talked on the phone with David Murray of the Australian newspaper about my suspicion that Ivan Milat was involved in the murders of these two girls.

On Wednesday 29th May 2019, I emailed the New South Wales police about the possibility of Ivan Milat being involved in these murders because there is no indication that the Queensland police would do this. I asked that should Milat come to a position of admitting his crimes, the NSW police should keep these cases in mind.

On 6th June 2019, Trudy Brown, editor of the Northern Miner in Charters Towers, published a very compelling article about my work with appropriate photographs about my belief that Ivan Milat was involved in these murders, which was also published in the Townsville Bulletin. The story was also republished in the southern newspapers of New South Wales and Victoria.

After these publications, Patrick Billings, a journalist with the Courier Mail, telephoned me for information, making out it was the first time he had spoken to me. He had phoned me previously and received information but did not do anything about publicising my work. I recognised his name and forwarded him the underneath email.

Mon 29/04/2019 11:55 AM

Dear Patrick,

Thank you for replying to my email to you.

There must not be much communication between staff at the Courier Mail for you not to know about my five-year battle to obtain justice for these murdered girls. Quite a lot of copies of my letters to the Commissioner of Police have been emailed as attachments to staff of the Courier Mail over an extended period including Sam Weir. Supporting letters or emails have also been sent to Sam Weir from David Cunningham.

However, as all that may be, the only one way for you to be fully acquainted with my work on this matter is for you to come to [redacted] and listen to two recorded phone interviews I did with the husband and daughter of a woman named Mearle Whyte who died in Townsville Hospital on 16th June 2014 (should have been 27th June 2014). She had not been interviewed by the police despite my informing them that she was dying and wished to be interviewed before she died, as well as her daughter contacting Crime Stoppers to request, she be interviewed before she died. She was not re-interviewed.

These interviews are each about forty-five minutes in length so you will need plenty of time for any visit plus hours of reading of letters etc.

I did these interviews, which are startling in their content and detail events that could only have come from a person with intimate knowledge of what had occurred at the Pentland Hotel in early July 1972 in wintertime.

If I was to try and send copies of numerous letters to the police and others, you would be swamped for days of reading as my file is now some three inches thick. The only support I have had is from David Cunningham and Peter Cameron who tried to get some publicity for my investigations by mentioning my work about sixteen times over four years in his traps column in the Sunday

Mail before he retired. He is of the same opinion as me that there is a concerted effort by the police to deny that investigations by police in 2003 and 2005 were severely flawed by the investigating police officer from Charters Towers at the time.

He vainly tried to obtain support from Peter Gleeson when he was editor of the Sunday Mail. I have had some support from Trudy Brown, editor of the Northern Miner Newspaper in Charters Towers who has published two large columns on my work. She has also interviewed one of the persons with whom I did the interview and has come to an informed position on my work after reading what I have uncovered.

I recently emailed Sam Weir that I was happy to work with his staff on this matter and hold no grudges.

I will attach a couple of the latest letters about this case as attachments as a sample of my investigations.

Hoping you will find the time and interest to follow up my invitation. David Cunningham has a Facebook page open about his sister's murder.

Regards,
Mick Gurn

AS USUAL WITH THE PRESS BILLINGS, THE COURIER MAIL GOT MY INFORMATION AND I HEARD NOTHING MORE FROM THEM AND HAD NO ASSISTANCE WITH ANY ARTICLE IN THE COURIER MAIL.

CHAPTER TWENTY-FOUR

During this break, the new Commissioner of Police for Queensland was announced by the government as Katerina Carroll. I believed that with a new commissioner, the case would be looked at with fresh eyes and believing that she had had some experience as a detective, I expected her to order police to look at the case based on the work I had done. Once again, I was sadly disappointed, and nothing occurred to indicate a change of heart by the police.

I wrote to her by express post to reach her on the day she started work on 9th July 2019, advising her of my work with emphasis on the mishandling of these cases by police over the years and asking for her support. I enclosed a personal handwritten letter to her in the same vein.

No reply was received from the commissioner herself to my letters. The usual non-informative letter was received from the police in response to this letter to the new commissioner.

The letter to the new police commissioner is shown below and is included here to keep telling this story as it unfolded. There are some new points of interest in this letter.

Dated 8th July 2019

Reference to the 1972 murders at Pentland of Robin Jeanne Hoinville-Bartram and Anita Cunningham.

Dear Ms Carroll

Firstly, let me congratulate you on your promotion to Commissioner and I wish you success in your new role.

However, this letter is one you probably would wish you did not receive as it contains very severe criticism of the work of members of the Police Force Service (as it is now called). I began investigating these murders in 2014 as the result of casual conversations with a person who lives at Homestead outside Charters Towers who mentioned that his sister-in-law, a Merle Whyte nee Madigan, was dying of stomach cancer in Townsville Hospital and who claimed she had met the two murdered girls at the Pentland Hotel in the winter of 1972. She died in June 2014, not interviewed by Police despite my advising Inspector 'Smith' she was dying and wished to tell her story to the Police and her daughter pleading with Crime Stoppers to interview her Mother before she died.

From then on since 2014 I have written numerous letters to the Commissioner of Police Ian Stewart supplying him with information about these murders which contained severe criticism of the work of former Police Officer 'Bob Black' of Charters Towers Police who had interviewed this person Merle Whyte in 2003 and 2005 and has apparently reported to his superiors that the informant was delusional and that her story was false.

There have been many twists and turns over these last five years in which I have investigated these murders and to go into every aspect would require me typing endless pages of previously written letters which are no doubt on file with Police.

As a result of an unsatisfactory reply from your Inspector 'Peter Smith' who was then in charge of the Cold Case Unit and is a close friend of former Officer 'Bob Black', I decided to interview the ex-husband of Merle Whyte in the person of John Kingstone Whyte of Charters Towers and 'Paula' Whyte, == year old daughter of Merle Whyte who lives in Townsville.

I conducted these interviews over the phone using the speaker mode and recorded the interviews on a device over about 45 to 50 minutes each on 2nd October 2014 and 4th October, 2014 respectively.

These interviews contained such specific and detailed information and criticism of 'Bob Black's' work that it is impossible to dismiss the claim that Merle Whyte did indeed meet these girls at the Pentland Hotel. Another person could not know this detail. They show a person named 'Ted West' placed the hitch-hiking murdered girl's luggage on the roof rack of a car of a band member who had played in a band at this Hotel this day, which was most probably a Friday and likely to be Friday 7th July 1972. This 'Ted West' had obtained a lift to Charters Towers for the girls with this band member and they left the Hotel in this car which was a Falcon Station Wagon and which I uncovered was owned and driven by a Walter (Wally) Barry. His vocalist de-facto Pam Barry is believed to have left in the same car from the Hotel.

Another person who left the Hotel in this car was a man who the girls only knew as Cowboy and who had established contact with the girls in Mount Isa and had travelled in a truck with them hitch hiking as far as Hughenden and then with them again in another truck as far as Pentland. This person, I have reason to believe may have been the serial killer Ivan MILAT. At least one other man left with the car whose first name seems to have been an ARTHUR somebody.

What transpired from then on is contained in my correspondence to Commissioner Ian Stewart and in recorded interviews. The decomposed body of Robin Hoinville-Bartram was discovered in a shallow grave under the railway bridge over Sensible Creek about 20 kms from Pentland towards Charters Towers.

My deductions in all this have been the subject as I said of numerous letters to Commissioner Ian Stewart who has not caused sufficient investigations into my claims to prove or try to disprove my assertions which are well founded common sense.

You will see from the correspondence I am enclosing with this letter, which are copies of previous correspondence to Commissioner Stewart that not only do I challenge his lack of ensuring my claims are properly investigated, I have unfortunately had to accuse Inspector 'Peter Smith ' of perverting the course of Justice and the reasons for these serious claims are well set out in the correspondence I am enclosing with this letter, of which copies have been forwarded to the Premier, the Attorney General, Leader of the Opposition in Parliament Honourable Deb Frecklington, Honourable Bob Katter, Honourable Robbie Katter and Honourable Shane Knuth.

My letters to the Attorney General are an effort to have her order an Inquest into the murder of Robin Hoinville-Bartram, which would encompass the missing and no doubt murdered Anita Cunningham. This Inquest has twice been denied by the Attorney General on the grounds that I am relying on second hand conversations. However, I have been able to substantiate points of reality in that Merle Whyte's brothers knew of her and her Mother Betty Madigan meeting the murdered girls at the Pentland Hotel.

I have confirming statements that Merle Whyte saw one of the murderers, Wally Barry at Pam List's house when she went there as Pam Barry (later LIST) was making Merle's wedding and bridesmaid dresses and she recognised him as the owner/driver of the band members car the girls had left the Pentland Hotel with this late evening. 'Paula' says that Pam Barry denied to 'Bob Black' according to her mother that this man was at her house. (This man would undoubtedly be Walter Barry.)

It is also a fact that Betty Madigan, Merle's Mother, cashed a cheque for cash at the Pentland Hotel with a 'Ted West' this fateful date and verifying this fact would go a long way to establishing the veracity of meeting the girls. This has not to my knowledge been done by the Police. I have been thwarted by the Westpac Bank refusing to search for this transaction in records because the Police will not support the search. I even asked the Managing Director of Westpac in Brisbane to order this search, and he has not done so and I would conclude that he inquired of Police about my request and they did not support my request which is very very odd to say the least.

David Cunningham, brother of Anita Cunningham has worked with me on this case and has a Face Book page about the murders. He has recently told me that he is having difficulty obtaining the Police file on this case under the Freedom of Information Act as the Sergeant he is dealing with told him it would be a long time before he got the information as the file is enormous, that they are overworked and that he would not answer any further emails from David. He said the Sergeant is abrupt and seems hostile.

I do not think it is necessary for me to continue dealing with every aspect of this unholy mess mishandled by the Police. Commissioner Stewart announced his retirement shortly after receiving my last letter of complaint to him which some people think is the reason for his retirement. I am of an open mind on that one, but I am of the opinion that he has dropped this in your lap to sort out as when the real story comes out about the Police investigations into these murders it will unfortunately be headline news throughout Australia. I suggest it would be in your interests to conduct your own review of the Police handling of this case.

The people who are shielding persons in this matter or have intimate knowledge of these two crimes are under pressure through publicity being given to my investigations in the Northern Miner Newspaper in Charters Towers. This Editor Trudy Brown has come to an informed position after reading my correspondence and speaking with one of my informants and using her common sense as to the likelihood of everything I have uncovered being correct.

A similar correct opinion has been formed by Peter Cameron, who mentioned my work in his Traps Column in the Sunday Mail on 16 occasions over 4 years before he retired. Unfortunately, the

Courier Mail and the Sunday Mail will not entertain that there could be another side to the story told them by Police who are relying on the reports of the investigating Officer 'Black', over which the recorded interviews I did with John and 'Paula' Whyte cast a very dark shadow concerning his conduct and investigating ability.

Similarly Channel Seven has been duped into believing there is nothing to my claims.

I am asking you to personally listen to the recorded telephone interviews I refer to in this letter and read the written notes taken by 'Paula' Whyte of what her mother told her about these murders whilst she was dying in Hospital. These notes were taken from 'Paula' by Inspector 'Smith' when he accosted her in Charters Towers in April 2015.

In relation to former Police Officer 'Bob Black's' investigations after being contacted by Merle Whyte it is reasonable to believe that he would have interviewed Merle's Mother, Betty Madigan, as she was with Merle when they met the murdered girls at the Pentland Hotel to confirm the story. The family do not have knowledge of Betty being interviewed by 'Black'.

Betty Madigan's attitude seems to have been that she did not wish to be involved, however her version is absolutely what would be required to back up or disprove Merle's version, especially as it relates to the cheque cashed by Betty with 'Ted West' at the bar in the Pentland Hotel this fateful day. Confirmation of this cheque transaction with a relevant date, could be expected from Brian Patrick Madigan, Betty's husband and Father of Merle.

Any appraisal of 'Black's' reporting as a review of the cold case would not be complete without Betty's version being known to the Police.

We have the attempt on Merle's life when shots were fired at her whilst she was on the veranda of a house in Charters Towers whilst cuddling 'Paula', which went through glass louvres. This was when a car drove past her house turned around and stopped in front of her house and shots were fired at her. Police attended, including 'Bob Black'. Police dismissed the occurrence. 'Paula' believes that a bullet may still be in the veranda wall of the house.

In 'Paula's' interview with me she says that her mother came face to face with one of the murderers at a rodeo in Charters Towers when she recognised him. Perhaps this meeting triggered the attempt on her life although 'Paula' believed that she was not born when Merle met the man at the Rodeo, but as she was only about five years old at the time she could be mistaken.

This incident is referred to by Inspector 'Smith' when he accosted 'Paula' in Charters Towers in April 2015 (to call his approach as an interview is a stretch too far) and forms part of an email from 'Paula' to me.

As I made the application for an Inquest under the Coroner's Act, I believe I would be entitled to request that I sit at the Bar Table and examine the witnesses at an Inquest which I reasonably hold would entitle me to a complete undoctored and uncensored complete copy of the entire Police file on these murders.

I bring to your attention that the most basic of investigative procedures in obtaining detailed written and signed statements from the informants could not have been done by 'Black' or this situation could not have occurred in the first place.

I can only hope that you will straighten this mess out quickly because no matter how long it takes or what has to be done by me, the truth will eventually be told. I have repeatedly told the Police to disregard everything that has been reported by 'Bob Black' and start from my recorded interviews, which the Police have, and you will obtain a favourable result.

Perhaps you could gain some confidence about my work if you were to contact former Commissioner of Police Bob Atkinson and former Detective Inspector Owen Lindemann, who know me well and may have an opinion on the value of my assessment of the case. These former Police served under me when I was in charge of ===== C. I. Branch.

It is absolutely frustrating to think that when Merle Whyte first contacted the Police that a Police Officer of ordinary ability by treating her with respect, would have obtained a detailed written and signed statement from her and her Mother Betty Madigan getting the full story, naming suspects, got their descriptions, clothing they wore and more importantly solved the case as some murderers were still alive with witnesses and connected people available to be interviewed.

Further to add to the botched investigations we have Inspector 'Smith's' actions stymieing the investigations for a further three years from 2015 to 2018 and during this time a principal suspect in the murders in the person of Pam List dying not interviewed fully by Police which is contrary to advice to me in writing from Assistant Commissioner Hogan that she and 'John Fox' and Band members, the ====, would be interviewed by Police.

How I linked Ivan Milat to these crimes is set out in a letter to Inspector Hansen dated 14th March 2017. The two murdered girls hitchhiked from Mount Isa with a man they only knew as 'Cowboy' which was one of Milat's nicknames according to a Producer of Channel Seven. At the Pentland Hotel he introduced himself to patrons as 'Richard', which is the name of one of his brothers and whose name he was known to have used from time to time.

Milat absconded on bail from a NSW court in 1971 on charges of rape and robbery. He eventually returned from New Zealand in 1974. When I interviewed Pam List over the phone before she died, she claimed that she and Wally Barry were not in Australia at the time of the murders but that they were both in New Zealand in 1972. I believe that after the murders some of the murderers went to New Zealand and probably with money from the murdered girls. Proper investigations should be able to still place Pam List in Charters Towers in July 1972 as she was a regular performer of country and western music in the District. She was also well known to many people in the town. There is also the two .22 bullet wounds to the back of Robin Bartram's head, a trait of Milat when carrying out his horrific attacks.

Merle Whyte also believed he was the person who travelled with the girls hitchhiking as related in 'Paula's' interview although she would have liked to have seen a photo of him clean shaven and without facial hair.

Below is a copy of an email I forwarded to David Murray of the Australian Newspaper on 28th May 2019 which in my mind puts paid to Police assertions that Ivan Milat was not involved in the murder of these girls.

""""""""""""""""""""""""David Re your article in the Australian Newspaper and Sunday Mail about Milat's possible involvement in the murder of David Letcher in 1987 and our phone conversation today.

David, I remember reading the book MILAT by Superintendent Clive Small and I recall him saying N.S.W.Police had no information about Milat's time in New Zealand somewhere in the book. At this time I have found the following------

On pages 61 and 62 the book reads, and I quote

'In 1971 he had been arrested with others and charged with armed robbery and later the same year with rape. Bailed, Ivan did not hang around. He fled to New Zealand, where he lived for about two years before returning to New South Wales following trouble with the New Zealand Police (WE COULD NEVER IDENTIFY WHAT THE TROUBLE WAS)'

Interesting isn't it that Small says Milat lived in New Zealand for about two years i.e. 1972 to 1974. The Pentland Murders occurred in July 1972 and the body of Robin was discovered in November, 1972 in a decomposed state.

This would indicate to me that Milat went to New Zealand in

1972. Clive Small has since confirmed that the NSW Police cannot establish when Milat went to New Zealand.

I intend to mark the posting envelope Private and Personal to ensure it gets to you personally before the Deniers get to you. Unfortunately, Inspector 'Peter Smith' has I believe stepped outside the boundary of Police trust, impartiality and confidentiality by his behaviour in Charters Towers in April 2015 when he went to Charters Towers.

I have further suspicion that whatever I report to Police is being conveyed to 'Bob Black by someone which has had a detrimental effect on the contribution of 'Paula' Whyte to this investigation. However in the interests of Justice I must inform you that on 24th June, 2019 I had a further long conversation with John Whyte in which he reveals that after his deceased wife had been accosted by the three men in Charters Towers the morning after the murdered girls left the Pentland Hotel with these same three men she was so frightened that she never went to town for two years. She was frightened of these men as she knew some of them lived in Charters Towers and that is the real reason she did not come forward to the Police earlier than she did.

Further that in 1985== (I have deleted this paragraph because it contains sensitive information about the identity of one of the offenders who is still alive. To disclose this information now will hinder any police action if it ever happens.)

I have identified the three men now as Walter Barry (deceased in a Brisbane Hospital of cancer), Ivan Milat (dying in prison) and 'John Fox' who is previously referred to in 'Paula's' recorded interview with me as ARTHUR.

John Whyte is a person who has had head injuries but if you know how to talk to him, he is a fountain of information. He just does not realise the value of the information he has but you have to prompt him with a direct question on a specific subject and his recall is very good. He described the Ford Falcon Station Wagon the girls left the Pentland Hotel in as pale blue, sun faded in parts with one of the rear (boot on other cars) doors painted grey, probably as a replacement for a damaged door. This is the vehicle that he saw parked at Pam List's house and owned by Wally Barry.

There is absolutely no doubt whatsoever that my information to the Police to help them solve these murders has been substantially correct throughout this five-year unreasonable struggle against Police inaction largely attributed to protecting the work of former Officer 'Bob Black' of Charters Towers and what he has reported.

I am including on the USB memory stick I am enclosing with this correspondence for your information, a personal conversation I had with John Whyte on 24.6.19. John rang me to discuss an aspect of the case, and I told him to hang up and I would ring him back and record the conversation. In this conversation 'John Fox' of ================ Charters Towers is clearly identified as one of the men who confronted Merle Whyte (then Madigan) outside the Betty Noonan's Hair Dressing Salon in Gill Street the morning after the murders.

I am delaying posting this letter and attachments until you take office after previous experience in giving information to the Police which has been disregarded. I have had replying letters from Police urging me to give them information, but I feel the aim of that offer is merely to know what I am going to do next.

I have asked the numbers of people following my work to obtain Justice for the murdered girls not to judge the Police on this one episode but value the outstanding work the Police do for us seven days a week, 24 hours a day.

Yours sincerely,

M. J. Gurn

CHAPTER TWENTY-FIVE

On the 30^{th of} November 2019, I sent a proposal to Adam Hegarty of Channel Nine offering to go to North Queensland with their backing to investigate these murders.

My offer to Channel Nine can be read as Appendix Number Five.

In a letter dated 17th January 2020, David Cunningham wrote to Detective Inspector Damien Hansen of Homicide Group.

David's letter can be read as Appendix Number Six.

Inspector Hansen replied to David that he was directing a detective to look at the circumstances.

Channel Nine made no response to my proposition but they did make a television programme after interviewing me on camera on Friday 14th February 2020. They put together a realistic simulated version of the girls in the Pentland Hotel, including some statements from me, which aired just before 7pm on Thursday 20th February 2020. Before the programme aired, the preambles advertised the forthcoming airing the night before and all during the Thursday about a police cover-up in this case but were not again mentioned during the actual programme for some reason.

After the television programme, one would normally expect some interest from the press and other television stations about my take on the cases or what I had uncovered but no one showed any interest and most certainly, I received no contact from the police whatsoever. To my way of thinking, this is extraordinary. All I can think of is that what I am saying is just so unbelievable that people are having trouble believing that what I am proposing could not possibly be happening but sadly

IT IS TRUE AND HAPPENING RIGHT BEFORE YOUR EYES.

On Saturday 7th March 2020, I spoke with another daughter of John Whyte in the person of Joan Whyte, who further confirmed that her mother Mearle Whyte and her grandmother Betty Madigan did meet the murdered girls at the Pentland Hotel before they were murdered.

Transcribing these recorded interviews requires listening to a few words of the recording, hitting pause and writing down in longhand what was said and then listening again to a few words and pausing again. Of course, this slow and tedious task takes many hours to complete each recording.

RECORDED INTERVIEW WITH JOAN WHYTE

I began, 'Your father told you I would be ringing this morning?'
'Yes, he did.'
We had trouble with the line and Joan rang back and said, 'Can you hear me now?'
I said, 'Yes, better this time. Well, you know my part in all this, don't you?'
She said, 'Yes. Dad told me.'
I said, 'It would be easier for me if I could email stuff to you.'
She said, 'Yes, that is alright.'
She gave me her email address.
I said, 'I am going to record this talk. Is that alright?'
She replied, 'Yes, that is okay.'

I said, 'What does your friend have to say about this whole episode?'

She replied, 'The other day I went to see Marco. He is a psychic. He has done a few cold cases. I just asked him. I hadn't really asked him. I see him every now and then. I asked him how she felt from Anita's point of view, and he just asked me. He didn't really ask me where did this take place and I told him out at Pentland and he was talking about one of the fellows, just three fellows. He said that were in on it, like killing stuff and he said one was a mechanic because he had grease on his fingers and it was pretty crazy, he was talking about, and she wasn't close to where Robin was. She was sort of away from where Robin was found, I am not sure.

'I know Mum was telling the story for years and years. I sort of half listened, but Paula knows a little more than what I do. He said there was a shed across from the rail line and he thinks she was around but not in the shed but placed around that. He said they weren't buried together basically. They put them apart because it was harder to find them, and he and he said one of them out of the pack has passed on but he said Anita died through blunt trauma to the head and she would have been raped by at least four of them.

'Then he said if I wanted, he could connect with her and find a little more. That's what I could find more. He said he did not think Dad was going to find her. He more or less said. I don't know if you believe that sort of stuff, but I do since my mum passed away.

'This fellow is not like one of them that just talks crap. He has told me stuff that no one other than myself could know. Sometimes they use mediums to try and solve stuff, cold cases, because they can connect with the person who has passed. You know it's pretty crazy, but I think he was on to something. I don't know about this shed, but he said it was located near but away from Robin.'

I said, 'Who is this fellow?'

She replied, 'His name is Marco Dellavalle.'

I said, 'Does he live in Charters Towers?'

She said, 'No, he lives in Townsville.'

I said, 'How do you contact him?'

She said, 'I've got his number, and I message him. He's on Facebook. I don't see him that often.'

I said, 'Where do you live?'

She told me her location.

I said, 'Are you single or married?'

She said, 'I am single.'

I said, 'How old?'

She answered.

I said, 'Joan, you were apparently with Paula when Inspector Smith came to Charters Towers in April 2015 apparently to investigate the recorded interviews I did with Paula and your father.'

She said, 'Yes.'

I said, 'When that was all over, I asked Paula to get you and her to make written notes of everything that transpired that day and what was said. Did you do that?'

She replied, 'No, I did not know that we had to do that. Paula did most of the talking because she knows the story inside and out sort of thing. Mum has been telling it for years and years. No, we didn't do any notes. We didn't know we had to.'

I said, 'What was your impression about Smith? What was your impression of him?'

She said, 'I think he was alright, but I don't think he really wanted to find her. I think from everything that transpired, they made Mum out to be a crazy person. I think they just sort of have given up in my opinion when they went out there. I don't think they really wanted to find her in my opinion.'

I said, 'No, that's right. Smith was supposed to take her through the record of interview with me and Paula said he did not do that. Do you know whether he did or did not?'

She said, 'No, I don't think he did.'

I said, 'Did you hear everything he said to her?'

She said, 'No, actually, she went upstairs with the lady. The other detective and I waited downstairs but when we were heading out to Pentland, he didn't go into any of that. I would have to speak to Paula and ask her if he did but from what I know, I don't think so.'

I said, 'What I will do is send you some information. I appeared on a TV interview just recently on 20th February and I have now got the means to send that interview to you. You could download it and show it to your father.'

She said, 'Yes, alright.'

I said, 'I have also written to Deb Frecklington, the leader of the LNP in Queensland, and have asked her that if she gets into power in the October election to order an inquest and to raise the reward money so we can get some other people interested. Do you know anything about Ted West at all?'

She said, 'No but Mum was talking about him and that he was involved in it. But what Dad told me. Yeah.'

I said, 'You did not discuss this matter with your mother as much as Paula from what I can gather?'

She said, 'Yes, I was young. Mum passed on when I was twenty or so I was probably a teenager and the only thing that Paula was more... but at the same time Mum was obviously telling the truth but no one would listen to her but they stuffed up by thinking they knew everything but it got to the point where it was too late and she passed and you know, they were like, you know you don't know what you are talking about and Bob Black. I can remember Mum saying he took her out to Pentland, and he said, "Why don't you show me where you think she is buried?" And Mum said, "I am not going to do that or you will say I had something to do with it."

'Mum said she was there that night, and they nearly pulled her up and if she hadn't kept driving, she would have been in the same boat as what those girls were. She would have been dead, and they did try and get her the next day in Charters Towers and from what Mum told me, it was a bit of a horror show, and she was half walking around and worrying he was going to catch up to her because she saw something she wasn't supposed to, and she knew these girls had been murdered.

'It was like there was nothing she could do and then for years she… not blamed herself, but she was going to give them a lift, but they had already left. She was thinking about it but my grandfather was quite a strict man, so he said, "No picking up any backpackers." She said she had a good think about it and decided that she would and by the time she walked out to tell the girls, they had already gone. She come across what she saw that night and the girls were missing and old mate turned up the next day with a big scratch down his face. If that doesn't say something is wrong, I don't know what does.'

I said, 'Did she say who that bloke was with the scratch?'

She said, 'No, I can't remember his name. I will have to talk to Dad because Dad will know, but I know he was one of the main ones in it.'

I said, 'Does Ivan Milat come into it?'

She said, 'Yeah, well, Mum said he was there, and he was the one with long hair.'

I said, 'He was the one with long hair. There was a bloke called Wally Barry involved.'

She said, 'Yes.'

I said, 'And he was supposed to have long hair. He had nothing at the front of his forehead and his hair went down to his shoulders at the back. Is that right?'

She said, 'From what I can remember, Wally Barry had long hair. Yes, it was kind of the in thing back then. They were all like hippies from what Mum was telling me.'

I said, 'And what about Pam List or Pam Barry? Pam List

was living with Wally Barry at the time. Do you know if she was involved at all?'

She said, 'I don't think she was involved as in as in firsthand but I think she covered it up from what I gather from Mum and Dad told me over the years she covered it up.'

I said, 'Well, you know I spoke to her on the telephone, and I put things to her and she got very upset about it all and it wasn't long after that she passed away.'

She said, 'Yeah, I know.'

I said, 'Yes alright and I will send you this material and you can download the show that was on TV and other stuff and is it alright if I send you stuff instead of having to go through the post to send to your father and you will give it to him.'

She said, 'Yeah, that's alright. I live out of town but Dad come down here quite a bit and I go up to the Towers so that shouldn't be an issue.'

I said, 'You have a car obviously.'

She said, 'Yes.'

I said, 'And Paula, I know now she has moved and your father has told me where she is so we won't say anything about her whereabouts because I am recording it so we will keep that to ourselves and I promised her not to name her in any of this which I have been fairly successful in doing but there have been times when it has come out and Paula is more confident now that she has moved away from Townsville. That is good that way.'

She said, 'Yes. It is good that way. I didn't know but there is still a couple of them who are alive, but I don't know if they would do much if they found out we were trying to solve it. God knows how old they would be now. But back in their day they were dangerous bastards. Mum lived in fear for a long time. Them coming around. A few things she told me over the years but when they went out on the property, and someone was crawling in the grass and her brother ran back to the house and they were shit scared. That sort of thing does not happen out of the blue. There has to be a reason behind it.'

I said, 'Was it the Twelve Mile Outstation on Wando Vale?'

She said, 'Yes.'

I said, 'You are happy to make your mother's words come true.'

She said, 'I can't see why not.'

I said, 'Well, it's nice if I can rely on you. I am not getting a lot of help really, but Paula does not want to get really involved any more, but she did give me a very good interview when I took an interview from her, which was very detailed and I am quite sure it is quite true.'

She said, 'Well, Paula knows the story inside and out.'

I said, 'Yes, if this gets to the inquest, she will have to give evidence in court and so it will all come out then.'

She said, 'Yes.'

I said, 'If you have anything to say, you can email me. I will send you this stuff and you will get my email address from that. You are free to contact me or by phone at any time.'

She said, 'Thanks. Have a good day.'

I said, 'Same to you.'

No doubt, like you, I do not know what to make of what the psychic told Joan about the whereabouts of Anita's body but there are some remarkable coincidences here. One is that one of the killers Wally Barry has passed as the psychic said. There is a shed near the railway line at Sensible Creek, which is not visible from the road and to which access is gained via tracks under the bridges at Sensible Creek according to my informants. One of the killers whose identity I have given to police is still alive and is a mechanic. As some pundits would say, 'This is not a bad batting average, is it?'

What do I think about people who allegedly talk to the dead? Well, I do not believe that anyone can talk to the dead. As far as I know, when you are dead, you're dead just like the billions of human beings who have lived and died on this planet over thousands of years.

However, having said that I have for many years held a belief that human beings have as yet undeveloped senses in addition to the five senses we do have and that these additional senses will develop through evolution in the thousands of years to come.

It is possible that some human beings already have this early development or part development of some of these senses which could explain the uncanny accurate forecasts that some people are able to make. I, myself, have been in situations in which I recall having previously seen the situation before in my dream many weeks, months, even years before.

In another instance, how does one explain that I dreamt one night that Robin (my partner metal detecting) who I have mentioned in this book was knocking at my front door? Later the same morning as usual, I went to my newsagent to buy my morning paper and the woman said to me, 'Do you know a Robin?'

I said, 'Yes I do but I have not seen her for six or more years.'

The news woman said, 'I had a phone call from a woman called Robin this morning who asked if a man named Mick Gurn had been in for his paper yet.' She said she replied, 'I know a Mick that comes in for his paper, but I don't know his last name. He has not been in yet.' Robin left no message with the newsagent. Robin knew the town I lived in but not my address.

I know Robin well enough to know that if she had come to my town, she would make enough inquiries to find me. I went to golf in the afternoon, but I left a note on the front door with my mobile number in case Robin called. Sure enough, she came to my place, found my note and rang me on my mobile phone. She was passing through on her way back to South Australia. Is this coincidence? Well, I am unable to explain it.

CHAPTER TWENTY-SIX

There is an aspect about these murders that has attracted little attention and probably because very little is known about the occurrence, but it is a fact that about two months after the body of Robin Bartram was discovered at Sensible Creek. A close friend of Anita Cunningham in the person of Althea Briers (now Bell) of North Baldwyn, Victoria 3102, received in the mail a letter addressed to her from Chillagoe in North Queensland.

Inside was an invoice document from Jack and Newell Pty Ltd, General Merchants, of Chillagoe dated 25th January 1973 for bread, 32 cents; 1 writing pad, 23 cents; 1 macaroni, 24 cents; 1 tin orange peach fruit drink, 33 cents and 1 packet of Bio Ad, 43 cents for a total of $1.55.

Written on the back of this invoice in longhand were the words:

I do not recommend that
you come here for long,
or unaccompanied. Tis verily
a dead hole madam, and
the station hands desperate.

There does not appear to be much mention about this letter

anywhere but in an email to Anita's mother on 12 September 2013 from Inspector Peter Smith. He stated:

'I have inquiries underway regarding the strange note sent to Anita's friend. I can confirm the note was written on a docket from a Chillagoe store. Chillagoe is located around 450kms north of Pentland. Police in 1972 attended Chillagoe with the docket and identified the shop. They showed pictures of both girls around the town and to the store owner; however, no one recognised the girls. Chillagoe was and remains a very small country town so the likelihood of them going unnoticed would be very low.

Our running sheet from 1972 also tells me the handwriting on the note was examined by handwriting experts both in Victoria and Queensland and both agreed the handwriting was not "identical" to Anita's handwriting and the note was dismissed.'

On 17th March 2020, I rang Althea Briers (now Bell) in Victoria who was quite cooperative but other than the fact that she had received the strange letter, she was unable to offer any explanation at all as to how the sender had come by her address. She agreed that in some way the sender must have had access to some personal records in the possession of Anita for the sender to obtain Althea's address in Victoria.

In 1972, Althea was surprised to learn of Anita's disappearance and obvious murder. She said that when Anita and Robin left Victoria in July 1972, she did not even know that they were going north to Bowen.

As a matter of interest, I obtained a sample of the handwriting of Ivan Milat and compared it to the handwriting on the note posted to Althea Briers. I could find no similarities but Ivan Milat in his letters to outside people from the jail, whenever he used the word **should,** for some strange reason, he underlined the word with two strokes. On the envelope addressed to Althea

Briers, the postcode 3102 is underlined with two strokes. I put this down to coincidence because my investigations are sufficient for me to believe that he went to New Zealand after the murders and the wording on the note seems to be from a person versed in poetry and unlike anything Milat wrote.

It is not likely that now fifty years after the murders, any new information surrounding this strange occurrence will be discovered. It is also strange that whoever posted this letter to Althea misspelt her name as Althaea but once again it is no help in discovering the author of the note.

Having said all that, I would point out to you that as this document posted to Althea Briers was an invoice it means that the document is the front page of the entry in an invoice book and therefore would leave a carbon copy of the transaction for compiling the account holder's statement and bill for the month and that would mean that the sender of the letter to Althea was the account holder and easily identified as such by the store owner.

I cannot believe that the store owner would not advise police of this when they made inquiries at his store so why has Inspector Smith said that police attended and located the store in 1972 with the docket. He makes no mention of the store owner identifying the invoice as written out by the store for a customer. Inspector Smith refers to the document posted to Althea as a docket. It is not a docket or a receipt. It is an invoice and in finer print at the base of the page it states it is an invoice and says, 'Please keep this invoice, as amount will only appear on statement.' The purchaser was clearly booking the goods up for payment later and therefore must have been well known to the storekeeper. So why was the purchaser not identified when police pursued this line of inquiry?

I say this despite the invoice saying it is a cash sale. It is more likely that the buyer was delaying paying for his goods. In any case, surely the person who wrote out the invoice would have offered information along these lines regarding the sale.

The cost of the purchase was $1.55, which may seem a small amount to us in 2023 but those same items now in 2023 may cost as much as $20.00 or more so in 1973 it was a costlier purchase.

Smith says the police showed the store owner pictures of the murdered girls, which they showed around town as well. **Something is not right here.** Police could not have located the store in 1972 or showed pictures of the girls around town in 1972 because the goods were not purchased until 25th January 1973 and the letter posted after that to Althea Briers. This could be a typographical error on the part of Inspector Smith, and he really meant 1973. However, it does not solve the questions I ask.

I deduce from the invoice that the account holder lived in Chillagoe or very close to Chillagoe because of the few items purchased. People living on cattle stations in the area travel long distances to get to a store and buy in greater quantity. I also deduce that the mailer of the letter had already addressed the envelope and stamped it with a seven-cent stamp before he bought the items, which included a writing pad.

To me, it seems that he bought the writing pad to send the letter with the brief comments to write on a page of the writing tablet but decided to use the back of the invoice anyway after making his purchases when that piece of paper became available.

A person with this ODD way of writing in poetry and maybe speaking that way would surely have been known to be a bit odd among residents of Chillagoe one could reasonably think.

The sender did not identify himself, but he must not have been very intelligent to use this invoice when sending the letter because the invoice should have identified him to police and the storekeeper when the store keeper saw the invoice.

The fact that the account holder's name is not on the invoice would indicate that the store did not have many account holders and that they knew who they were by name individually and added the transaction to their statement immediately.

Is this an example of the shoddy way this case has been handled since 1972?

We will have to wait and see.

These are matters for further inquiry by police and delving into by a Commission of Inquiry.

The invoice, envelope, message on back of invoice is below.

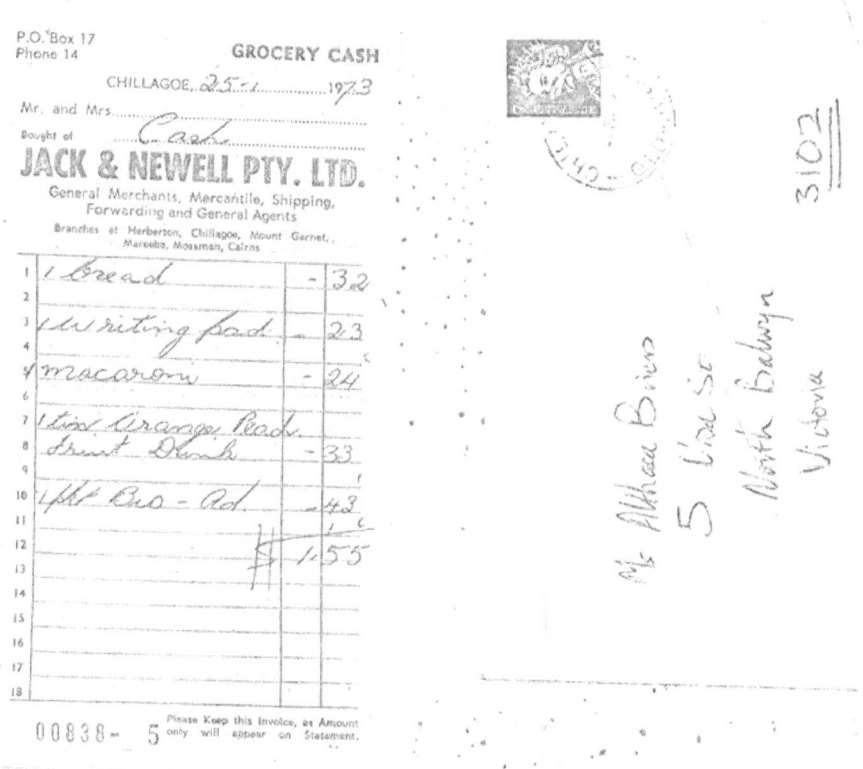

Another matter to consider is that in the communications from Inspector Smith, you may notice that Mearle Whyte's Christian name is spelt by him as MERLE. I have more recently found out that she spelt her name MEARLE.

If Bob Black had taken any statement from Mearle, then you

would expect that he would have found out how to spell her name correctly. This little snippet further confirms my beliefs that Officer Black never took anything in writing from Mearle Whyte when he interviewed her, which is most peculiar to say the least and a departure from normal police procedure.

I have seen the gravestone of Robin on TV. Her full name is Robin Jeanne Hoinville-Bartram.

CHAPTER TWENTY-SEVEN

The following letter was posted to the Commissioner of Police Katerina Carroll on Friday 23rd October 2020. The interview with Joan Whyte mentioned in this letter was shown in chapter twenty-five.

Commissioner of Police
Brisbane
Dated 22nd October 2020.
Dear Ms Carroll,
In respect to the unsolved murders of Anita Cunningham and Robin Jeanne Hoinville-Bartram at Pentland in 1972, I am enclosing extracts from a book I am writing about these cases with a view to having the government order a Commission of Inquiry into the police handling of these cases.

This letter contains particulars of a recorded telephone interview I had with Joan Whyte on 7th March 2020, who is another daughter of Mearle and John Whyte, which corroborates the recorded phone interviews I did with John and Paula Whyte on the 2nd and 4th October 2014, which prove that Mearle Whyte and her mother Betty Madigan did meet the murdered girls at the Pentland Hotel in 1972.

This interview throws new light on the possible location of the remains of the murdered Anita Cunningham and in my opinion throws some suspicion on another man who could have been involved in these murders.

Another chapter of my book deals with the missed opportunity by police to identify a person who posted a peculiar note to a friend of Anita Cunningham in 1973, who must have had some item from the possessions of Anita, which gave that person the address for him to post the note to Victoria.

I then pasted into this letter chapter twenty-five from my draft book, which detailed the recorded telephone interview I did with this daughter of John and Mearle Whyte.

In another chapter I write,

'Further, Joan Whyte is so moved by the terrible treatment handed out to her mother by the police that she is studying law and is pursuing a career where she hopes to be able to make a difference, so this type of thing does not happen to anyone else's mother.'

I then pasted from my draft book chapter twenty-six which deals with the mysterious letter posted from Chillagoe, North Queensland to Althea Briers in Victoria with the invoice for goods dated 23rd February 1973.

I then continued my letter to the Commissioner of Police as under.

'I have not previously forwarded you this information because it has been a waste of my time and money giving police information from my investigations, which is very sad. It is to be hoped that there is a change of attitude and that you dismiss everything that has been reported by former Police Officer Bob Black and begin the investigation of these murders from my interviews with John and Paula Whyte on 2nd and 4th October 2014 as I have told the police repeatedly and repeatedly over the years.

I have told the police and principally your predecessor, Commissioner Ian Stewart, years ago, that whatever I have to do to get justice for these murdered girls I will do. This reluctance of *the police to admit the reality of the situation is just making them look sillier and sillier which is an embarrassment to me, being a former detective sergeant myself.*

Yours faithfully,
M.J. Gurn

On 6th December 2020, I wrote to the new attorney general Ms Shannon Fentiman requesting a Commission of Inquiry into the mishandling of investigations by police into the murders of these two girls. This letter contained the questions I asked the attorney general to ask police so that she could make an informed decision on my application. She obviously did not ask police.

The main body of this application can be read as Appendix Number Ten, which totalled forty-five pages in all.

A reply from the attorney general denying my application for a Commission of Inquiry dated 19th April 2021 appears as under:

I replied to the Attorney General in an email as under:

Our ref: 596004/1, 5458911

19 APR 2021

Mr Mick Gurn
mickgurn@hotmail.com

Dear Mr Gurn

Thank you for your correspondence dated 6 December 2020 and 11 February 2021. I also acknowledge your correspondence to Mr David Crisafulli MP, Member for Broadwater, dated 11 January 2021 and 11 March 2021, which Mr Crisafulli sent to me for my consideration as the Attorney-General and Minister for Justice, Minister for Women and Minister for the Prevention of Domestic and Violence, on 22 March 2021.

I note your requests to the Honourable Yvette D'Ath MP, previous Attorney-General and Minister for Justice, who decided not to direct the State Coroner to hold inquests into the death of Ms Robin Jeanne Hoinville-Bartram and the suspected death of Ms Anita Cunningham, which remain under investigation by the Queensland Police Service. I note that a reward of $250,000 remains on offer for information that leads to the apprehension and conviction of the person or persons responsible for the death of Ms Hoinville-Bartram and the suspected death of Ms Cunningham.

The previous Attorney-General and her staff have informed you of the role of the Crime and Corruption Commission (CCC), which is a standing commission of inquiry into allegations of corruption by police officers. I note that you have views on the actions that you consider various police officers have taken (or have failed to take) in these investigations. If you wish to pursue these matters, the appropriate course would be for you to write directly to the CCC detailing your concerns.

A coroner acting under the *Coroners Act 2003* has the same powers as a commission of inquiry when investigating deaths and suspected deaths in Queensland. I appreciate the analysis you have undertaken over many years in relation to the death of Ms Hoinville-Bartram and the suspected death of Ms Cunningham. I understand the grief and distress that family, friends and persons concerned in the investigation of these matters feel when the persons responsible for these crimes have not been charged. The position remains however that there is no cogent, reliable evidence or new evidence concerning the death of Ms Hoinville-Bartram and the suspected death of Ms Cunningham which may be considered by a coronial investigation and inquest process.

I appreciate that this is not the outcome you were expecting, but cogent, reliable or new evidence is required before I will consider exercising my discretion to direct the State Coroner to conduct investigations or inquests into the death of Ms Hoinville-Bartram and the suspected death of Ms Cunningham.

Dear Ms Fentiman,

Thank you for your reply to my application for a Commission of Inquiry into the rapes and murders of Robin Jeanne Hoinville-Bartram and Anita Cunningham at Pentland in 1972.

Your reply is absolutely gut-wrenching after seven years trying to obtain justice for these girls and to find the remains of Anita Cunningham. I am sure that the dozens of persons who are following me on this journey will have similar sentiments to me with your reply not to say the utter disappointment of David Cunningham, his mother Eileen and the other brothers of Anita.

The very purpose of my application to you is to provide you with the evidence I have uncovered over seven years, which does, in the minds of most ordinary citizens, provide you with sufficient material to effectively form a view that police investigations to date have been seriously mishandled and that there has been a cover up to stop embarrassment to the Queensland police service.

The examination of witnesses is where the grounds would come from to prove this cover up. How on earth are these cases going to be solved if the very persons who can provide evidence that the girls were at the Pentland Hotel and is where they left from with the men who raped and killed them if these witnesses are not examined in the witness box because police are unwilling to admit that their investigations have been very poorly conducted. I speak from experience, and I know that these investigations should have been handled differently from 2003 to now and that the supposed investigations at Charters Towers in 2015 by an inspector were an absolute disgrace and are grounds for my claiming that those actions amount to perverting the course of justice.

You say that I should deal with the Crime and Corruption Commission, but I have already dealt with them on these matters, and they will not investigate. I have forwarded my concerns to the Police Integrity Squad, which also failed to take any action, which was the result I foretold.

It seems that the only way the crimes will be solved, and the real truth will surface is with pressure from the public for a Commission of Inquiry, which I will do my utmost to encourage.

In my application to you for a Commission of Inquiry, I asked you to ask the police a number of questions. I am asking you to forward to me the response you received from the police service concerning my application please.

Yours sincerely,

M.J. Gurn

I did not receive a copy of the police response to the attorney general, which she should have forwarded to them for an opinion on my application for a Commission of Inquiry.

David Crisafulli, Leader of the LNP in Queensland Parliament, did write a letter to the attorney general supporting my application for a Commission of Inquiry and the attorney general replied to him in the same vein as she replied to me.

My investigations into these crimes took an unexpected turn when John Whyte telephoned me on Friday 30th April 2021 to say that he had been lying in bed the night before when it came to him that in about 1998/9 he and his wife Mearle were trying to obtain a rental house through the housing commission or some council scheme and that their applications were handled by a clerk in the Charters Towers court house.

He remembered that Mearle informed him that the clerk was a man named [redacted] and that this man had been a member of the band that had played at the Pentland Hotel the day the murdered girls were there. She said that this man was singing in the band. John was very disappointed with himself that he had not remembered this information earlier. (In some circumstances you may think that this information was very convenient from John Whyte but one has to remember that he has suffered severe head injuries, and his memory is patchy.)

I confirmed with someone in Charters Towers that this man had been a clerk in the Magistrates Court House at Charters Towers about 1998/9.

I prepared a letter for the Commissioner of Police Katerina Carroll, which I posted by Express Post to her on Monday 10th May 2021 with this additional information and emphasising points of my arguments.

Commissioner of Police
Brisbane.
Dated 9th May 2021
Dear Ms Carroll,
When you took office, I wrote to you officially and personally concerning the inadequate investigations into the rapes and murders of Robin Jeanne Hoinville-Bartram and Anita Cunningham at Pentland in 1972 wherein I asked and expected that you would take action to see that justice for the murder of these girls would be carried out but unfortunately nothing changed. At least one of the killers remains at large living in Charters Towers despite the information I have given you over these years and more recently with more information from another recorded interview with a credible witness corroborating previous information.

When your Inspector Peter Smith went to Charters Towers in April 2015, his mission was to interview persons who I was informed by Assistant Commissioner Hogan in her letter dated 8th January 2015 would be interviewed as well as him establishing the truth or otherwise of the recorded telephone interviews I had done with witnesses on 2nd and 4th October 2014.

She also said that Inspector Smith had reviewed the original investigation and that it was being reviewed by the Homicide Cold Case Unit. Smith was in charge of this unit. Assistant Commissioner Hogan also said, 'The Homicide Cold Case unit has investigated information provided by Merle Whyte, prior to her passing in June

2014. The outcomes of these investigations have been provided to you in the response by Inspector Smith.'

Smith had replied to me in a letter dated 15th September 2014 with the crux of it being that Mearle Whyte was mistaken in her belief of having met the murdered girls at the Pentland Hotel. You will see that this cannot possibly be Smith's real view in light of the following information I provide.

The result of his visit to Charters Towers in April 2015 was that he did not pursue any investigations into the veracity of the recorded telephone interviews with me by witnesses or interview the persons he was charged with interviewing by Assistant Commissioner Hogan.

From Charters Towers in April 2015, he emailed me that I would receive his review about the investigations he had made but this review advice was never received by me despite repeated requests for same to the then Commissioner Ian Stewart. The result of his mission to Charters Towers resulted in me advising you that his actions in Charters Towers in not carrying out his duties effectively amounted to perverting the course of justice but no investigations or interviews with witnesses have been carried out by other detectives to substantiate my charge. Smith has not been held accountable. It is reasonable for me and others to ask WHY?

When Smith was in Charters Towers, he let the cat out of the bag by telling a witness that men involved in this sordid business (as he put it) were 'friends of the police' and 'were persons of influence who did not want their involvement known' as shown in following information.

On 29th April 2018, David Cunningham spoke to one of my witnesses who has provided one of my recorded telephone interviews where she told him that Smith had told her that her mother must have a mental problem, that the family's story was 'fiddlesticks' and to 'give it up' and 'don't even try to go there' as the young men implicated are now 'good people' with friends in the police force. That the young men have now become magistrates, lawyers and bailiffs. That they are people of influence who don't want this sordid story to come to light.

After some email contact with this witness, she emailed me in her own hand so it cannot be denied that Smith had said to her that her mother did not know what she was talking about and that the men who were involved that night are upholding citizens and that they would never do a thing like that and that her mother's accusations could get good people in trouble. He had gone on to say that Bob Black was a great man and raised his voice and overpowered her at the time. Later, when showing Smith where her mother thought the body of Anita Cunningham was buried on the Flinders Highway, Smith told her in a way of speaking, 'That I could get myself hurt and that I should let the story go and be buried with my mother.' He said that like Bob Black, he had belittled her mother and that she and her mother had made this shit up and that they were mad.

Why would a senior police officer make such stupid statements admitting that he knew who they were and that they were involved to some degree but does not pursue them to establish what they know and bring the offenders to justice. By his own words, he knows who they are so why has he not established what they know about them being in the band performing at Pentland when the murdered girls were there when they met Mearle and Betty Madigan?

This is the same officer who was in charge of the Cold Case Unit and finds in his and his unit's review of the cases that Mearle Whyte story of meeting the girls at the Pentland Hotel is wrong or that she is mistaken when all the time he knows who the other band members were who played their instruments and sang at the Pentland Hotel on the day Mearle met the murdered girls. If this does not prove my case of perverting the course of justice, I do not know what does. Making this accusation hurts me more than you can know but my loyalties lie with the murdered girls.

I have now ascertained the identity of one band member who was singing in the band this day and who went on in life to have a career as a magistrate in Queensland. He is [redacted], retired and who lives in [redacted].

I have to ask is the real reason for this cover up of one member protecting another because of loyalties outside police loyalties, which I foolishly believed was dead and buried years ago? This amounts to saying, 'To hell with justice for the murdered girls, just protect our own hides.'

Former Police Officer Bob Black is the problem here and his reporting of not believing a woman who met the girls at the Pentland Hotel in July 1972. His reporting is not believable in view of information I have given you. Then when I stir the pot, Smith protects Black. I ask who is protecting Smith because if ever there exists a case of perverting the course of justice and a cover up, this is it. As I said before, no amount of soft soaping it will change the truth. The CCC do not want to know about it and flicked it to the police integrity unit who did zilch. So just how deep does this cancer run?

Your Detective Inspector Hansen appointed a detective to review these cases after complaints from David Cunningham, brother of the murdered Anita Cunningham. This detective contacted David initially but since then has not contacted David with any information and has been missing in action with any information to David Cunningham. WHY? David and I are entitled to ask.

I have previously advised you that one of the killers still alive is John Fox, who has spread rumours around Charters Towers trying to involve my informant John Whyte as guilty in these crimes, which is a despicable act trying to throw suspicion away from himself.

I told you in my letter to you when you took office how to

obtain evidence to arrest and charge John Fox with these rapes and murders but twenty-one months later nothing has happened.

There is a simple way to put a stop to this charade and that is to appoint two detectives you trust who have not previously been involved in any way with this case and give them unfettered authority to pursue my authentic information.

It is with deep regret that I raise this dreadful topic, forcing me to complain about a fellow police officer, albeit from a retired one with twenty-three years' service to back up his credentials and experience and appointed a Justice of the Peace in 1979.

For my own safety, I have spread my thoughts on all this far and wide among my relatives and friends and sympathetic press and will be included in the book titled HEAR OUR CRY I am writing.

Sincerely,

M. J. Gurn

On the morning of Tuesday 11th May 2021, John Whyte rang me to say he had been talking to a woman who had a connection with the Ted West who is mentioned in these investigations as being the person who had cashed the cheque for Betty Madigan in the Pentland Hotel on the day she had met the murdered girls and who was the person who arranged the lift to Charters Towers for the girls with a member of the band. West was also seen to place the murdered girl's luggage on the roof rank of the band members car.

John had information that Ted West had recently been hospitalised but was home on the Gold Coast but bedridden and not expected to live.

This information was of such importance that I immediately posted another letter to the Commissioner of Police Katerina Carroll by Express Post as I considered it imperative that urgent action was necessary for police to interview this man before he died. This brief letter is shown below.

Commissioner of Police
Brisbane
11th May 2021
Dear Ms Carroll,

If this was not urgent, I would not be writing Express Post twice in two days at the expensive $7.65 each time.

I will try to be brief. The murders of Robin Jeanne Hoinville-Bartram and Anita Cunningham at Pentland in 1972 occurred after they left the Pentland Hotel in a car with men. They were tricked into believing they were being given a lift to Charters Towers. The lift was arranged by a man named Ted West or similar spelling who was actually seen putting the murdered girl's luggage onto the roof rack of the car. This is also the man who cashed a cheque for Betty Madigan at the Pentland Hotel when Mearle Whyte (later Madigan) and her mother Betty Madigan met the girls there.

If former Police Officer Bob Black actually interviewed this man at any time is unknown but it has been said that he has denied any involvement at all.

Yesterday in my letter to you, I mentioned that I had told you how to obtain the evidence to arrest and charge John Fox with these crimes. That was by getting the truth out of this Ted West. Obtaining the truth from this man has been critical in proving Mearle Whyte's story of meeting the murdered girls. Today I learned from John Whyte that he has information that West has been hospitalised and is now home somewhere on the Gold Coast but bedridden. John believes that he is dying but what the health problem is, he does not know.

I am asking you to immediately cause this man to be interviewed by police before he should die as we do not want another episode like that of police failing to interview Mearle Whyte in Townsville Hospital before she died on 16th June 2014 (should be 27th June, 2014) not interviewed by your Inspector Smith although I had told *him she was dying on 9th May 2014 and wished to be interviewed by police and tell the full and truthful story about meeting the murdered girls. He had five weeks to interview her.*

This man West is well known in Charters Towers. He owns houses there I believe. He was a boner at the Cape River Meatworks in 1972. It should not be difficult to get his address on the Gold Coast from Charters Towers Police. His wife was a teacher at one time at a local school and she is well known there too.

David Cunningham, brother of the murdered Anita, is trying to contact Detective Inspector Hansen with a similar request for him to arrange for West to be interviewed as a matter of urgency.

I leave this in your hands.
Yours faithfully.
M. J. Gurn

A reply from the Attorney General to my application for a Commission of Inquiry is as follows:

2 8 MAY 2021

Mr Mick Gurn
mickgurn@hotmail.com

Dear Mr Gurn

Thank you for your correspondence dated 19 April 2021 regarding your application for a commission of inquiry.

I understand your desire for further investigations to be undertaken into suspected corrupt conduct by police investigating the death of Ms Hoinville-Bartram and the suspected death of Ms Anita Cunningham.

The Crime and Corruption Commission (CCC), a standing commission of inquiry, remains available to investigate your concerns about alleged police corruption. The Parliamentary Crime and Conduct Committee has oversight of the CCC to ensure that the CCC handles complaints in an appropriate manner.

I understand that you have contacted the CCC before and that they have taken no action, but I strongly encourage you to approach the CCC to present the totality of evidence you have collated which you allege demonstrates a cover up of police corruption. It is very important that your correspondence to the CCC details each allegation against each specific police officer, including the evidence you have collated to substantiate each allegation.

I understand your reticence to approach the CCC again. However, as I have noted above, the CCC is a standing commission of inquiry which examines allegations of police corruption and is therefore the entity responsible for investigating your concerns.

Yours sincerely

[signature]

Shannon Fentiman MP
Attorney-General and Minister for Justice
Minister for Women and Minister for the Prevention of Domestic and Family Violence
Member for Waterford

My reply to the attorney general is as follows:

Dear Ms Fentiman
Attorney General
3rd June 2021

Your email of 2nd instant has been received. Thank you urging me to again further contact the CCC.

First, let's go back a bit. I replied to your official refusal to order a Commission of Inquiry in your email to me dated 19th April 2021. My application for this inquiry was for (1) The incompetent police handling of investigations into the murders of Robin Jeanne Hoinville-Bartram and Anita Cunningham at Pentland in 1972. (2) The way the justice system has been manipulated to keep the circumstances from the public.

My forty-five odd page application to you for such an inquiry set out all the information at my disposal and which fully informed you of all the facts within my knowledge. I did not embellish any part of that information in any way. I do not know how I could have been more explicit.

A paragraph from page six of that application reads as follows:

*'Despite all this, the Brisbane Newspapers, the Courier Mail and Sunday Mail have not supported me or David Cunningham and have not even had the decency to reply to correspondence from us. Why have the editors of these newspapers blackballed David Cunningham and me and stopped us from gaining traction in our efforts to see justice for these murdered girls? How they have been hoodwinked in this day and age is remarkable to say the least when their editors claim from time to time, they are all about truth and justice. I hope the people or entity behind this abuse of the justice system protecting certain individuals will be revealed to the general public with a Commission of Inquiry **because anything less than this official procedure is unlikely to uncover and expose their identities.**'*

You replied yesterday, 2nd instant, advising me that the Parliamentary Crime and Conduct Committee has oversight over the Crime and Corruption Committee and urging me to make another application to the CCC.

In two recent replies to you, I asked you for the answers you received from the police. I asked you to ask the police about their stance in their investigations into these murders. In each reply from you since then, I have had no acknowledgment from you to my requests for these answers in the two email replies from you.

I must ask why? Could it be that you did not ask these questions? The next question that arises is how could you possibly make a decision to deny my application for a Commission of Inquiry if you did not know the answers to these questions from the police?

Again, I say that there were two matters raised in my application for a Commission of Inquiry. One was about ascertaining who murdered these girls and why the case has not been solved despite my very believable information concerning the identities of the possible offenders. I pointed out that examination of witnesses who can throw light on the murders would be adduced from them in the witness box during the inquiry.

The second matter for investigation by a Commission of Inquiry was how the press and media have been hoodwinked into believing that there was nothing to see here and how David Cunningham and I have been treated as lepers by the press to get the story out into the public arena with the exception of the Northern Miner newspaper and the Townsville Bulletin and from Peter Cameron in his traps column over four years in the Sunday Mail.

Do not forget that any interest in this investigation by Channel Seven in 2015 ended abruptly after Inspector Peter Smith went to Charters Towers in April 2015 to inquire into my recorded telephone interviews with witnesses who said in his email to me from Charters Towers that he had told their representative Alex Cullen something that was sufficient for that commercial television channel to lose all interest in my investigations, which is just another example of how no exposure to this cover up has been successfully accomplished. What Smith told Cullen is not known to me and would have to come from Cullen in the witness box.

These are the actual words in the inspector's email to me that he says he told Cullen, 'I have personally advised Alex Cullen of Channel 7 of the outcome of our further review.'

My belief here is that the justice system has been corrupted over the past seven years but who or what is responsible for this situation is not known to me but would be revealed with a Commission of Inquiry. I said that I have been up against a very powerful force, but I do not know the identity of that force. If I had the information, then I could approach the CCC again. All I have is what is so blindingly obvious to me, many others and to the professional journalists who support me.

Of course, one has to wonder how when Peter Cameron's articles about my work on this case is published in his traps column in the Sunday Mail. There was no follow up investigation by the editor of the Sunday Mail and the complete lack of interest from other newspapers or the radio and television stations yet people I know were asking me about the cases and asking why the police have not solved the cases. Knowing the press as we do, I cannot imagine for a second that they would not have contacted the police media section for information and must have been told convincingly sufficient information for them to take no further interest in these cases.

I am not the only one believing there has been a cover up by police to hide the true facts from the public. Channel Nine used those words over two days a number of times in their preamble build up to the airing of their program on my interview with them in 2019.

I will not make any further application to the CCC because I do not know who or what is behind these circumstances outlined here. That is what the Commission of Inquiry could establish by questioning the persons who I have told you need to be questioned in the witness box to get to the heart of the corruption.

As to the Detective Inspector I have mentioned previously involved in this case, I have given all relevant information to the Commissioner of Police, and it is her job to take whatever action is appropriate. You have a copy of this information to the commissioner in my letter to her of 9th May 2021, which you have acknowledged receiving in your reply yesterday.

Yours faithfully

M.J. Gurn

Copies to relevant parties for their information.

CHAPTER TWENTY-EIGHT

When you are reading the history of my investigations, you will of course notice that John Whyte conveniently, it might seem to some people, just comes up with additional information out of nowhere. Well, there is an explanation and that is that John's memory of events has been impaired due to head injuries he received about 1977 when he was involved in a fight with one of brothers who hit him over the head with some hard object, causing him to lose consciousness and waking up in hospital seventeen days later from a deep coma.

Doctors have told him that his memory of events in his life will probably get worse as he gets older. John did phone me on 30th April 2021, informing me that he had recalled that Mearle had told him that one of the band members who sang in the band at the Pentland Hotel on the day the girls left there with their murderers was a man who had worked at the Charters Towers Court House and who went on to be a magistrate. This came about because John and Mearle were endeavouring to obtain a government rental house, but their application seemed to be always down the list handled by this man at the Charters Towers Court House. Mearle challenged this man as to why they had not been given a rental house.

Mearle believed that this man was deliberately withholding

their opportunity for a rental house as he also knew who Mearle was as it related to the Pentland murders.

Similarly he recalled that he had left his motor vehicle at a garage in Charters Towers for service and asked Mearle to pick the car up later in the day but she refused, telling John that a person at the garage was in fact one of the men who had left the Pentland Hotel with the murdered girls in the band members car and was one of the three men who had tried to get her to Townsville with them the next day.

On Tuesday 11th May 2021, John advised me that he had information that Ted West had been hospitalised and in danger of death as far as he could make out.

This information was urgently conveyed to the Commissioner of Police and David Cunningham received four phone calls from different police who assured him that Ted West would be interviewed. This happened after I told David about West's condition and which he conveyed to the Homicide Squad urgently.

It would seem that West would have been interviewed by police but as usual, neither David Cunningham nor I have been advised what West's position is now. It is to be hoped that he now tells the truth and admits his part in these events.

On 16th November 2021, during a phone call from John Whyte, he told me that he had tried unsuccessfully many times to get his wife to go to the police prior to 2003 when she eventually did make contact with Officer Bob Black. He said that Mearle was just too frightened of the killers who were still living in Charters Towers and knew her identity.

This fear for Mearle, which prevented her coming forward, was borne out specifically in Paula Whyte's recorded phone conversation with me which corroborates the information John has supplied.

It will be interesting when other members of the Whyte

family give evidence, hopefully in an inquiry, about Mearle's fears for her life from the murderers of the two girls.

John said that he was friendly with a policeman in Charters Towers at the time named Des Whelan or similar name. He discussed Mearle's position with Whelan, but Whelan told John that the police were powerless to assist unless Mearle was prepared to provide her information to them. John believes this man Whelan may now be deceased. To me, whichever police were serving in Charters Towers at the time Whelan was there may be in a position to say that Whelan advised them of the situation. Whelan is unlikely to have kept this information to himself in my opinion.

It is also very likely that that whoever was in charge of Charters Towers Police Station when Whelan was there was consulted on this matter and efforts should be made to see if this occurred.

CHAPTER TWENTY-NINE

In a letter to the Attorney General I said I have had tremendous support for my investigations from Peter Cameron who mentioned my endeavours to gain justice for these murdered girls on a least sixteen occasions in his traps column in the Sunday Mail newspaper over four years until he retired. I also had huge support of my efforts from Trudy Brown, editor of the Northern Miner newspaper in Charters Towers and through her efforts by the Townsville Bulletin newspaper. Channel Nine showed a segment about the case on Queensland Television in a program on 20th February 2020 in which I was interviewed on television for which I am appreciative.

I write that despite all this, the Brisbane newspapers, the Courier Mail and Sunday Mail have not supported me or David Cunningham and have not even had the decency to reply to correspondence from us. I asked why have the editors of these newspapers blackballed David Cunningham and me and stopped us from gaining traction in our efforts to see justice for these murdered girls. How these editors have been hoodwinked in this day and age is remarkable to say the least when these editors claim from time to time they are all about truth and justice.

I hope that the people or entity behind this abuse of the justice system protecting certain individuals will be revealed to the public with a Commission of Inquiry because anything less than this official procedure is unlikely to uncover and expose their identities.

I say that these crimes are solvable with at least one offender still alive and named by me to the police. I said I had told the police how to go about solving this case and that from other citizens this may sound presumptuous on my part but that I had the knowledge and experience to make the claim. I also had told the police the names of two other male offenders who are now deceased.

I implored the attorney general to correct this abuse of the justice system.

I attached to this application copies of my recorded interviews with witnesses including the foreword to this book from David Cunningham, which explained the pain and suffering of his mother and family in losing Anita and the frustration the family felt with the lack of police activity in solving the cases despite the extraordinary amount of sound evidence I had supplied them with. I asked the attorney general to see reason for the sake of justice in this state and to order a Commission of Inquiry in line with my suggestions.

I suggested to the attorney general that she will probably follow custom and forward my application to the police for comment. I urged her to disregard the anticipated comments from police, which would be along the following lines.

'That extensive investigations have been made into the claims of Mr Gurn and evidence has not been uncovered to support his claims against the inactivity of police in solving these crimes.'

I suggested they will further say, 'All persons whose identities were made known to former Officer Black have been questioned and deny all knowledge of involvement in these crimes. There is no evidence to connect any such person.'

Further that the claims by Mr Gurn regarding the

perverting of the course of justice by Inspector Smith are being considered.

I said to the attorney general that for her to make a judgment on whether she would order a Commission of Inquiry, she would need answers from the police to a number of questions such as 'is the police position still that the murdered girls were never at the Pentland Hotel before they were murdered?'

I asked her to ask police why Mr Gurn had not been forwarded the review Inspector Smith said he would forward to Mr Gurn, which concerned the recorded interviews Mr Gurn did with John and Paula Whyte, which Mr Gurn had requested from the Commissioner of Police on a number of occasions.

I asked her to ask the police why they had not supported Mr Gurn's attempts to trace particulars of the cheque transaction by Betty Madigan at the Pentland Hotel most likely in July, 1972 when she met the murdered girls which would support her and her daughters claims of meeting the murdered girls and establish the date of the transaction and the meeting, which was the day the murders and rapes were committed.

I asked her to ask police how the investigation into the letter sent on 23rd February 1973 from Chillagoe to a friend of Anita Cunningham was so bungled. I pointed out that this bungling had failed to identify the person who posted this letter to a friend of Anita Cunningham who must have been in possession of some article from the possessions of Anita for her to obtain this friend's address in Victoria. I pointed out that this mishandling could have solved the murders and obtained vital information about the killers eight months after the murders and rapes.

I asked her to ask police if they had searched areas Mr Gurn had asked to be searched to find Anita Cunningham's body which involved more recent information, he had obtained from the recorded interview he had with Joan Whyte in March 2020.

I asked her to asked police who were the police present at any time Bob Black interviewed Mearle Whyte and if they supported Black's opinion of meeting the murdered girls.

I said she should ask if detailed statements were obtained by Black from Mearle Whyte and Betty Madigan when Mearle first approached the police in 2003 with information and if so, make these statements available to her as part of her deliberations. I pointed out that obtaining these statements is fundamental practice in police investigations.

I asked her to ask if Queensland police had made inquiries of police in New Zealand in an attempt to discover if Ivan Milat was in New Zealand and the dates he was there adding that I had done that.

I asked her to ask if police had contacted New South Wales police to see if any of the 400 odd recovered items in the arrest of Ivan Milat could be connected to the murdered girls Bartram and Cunningham. I said I had done that.

I asked her to ask if police had advised New South Wales Police to keep in mind these crimes should Ivan Milat make any admissions in his final days, which I had also done.

I suggested that she should inquire if any DNA was found on the clothing of Robin Bartram's body, not consistent with her own DNA and if any such sample had been tested against Ivan Milat's DNA.

I asked her to ask if inquiries had been made into whether Walter (Wally) Barry could be connected to these murders and what was the information from Mount Isa Police, which caused Inspector Nikola in charge of the Townsville District to order a new search around Sensible Creek to try and find the remains of Anita Cunningham.

I told the attorney general that examination and cross-examination of all police involved and a long list of witnesses I could provide who would be called to the witness stand in a Commission of Inquiry would get to the truth of the many aspects of why these cases had not been solved and why the failure of police to act professionally had allowed murderers and rapists to enjoy years of freedom since 2003 when they should have been behind bars had he cases been handled by more competent police.

Other comments were made in this letter.

I wrote to the attorney general on 11th February 2021 saying that I had applied to her for a Commission of Inquiry and that there was an urgency for this matter to be resolved.

The application by me was made on 6th December 2020 and there had not been a response so on 14th March 2021, I wrote a letter to the attorney general and told her that I found it most disturbing and disappointing that I had not even had the courtesy of an acknowledgment of my letters to her let alone a comprehensive assessment of my request after three months, which was not the way I and many others following me on this journey for justice think government business should be conducted.

I said in that letter that I pointed out to her and David Crisafulli that a detective inspector had said to an informant that people involved in these crimes are people of influence who do not want their involvement disclosed as they went on in life to become a magistrate, a solicitor and a bailiff. I said that those words should send a chill up the spine of people looking for justice for these girls and to anyone interested in our justice system.

The attorney general replied to me in a letter dated 19th April 2021 acknowledging my correspondence and that which Mr Crisafulli had sent to her, which he done after my request to him for support.

She went on quoting various matters, which included, 'The position remains, however, there is no cogent, reliable evidence or new evidence concerning the death of Ms Hoinville-Bartram and the suspected death of Ms Cunningham which may be considered by a coronial investigation and inquest process.'

I replied to the attorney general on 11th May 2021 that she had obviously not asked the questions I had asked her to ask the police so she could make an informed decision and that I therefore could not see how she could make an informed decision without this information.

Then on 28th May, the attorney general wrote to me thanking me for my correspondence. She said she understood my desire for further investigations be undertaken into suspected corrupt conduct by police investigating the death of Ms Hoinville-Bartram and the suspected death of Ms Anita Cunningham.

She said that the Crime and Corruption (CCC), a standing commission of inquiry, remains available to investigate my concerns about alleged police corruption and that the Parliamentary Crime and Conduct Committee has oversight of the CCC to ensure that the CCC handles complaints in an appropriate manner.

She continued that she understood that I had contacted the CCC before and that they have taken no action, but she strongly encouraged me to approach the CCC to present the totality of evidence I had collated which I alleged had demonstrated a cover up of police corruption. She said it is very important that my correspondence to the CCC detailed each allegation against each specific police officer, including the evidence I had collated to substantiate each allegation.

She said she understood my reluctance to approach the CCC again, but that as she had noted above in her letter that the CCC is a standing commission of inquiry which examines allegations of police corruption and is therefore the entity responsible for investigating my concerns.

I replied to the attorney general that I would have to think carefully before I would approach the CCC again as I did not know who was behind the corruption.

Time passed and matters were reported in the daily press, which seemed to indicate that matters about police were not achieving good results when the CCC referred complaints to the Police Integrity Unit, plus the fact that there had been a change of Chairmanship of the CCC, so on 7th August 2022 I lodged another complaint with the CCC stating that I had previously reported the same matters to them without them investigating the matters I had raised with them but that I was again contacting them because it was at the suggestion of the attorney general.

In that letter to the CCC after outlining what I was complaining about, I said I would not contribute further unless I received some sort of indication that they would take some action.

This letter very quickly elicited a reply from the CCC that they would take no action and their position was unaltered.

On 17th August 2022, I sent an email to the attorney general of which a copy is pasted below.

Dear Ms Fentiman,

On 9th instant, I forwarded you a CC of the email I sent to the Crime and Corruption Commission requesting their assistance in delving into why investigations by police into the murders of Robin Jeanne Hoinville-Bartram and Anita Cunningham at Pentland, Queensland in 1972 have not achieved a positive result in respect to solving these crimes among other matters of corruption with which you are fully aware through correspondence from me and my applications for a Commission of Inquiry to get to the heart of the matter.

In a letter from you on 28th May 2021, you urged me to again complain to the Crime and Corruption Commission, but I did not comply with your request until the 9th instant for reasons which I have explained in my email complaint to the Crime and Corruption Commission and to you.

This morning, I received an email from the CCC to the effect that they will take no action on my complaint.

Your office will receive the email from the CCC to me as a forwarded email today. The CCC again are suggesting that I further complain to the Ethical Standards Command of the Queensland Police Service, but I have been there before and I have no faith understandably in that body to take any action as they, like the CCC, previously advised me they will take no action on the detailed matters I raise.

If the perpetrators of these crimes are ever going to be identified and if still alive by the time a proper inquiry is under way and they are brought to justice, then it is up to you to order the Commission of Inquiry I have repeatedly requested from you. I respectfully submit to you that your reasons for not ordering a Commission of Inquiry pale into insignificance when stood alongside the abundance of credible evidence I have unfolded and brought under your notice plus the fact that your reluctance to order this inquiry is done without you knowing answers to the questions I asked you to ask police so that you could make an informed decision on my request.

It is regrettable that the CCC will not take up these cases despite my clearly informing them that I was making my complaint again to them on your request.

Then on 22nd August 2022, I sent a letter as an attachment to an email to the attorney general as under.

Ms S. Fentiman
Attorney General
Brisbane
Dated 22nd August 2022
Your Reference number 596004/.5590258

Dear Ms Fentiman,

On 17th instant I sent you an email, which is basically another request to you for a Commission of Inquiry into the murders of Robin Jeanne Hoinville-Bartram and Anita Cunningham at Pentland in 1972 wherein I tried to point out to you that the reasons for your reluctance to order this inquiry pale into insignificance when laid beside the credible evidence I have placed before you over a very long time coupled with the fact that I have every reason to believe that you do not know the answers to the questions I asked you to ask police so that you could make an informed decision.

I wish to further bring to you attention what I fear has been forgotten to same extent that the actions of Detective Inspector Peter Smith in Charters Towers in April 2015 were of such a nature that constituted perverting the course of justice.

I pointed out all the facts supporting this statement to the previous Police Commissioner Ian Stewart and expected that he would immediately cause an investigation into my allegations based on what Smith told the witness Paula Whyte when he spoke to her, which have been fully detailed in previous correspondence from me to you.

I even alerted Paula Whyte with information that she should expect to be interviewed by detectives not associated with the Cold Case Squad as a result of the then Commissioner ordering such an investigation and gave her certain advice.

To my utter astonishment, no such investigation was ordered by that commissioner. However, we have the extraordinary result of my letter to Commissioner Stewart about 13th February 2019 wherein I tell him that I hold him totally responsible for the manner these murders have been investigated and that an experienced person is formulating a social media campaign in Victoria about these cases.

Twelve days later, Commissioner Stewart announces his early retirement as Commissioner of Police in Queensland but only a short time later accepts another position with your government. You would have to be very naive to believe that his actions are not related to my letter to him. In my opinion, he could see the writing on the wall, so to speak.

Then Katerina Carroll is appointed as Commissioner of Police. On her first day in the job, my letter about the obvious corruption of the investigations into these crimes' lands on her desk, setting out all pertinent facts.

Naively, I believed that this new broom will sweep all previous obstructions to justice aside and she will order an investigation into Detective Inspector Smith's actions and words spoken by him, which clearly indicate that he already knows the identities of persons involved in some way in these crimes but tells Paula Whyte amongst a lot of other curious statements that the men involved are 'good people with friends in the police force. That the men implicated have now become magistrates, lawyers and bailiffs. That they are people of influence who don't want this sordid story to come to light.'

But to my amazement again, she does not order an obvious investigation to get to the heart of the inspector's actions and words. Nothing happens at all to clarify the position, and I am given no information on my complaint.

Now, this is no small matter. This very corruption of the justice system is taken apart here and to illustrate how this has happened occurs when the press and media make inquiries of the Police Media Section, they must have been convincingly told sufficient information to cause them to lose all interest in trying to find out whether my claims of police failure to properly investigate these crimes is made by me I am ignored.

It would seem to me that I have been branded as a nutter or some of other type of disgruntled person despite the fact that journalists Peter Cameron and Trudy Brown write continuous articles in their newspapers over years supporting me. In fact,

Trudy Brown interviewed one of my informants and listened to the recorded conversations and very convincingly formed an opinion that my assertions of how this whole debacle has been achieved is correct.

We have the same treatment handed out to David Cunningham, brother of the missing and no doubt murdered Anita, who, like me, his letters to the press are ignored and unanswered.

All of this stems from the inaction of the topmost post in the Queensland Police Service, in other words the commissioners past and present. Even if other police can see clearly what is happening here, they must be fearful of taking any actions themselves for fear of retribution. They must be treading water, in other words.

There must be other police awake to what has happened here irrespective of the initial cause of this debacle by the original investigating officer in 2003 when Mearle Whyte first came forward with information which set in train a disgraceful chain of events setting decent police up to supporting that officer and I suspect against their better judgment.

I have not even mentioned the bungling of investigations into the mysterious letter from Chillagoe to a friend of Anita in Victoria two months after Robin's body is discovered where the writer had some possession of Anita's to get the address of the person in Victoria. I have previously covered this bungling, which resulted in a missed opportunity to identify the killers.

Then we have Detective Inspector Smith and retired former Officer Black showing David Cunningham and Alex Cullen of Channel Seven the incorrect position of the discovery of Robin's decomposed body in 2014 on public television. Not one word about the claims of Mearle Whyte and her mother Betty Madigan meeting the murdered girls at the Pentland Hotel in July 1972 is ever mentioned by these police to David Cunningham and his mother Eileen whilst in the company of these police, which must have been close contact over some days.

These close relatives of the murdered girl Anita never knew anything about the girls being at the Pentland Hotel until I contacted them in Victoria in 2015.

I have tried to compress this letter down as far as possible as you have heaps of previous material to consult if you want clarification of some points, but I should point out the relationship between the government and the police commissioner the government employs.

As I understand, the position it is that the government employs the commissioner, and the commissioner employs all other police personnel. It is generally assumed that the so-called buck stops with the commissioner but in reality, in Queensland, the buck stops with the government which employs the commissioner in Queensland.

Now, one way or another the truth about the way these crimes have been investigated and handled will eventually be brought to public attention.

I have been fighting for justice for these murdered girls for over eight years and whilst I am able, I will continue to try and get assistance to correct and bring to light this corruption of the justice system and identify the offenders deceased and still alive.

I hope it does not sound too impertinent of me to suggest that Tony Fitzgerald would seem to be the logical person to conduct a Commission of Inquiry into the manner these crimes have been handled by police as it is not impossible that some fragment of these crimes has already come to light in his previous inquiry into the police culture in Queensland, not that I have any such information.

Yours faithfully,
M.J. Gurn

On the 28th of September 2022 I sent this email to the attorney general as under:

Letter Attorney General, Shannon Fentiman
Dated 28th September 2022
Dear Attorney, General,
Your reference no. 596004/5590258

I am writing this time to acquaint you with the latest information I have imparted to Queensland Police in an attempt to solve the crimes against the murdered girls Robin Jeanne Hoinville-Bartram and Anita Cunningham at Pentland, Queensland in the winter of 1972.

I will follow up with the reasons for me asking for a Commission of Inquiry into the police handling of these crimes in lay man's terms and not mentioning names where possible as I intend to then forward this letter to the press to once again seek their assistance to bring under the public notice the mishandling of the case by police.

I will paste here particulars of the email advice I gave to Detective Senior Sergeant Tara Kentwell of the Cold Case Division on 22nd instant before going into the results of my investigations into these crimes in as brief a way as possible. She acknowledged my email and forwarded it on to Detective Senior Sergeant Justin Anderson and Detective Inspector Damien Hansen.

Detective Senior Sergeant Kentwell,
Dear Tara,

I have more recently again complained to the attorney general regarding the lack of action of the present and the previous police commissioners in not ordering an investigation into the actions of a detective inspector at Charters Towers in 2015 when he was supposed to investigate the recorded telephone interviews I had had with [redacted] and [redacted] in October 2014. He was also supposed to interview certain people which he did not do. At Charters Towers, he made some astounding references to persons who he said were involved in these crimes (in some way) and who went on in life to hold positions as a magistrate, a solicitor and a bailiff. Quite a *number of other comments were made by the inspector, which, in my mind and I believe any reasonable person's mind, would amount to perverting the course of justice.*

I have not heard back from the attorney general yet.

As you have been told by me all I want is to finalise these crimes with the killers being brought to justice and to that end I will keep requesting a Commission of Inquiry to get truthful answers from persons who are without doubt involved and obviously have denied involvement, which has seen them escape more intense scrutiny. The claims that no new evidence has come forward is just a play on words and it is my opinion that all I have uncovered is new evidence, which I will not go over again and again.

My actual purpose in sending you this email is to bring under your notice the involvement of the persons(s) who use the tracks under the railway bridge and road bridge at Sensible Creek to get to the property I have previously advised you about which I am told is owned by a [redacted] but that may not be correct. Whether he is the owner of not, it is the person who uses and used this track in 1972 who must have been aware of the decaying body of Robin Bartram under the railway bridge. He could not have avoided the smell going back and forth to his property whether he had previous knowledge of the location of the body or not so why did he not report the body to police.

The answer is obvious and, in my mind, this would make him the prime suspect for placing the decaying bush turkeys to allay any inquisitive person from looking further to find the body. I have suggested before that this person might well be involved in the actual crimes.

You will also recall that the property I speak of is the possible location of the body of Anita Cunningham as I have explained to you previously.

I suggest you look further into whether this line of inquiry has been previously properly fully explored.

It might be a futile request, but I would like to know the outcome of any investigations.

This email to you will probably feature in further correspondence I send to senior police and the attorney general, and no doubt will feature prominently in any official inquiry if I am successful in that regard.

Regards,
Mick Gurn

I continued to the attorney general.

Now, as briefly as possible but condensing eight years of investigations is not easy in a few words.

1. After being informed about February/March 2014 about a woman and her mother meeting the murdered girls at the Pentland Hotel in the winter of 1972 I received information about the expected death of this woman in Townsville Hospital. So, I advised a detective inspector of Cold Case Squad on 9th May 2014 of this information who said he would probably get someone to interview her. She was not interviewed despite my advice plus a letter from me, unreturned phone calls to this officer and pleas to Crime Stoppers by her daughter for her mother to be interviewed. The woman died on 16th June 2014 (should have been 27th June 2014). The grandmother had died in March 2014. The decomposed body of Robin Bartram was discovered in a shallow grave at Sensible Creek about eight to eleven kilometres towards Charters Towers from Pentland on 15th November 1972.

2. I complained to the Commissioner of Police Ian Stewart about the disparity of information from the inspector and the information I was given by an informant. In September 2014, this inspector wrote to me that the woman who had claimed she and her mother had met the murdered girls was mistaken in her claims to have met them at the Pentland Hotel.

3. The inspector's letter did not add up to my way of thinking, so I purchased voice a recorder and recorded a phone call with the deceased woman's husband on 2nd October 2014 and then with the woman's daughter on 4th October 2014. These interviews left me in no doubt that the deceased woman and her mother had met the girls at the Pentland Hotel and that she had seen the girls leave the hotel with men in the car of a band member, which band had played for patrons in the hotel earlier in the day.

4. When this woman and her mother were at the Pentland Hotel, the mother cashed a cheque with a man in the bar, which would most likely tell us the date the girls were murdered as it was the same day the girls left the hotel with their killer rapists. All my efforts to have this transaction verified have been denied by the bank and police have refused to pursue this line of investigation to the best of my knowledge. I suspect this date would be Friday 7th July 1972 or Friday 14th July 1972.

5. The letter from police to me stated that the deceased woman had come forward on 29th May 2003 and again in 2005 and that she had been interviewed by Charters Towers Police who did not believe she had met the murdered girls. She claimed that she had been humiliated by police and provided a mixture of true and some false information, which she gave them to try and make a fool of the main interviewer a detective as some sort of payback for the way she had been treated by police. This, of course, contributed to the police assessment that she was untruthful, unfortunately.

6. At the time I interviewed the informants, I did not know that police had taken part in a Channel Seven program aired on television in May 2014 where they pointed out to David Cunningham, brother of Anita Cunningham, and the representative of Channel Seven where the decayed body of Robin Bartram had been discovered. Unfortunately, these police indicated the body was found under the road bridge over Sensible Creek but in fact,

the body had been discovered under the railway bridge a short distance away.

7. About May in 2003, police conducted a thorough search around Sensible Creek for the body of Anita Cunningham, where the decomposed body of Robin Bartram had been discovered in a shallow grave. Information on the internet stated that police had information from Melbourne and that Mount Isa detectives were assisting. The search proved fruitless, however. The mention of Mount Isa Detectives is significant as I went on the establish that one of the offenders had gone to live in Mount Isa after splitting with a woman in Charters Towers, which obviously leads to a conclusion that there must be a connection here.

I have established the identity of the owner of the car the girls left the hotel in and is the man who had gone to Mount Isa. I believe he was one of the killers, along with a person who still resides in Charters Towers and a strong possibility that of these three killers from the car in Charters Towers on the day after the girls had left the hotel with men that this person was the infamous recidivist killer Ivan Milat. There are likely to be other men involved not yet identified by my investigations.

8. My recorded phone calls established that three of the men who had left the hotel with the murdered girls had confronted the deceased woman in front of a hairdresser's salon in Gill St. Charters Towers the next morning (a Saturday) travelling in the same car the girls had left the hotel in. I further established that one of the men was the man who had hitchhiked with the girls from Mount Isa the previous day and that at this time he had a long fingernail scratch down the side of his face. The girls only knew this man as 'Cowboy'. These men tried to entice the deceased woman to go with them to Townsville, which she declined thankfully. The man with the scratch I believe was Ivan Milat.

9. The deceased woman and her mother returned to the Twelve Mile Outstation on Wando Vale Cattle Station where a night or

two later her fifteen-year-old brother was outside at night trying to shoot wild pigs when he stumbled across a man hiding in grass. This man ran away as the brother had pointed his rifle at the man thinking he was a pig. The women saw a car parked not far away. They spent a restless frightening night waiting for the father to return home from mustering cattle. It seems reasonable to think that not content with murdering the girls, they then tried to get the deceased woman into their clutches in Charters Towers the next day. When that was not successful, they hunted the deceased and mother down to their home at the Twelve Mile Outstation to silence them.

10. I received no satisfaction with the way the cases were being handled by police or that my information was being taken seriously. I initially tried to contact Channel Seven in Sydney with a view to making contact with the families of Anita Cunningham and Robin Bartram. This contact resulted in me being interviewed by a reporter from that company who interviewed me at my home on 21st March 2015. He was given the entire information I had gleaned. This reporter claimed that the Head of the Cold Case Unit had requested a month's grace before Channel Seven did anything on the story.

11. In April 2015, the detective inspector went to Charters Towers allegedly to investigate the truthfulness of my recorded phone calls with the deceased woman's husband and daughter and to interview three persons I was told by an assistant commissioner would be interviewed and after which I decided to contact Channel Seven for the dual purpose I have mentioned. These investigations by the inspector could only be described as cursory, bullying and lacking serious intent of purpose. He made the references I have previously referred to in my email to DSS Kentwell. His actions and words spoken to my informants could only be described as perverting the course of justice and there is no reason for me to go over these actions again in detail. He also failed to interview the

three persons I refer to who I was told would be interviewed by the assistant commissioner.

12. As a result of the inspector giving information to Channel Seven's reporter about his investigations in Charters Towers, Channel Seven lost all interest in my information and the case. The inspector emailed me from Charters Towers on 24th April 2015, advising me not to contact my informant, the daughter again, saying it was at her request. He also said I would receive information from him about his investigations in Charters Towers this April 2015. This information was never given to me despite my several requests for same to the commissioner of police. In his email, he said that the officer who had interviewed the deceased woman was considering taking legal action against me for the disparaging remarks I had made to the police commissioner regarding his incompetence.

13. This development stymied investigations for three years until April 2018 when I asked Anita Cunningham's brother, David, who I was then in contact with, to phone the deceased woman's daughter and have her measure the distance from Sensible Creek to a place on the Flinders Highway where her mother had seen the car the murdered girls had left the hotel in sideways across the road the same evening the girls had left the hotel.

This phone call by David to this daughter revealed the true details of the inspector's actions in April 2015 when the daughter opened up to David about the inspector's conduct. This also led to this daughter confiding in me in emails about the entire circumstances of the inspector's visit to Charters Towers, which clearly established a case of perverting justice.

14. Apparently, the visit to the Sensible Creek area to make the Channel Seven program occurred in 2013 and some months before the program was aired in May 2014 because on 12th September 2013, the Head of the Cold Case Unit emailed Anita Cunningham's mother Eileen and her brother David where he said

he had inquiries underway concerning the strange letter posted to a friend of Anita Cunningham in Victoria in February 1973 from an unknown person in Chillagoe, Queensland. The inspector in this email refers to the letter contents with strange writing as a docket or a note from a store in Chillagoe for some goods purchased with the writing on the back of the docket as he called it. He said that all inquiries in Chillagoe were unsuccessful in establishing the writer of the letter who must have been in possession of some article from the possessions of Anita Cunningham to obtain the friends address in Victoria.

15. When I saw a photocopy of this document, I saw that it was the front page from an invoice book where goods purchased by a customer were recorded to compile a monthly statement for the purchaser of the goods. There would have been a carbon copy of this front page in the invoice book to charge the customer. It is therefore unfathomable why police did not discover the writer and poster of the letter as he or she must have been a customer of the Chillagoe store. Bungling of this clue to the identity of the killers clearly needs a lot of explaining. I even interviewed the addressee of the letter over the phone, but she could not assist in identifying the poster of the letter.

16. The husband of the deceased woman I refer to has had severe head injuries, which saw him in a seventeen-day coma in hospital in the 1980s, which has left him with a patchy memory of events that come to him in stages. He more recently supplied me with information about one of the killers with a business in Charters Towers and also the identity of one of the band members who had played in the Pentland Hotel on the day the murders were committed.

17. As a result of the husband informing me that another of his daughters had visited a person who is a person who claims he can communicate with the dead and although his information to this daughter seems incredulous and unbelievable, what he says

is verified by certain details he supplied regarding the possible burial place of the remains of Anita Cunningham and information concerning the identity of the business person in Charters Towers. All very strange but remarkable. That information was given to DSS Kentwell for passing on to investigating detectives as we are told the case is being constantly investigated as an open case. What they are investigating is a mystery as I am given no information, which is odd as my contacts in the Pentland area might be able to help inquiries.

18. This other daughter I refer to in item 17 was interviewed by me over the phone in March 2020 and I recorded the conversation with this impressive woman. The recorded information completely corroborates her father and her sister that her mother, the deceased woman, and her grandmother did in fact meet the murdered girls at the Pentland Hotel in 1972.

We now have three persons close to the deceased woman who corroborate her story plus the word of three of her brothers who also state sufficient recall to substantiate the deceased woman's version of meeting the murdered girls. There is another brother who was more closely involved with the deceased who I am told has a lot more knowledge of the circumstances and whose evidence in a Commission of Inquiry will be eagerly anticipated.

I have had requests for an inquest denied by the previous attorney general Y'vette D'Ath and similar refusals from you. These refusals centre around the claim 'That there is no new reliable evidence to warrant a Commission of Inquiry.' (In short.)

I first applied to you for a Commission of Inquiry because a journalist told me that I could expect fairer treatment from you than I had previously received.

To my mind, the totality of what I have discovered is new evidence. Inferring that the people supplying the recorded phone conversations are not sufficiently reliable to be believed is merely a play on words. It is not just one voice; it is corroborating voices.

Until they are discredited, they are, in my mind, very reliable. There is not one word from anyone to discredit them despite the attitude of the police who have obviously not adopted the information in my recorded interviews. Discrediting remarks about these recorded conversations is what I would expect from people who do not want the stance of the police throughout this entire debacle to become public knowledge.

This stance is highlighted by the successful campaign conducted by the Queensland police service to stop me from gaining any traction in the media or press to bring this cover up of police inaction and mishandling in solving these crimes into public knowledge which unfortunately involves two police commissioners failing to order investigations into the actions of a detective inspector, which clearly involve perverting the course of justice for whom I have genuine regrets having to mention him here in this light but my first loyalties must lie with the deceased girls above all else.

The actions of the initial investigating officer in Charters Towers when the deceased lady came forward began this horrid affair. Then we have the inspector failing to have the deceased woman interviewed before she died. Then the bungling of the investigation into the letter from Chillagoe. Then indicating to the public, the wrong place Robin's body was located. Then his failures to do his job properly in Charters Towers in April 2015 but which saw him successful in terminating Channel Seven's interest in these cases coupled, of course, with the failure to inform me as he said he would the result of his review in Charters Towers.

I have to ask just how many breaches of the justice system does it take to warrant a Commission of Inquiry to get to the truth.

I am asking for a Commission of Inquiry where persons involved would get their chance to support their statements and to examine the actions of police throughout the entire police investigations into these crimes especially since 2003, which leave a lot to be desired as I have pointed out. I further again point out that you do not know the answers to the questions I asked you to ask police so you could make an informed decision.

We also have the very uncomfortable and curious stance of the Crime and Corruption Commission who refuse to take any part in bringing the mishandling of certain aspects of these crimes into the open.

I will not bother to comment in much detail on the stance of the Police Integrity Unit when they failed to act on the matters of impartiality and misplaced loyalties, which have become evident throughout my investigations over the past eight years.

This letter is as small as I can make my request, which, if everything I could say was said, the letter would be many pages more and form part of the many reams of A4 paper I have used up over the last eight years.

I am trying very hard to resist giving all this inside information to the press and media in case the information in some way hinders investigations, but my patience is running thin with alternatives on how to handle this situation. The body I would ordinarily rely on is the body subject of this letter.

I would urge you to accede to my reasonable request now please.

Yours faithfully,
M.J. Gurn

On 29th September 2022, DSS Kentwell replied that she had forwarded my information to Detective Senior Sergeant Justin Anderson who is currently managing this investigation.

CHAPTER THIRTY

As I continue writing this book and adding to it as events occur, I have to tell readers that on 31st October 2022, I received an email from the attorney general's office advising me that unfortunately the attorney general was unable to meet with me at that time; however, the attorney's senior policy advisor, Isabelle Shoshani, would be pleased to attend the meeting on her behalf.

This email was a surprise as I had not requested a meeting with the attorney general so I replied in an email that I had not requested any such meeting but that I would be honoured to have such a meeting and personally explain further the absolute necessity for a Commission of Inquiry into these crimes etc.

I further explained that as I was nearly ninety years of age, it would be difficult for me to attend and suggested a meeting at my home address.

Nothing further transpired about any meeting, but a very substantial event occurred on 1st November 2022 as David Cunningham sent emails and letters to various identities including the attorney general, the commissioner of police, David Crisafulli and others, which highlighted the mishandling of the cases by police and exposed an admission by police of a cover up in their handling of the cases.

The email from David Cunningham is shown hereunder.

Dear Attorney, General,

I am David Cunningham, elder brother of Anita Cunningham, who is missing, presumed murdered along with her murdered travelling companion Robin Hoinville-Bartram near Pentland in 1972.

I write here in reference to:

CRIMINAL CODE 1899 - SECTION 140

Attempting to pervert justice

(1) A person who attempts to obstruct, prevent, pervert, or defeat the course of justice is guilty of a crime. Maximum penalty—7 years' imprisonment.

I write in disgust at the continuing and ongoing police cover-up, a cover-up to which police have freely admitted.

That admission was made during a phone call between [redacted] and me.

During the phone call, I had mentioned the shabby, unprofessional, untrustworthy behaviour of QLD Police RTI, who, after months of other attempts to fob me off had failed, suddenly denied my application on the fresh grounds that the case was now suddenly 'under investigation'.

So I responded by asking [redacted] and [redacted] why and how can the case be 'Under Investigation', when the police have said they only have two facts in this case and no new information?

When I asked why police are still using the blocking tactic of 'Case Under Investigation' and refusing to cooperate with one of their finest, (retired), in helping to pursue the most pertinent questions in the case, this person replied verbatim, because 'people write books.'

With due respect, aside from the serious fact that in freely admitting the reason for the cover-up, Mr [redacted] has now made the blatant admission that the police are in fact engaged in a cover-up! Aside from that, it seems like a very unwise answer because a book or other publicity only casts the police in an even worse light when they openly admit they are trying to avoid scrutiny.

If you were worried about a book being published, which might bring you into disrepute, surely it would be better to be seen to be doing your job and start pursuing justice, rather than attempting to justify the police preventing the course of justice being pursued.

'The prosecution does not have to prove that the course of justice was perverted or would have been perverted. It is sufficient that the prosecution established that there was a real risk that injustice might result.' (Meissner v The Queen (1995) 184 CLR 132)

I allege that the guilty party in this foul and continuous obstruction of the proper course of justice is the Queensland police in their failure to examine not only the evidence and the leads, but their failure to examine themselves and their members, and their continued insistence on blocking any progress towards and in the interests of justice.

I also write to express my heartfelt admiration and total support for Retired Senior Detective Mr Michael Gurn in his quest to obtain justice for these two beautiful young girls in the flower of their teenage youth, cruelly destroyed and discarded, and then deliberately denied justice by a police force clandestinely trying to protect their own members.

Well, Mick Gurn is one of their own members and one with a proud and impeccable reputation. Why is he getting treated as an enemy by the Queensland police? What are the Queensland police afraid of? What are the Queensland police hiding?

With the investigative skills he employed so successfully as a senior detective in charge of his own squad, Mick has single-handedly almost solved this case while the police claim there is nothing to be known. I won't go into it here, as so much has already been written and sent to police, the coroner, the attorney general and ministers, I don't intend to reiterate the whole astounding story here.

I am writing to you. You are the people who need to pay attention and you are the ones who need to take the bull by the horns, pursue the truth fearlessly and honestly and act, before the whole sorry tale of suppression of the truth blows up and everyone gets egg on their face.

Readers of this book will immediately see the significance of this email from David Cunningham, which gives unchallenged confirmation of a cover up by Queensland Police in this case that requires urgent investigation of police practices and explanations as to why this has been allowed to have occurred.

On the 13th of November 2022, I wrote to the attorney general in an email as follows:

Attorney General Shannon Fentiman
Dated 13th November 2022
Dear Ms Fentiman,
My applications for a Commission of Inquiry into the murders of Robin Jeanne Hoinville-Bartram and Anita Cunningham at Pentland in 1972 have now been substantially fortified by the letter from David Cunningham to you recently wherein he confirms that police have actually admitted to him that there has been a cover up of police failings in their investigations into these murders.

This was a recorded three-way conversation so there is proof what I am telling you.

This proof of what I have been telling you for quite a long time now in various written documents over a long period of time must surely convince you that a Commission of Inquiry is the only successful manner in which the truth of the way these crimes have been handled by police will be exposed.

The longer you leave the authorisation of this inquiry, the harder it becomes for justice to be granted for the murdered girls for the wicked fate that befell them from men who saw an opportunity for self-gratification without any thought or consideration for these young women who did not deserve such treatment.

The perpetrators of these crimes have enjoyed a long life when they should have been brought to justice, but it is never too late to expose these criminals whether alive or dead for what they did to these women.

Please do not wait until there is an upsurge of public support for this inquiry which David Cunningham with his Victorian contacts and I will continue to fight for in the murdered girls interests and very definitely in the public interest in any way that we can find.

Yours sincerely,

M.J. Gurn

On 15th November 2022, I forwarded an email to the editor of the Courier Mail newspaper in Brisbane enclosing David Cunningham's letter to the attorney general and others pointing out the police admission that a cover up of investigations into the police handling of these crimes is admitted.

I requested the newspaper's assistance in obtaining a Commission of Inquiry.

To take advantage of the letter from David Cunningham and try to enlist help in obtaining a Commission of Inquiry into these crimes, I wrote to Ian Kaye on 23rd November 2022, who is closely aligned with David Crissafulli the Leader of the LNP in Queensland, which is the opposition in government in Queensland.

This letter contained a pasted copy of the email I had forwarded to Peta Credlin of Sky News asking her to assist in obtaining this inquiry from the attorney general.

Pasted hereunder is a copy of the email to Ian Kaye with a copy of the email to Peta Credlin who I had contacted previously from time to time seeking her assistance in obtaining publicity to give weight to applications to the attorney general to order a Commission of Inquiry.

Pasted hereunder is a copy of an email I sent to Peta Credlin yesterday as further encouragement for her to assist me in bringing to the public's attention this serious attempt to defeat justice in this state.

When you and David Crisafulli are pondering when or if you should step into and publicly support my efforts for a Commission of Inquiry, you would do well to consider this information to Peta Credlin in your own assessment of where the cases stand. If you can think of any reason why the Sunday Mail would allow the paper to be used to publish my work in Peter Cameron's traps column over four years and not want to know the truth about my work I would like to know because I cannot find a reason that stacks up as contributing or assisting justice in any way.

I have now decided not to include in this work the information I conveyed to Peta Credlin as the information may be contested and a distraction from the effectiveness of my efforts for justice for these murdered girls. The information dealt with why the Sunday Mail published Peter Cameron's articles on my investigations but did not pursue any inquiries by one of their own reporters.

In order to try and obtain further assistance in obtaining a Commission of Inquiry, I also requested assistance from the Townsville Bulletin in this endeavour on the 19th of November 2022 in an email. This paper has been very helpful throughout the last eight and a half years by publishing articles querying the police stance on these crimes.

On the 18th November 2022, I also emailed Adam Hegarty of Channel Nine suggesting that the channel might consider doing another program on these crimes as a follow up to the program they put to air in February 2020, having in mind that I now had evidence of a cover-up of mishandling of investigations by police into these crimes as evidenced by David Cunningham to the attorney general on 1st November 2022.

As quite a surprise, I received an email from Isabella Shoshani, Chief Policy Adviser to Attorney General Shannon Fentiman on 23rd November 2022 about meeting with me. I replied that this presented difficulties for me and suggested the meeting should be at my home or Toowoomba.

Nothing further was heard until Tuesday 31st January 2023 when I received an email from Isabella Shoshani saying she was hoping to organise a time to meet. She said it would be best if the meeting could be over Zoom or Microsoft Teams and supplied the times she had available.

I replied as follows the same day,

Dear Isabella,

I have replied to your first email about a meeting in November 2022 and I told you the difficulties that posed for me living in Pittsworth and organising Zoom or like meetings due to my incompetent computer skills. I suggested that any meeting should be in Toowoomba. I also informed you that David Cunningham wished to be present at any meeting.

Now I will go to any lengths to get a Commission of Inquiry into the mishandling of investigations by police into the Pentland Murders of 1972 and I must ask you why you want this meeting seeing as how I did not request a meeting with the attorney general?

What do you hope to achieve by a meeting as my requests to the attorney general are very clear. They are supported by sound reasoning and more so now that David Cunningham has exposed a verifiable cover-up by police in their failures in their investigations by admitting a blatant perversion of the course of justice by a detective inspector., This involves two police commissioners failing to order investigations to get to the bottom of his extraordinary conduct in April 2015 at Charters Towers, which, in my opinion, places these two police commissioners in positions where they will have great difficulty justifying their actions when questioned in the witness box. This may have repercussions for the government I would think.

The truth is that the police have dug themselves into a hole and cannot find a way out.

Sooner or later, the truth about this whole debacle will surface as truth always seems to prevail in the end. I must also tell you of my displeasure with the speed or really the lack of speed that the government deals with this issue because fifty years later, those people who have knowledge and who can supply information to see offenders arrested are growing older and older, including me.

One could be forgiven for thinking that some people are just waiting for me and those who can corroborate the available and real evidence to conveniently pass on and the whole debacle will pass off into the never never. Well, that is not going to happen if I can avoid it. It will take just one crack in the lies at present taking precedence to blow this whole thing wide open.

I do thank you for your interest on behalf of the attorney general.

For nine years, I have pursued justice for these raped and slain girls, which is why I have done what I have done, probably because of my experience as a detective over so many years I can see straight through the falsehoods that exist. This is the same for experienced journalists Peter Cameron and Trudy Brown who have resolutely supported me.

I look forward to your reply.
Yours sincerely,
M.J. (Mick) Gurn

On 3rd February 2023 I incorporated the email reply you have just read to Isabella Shoshani into another application to the attorney general for a Commission of Inquiry that followed that email.

    I can assure you that I have no hesitation at all in meeting you or your representative but at ninety years of age, I just do not have the skills to work with Zoom or any similar platform. I prefer to meet in person and as I live in Pittsworth here or maybe Toowoomba could be arranged. Just what the purpose of a requested meeting is I have not yet been informed and await Ms Shoshani's reply to my email reply to her for such information.

    I would like to bring to your attention if you have not yet realised it that the cover up in police investigations referred to by David Cunningham in his email to you and others is proved by the actions of the detective inspector in 2015 when he did not properly interview the persons who gave me the interviews I recorded on 2nd and 4th October 2014, which has been dealt with in previous correspondence to you.

    Then we have, of all people, two police commissioners failing to order an investigation into the detective inspector's conduct in April 2015 when he went to Charters Towers to investigate my recorded interviews with John Whyte and Paula Whyte, plus not interviewing three persons I was told would be interviewed, which has not happened.

    If that failure by police commissioners does not prove this cover up by police, I do not know what does.

    The police have dug themselves into a hole and cannot get out.

    It will be interesting to see at an inquiry how many of the various lines of inquiry I have pointed out to police have been followed up such as the cheque cashed by Betty Madigan at the Pentland Hotel the day the girls were raped and murdered. Even to the extent of not supporting my application to Westpac Bank for details of the transaction.

    Such as the bungling of investigations into the strange letter from

Chillagoe to a friend of Anita Cunningham in Victoria not long after the discovery of Robin Bartram's decomposed corpse. Such as why the person(s) using the track under the road and rail bridge over Sensible Creek did not report the smell of the decomposing body, which was unavoidable. To my mind, that person would be the main suspect for placing the dead bush turkeys in a position to try to satisfy any inquisitive person following the smell to not discover the body.

Such as verifying that years ago John Whyte asked help from a police officer named Whelan who he was friendly with about Mearle coming forward to police about her meeting the murdered girls at the Pentland Hotel with Whelan saying police were helpless unless Mearle came forward herself. It is likely that whoever was in charge of Charters Towers Police at the time would have been consulted on such a matter.

It will be very interesting to see at an inquiry how much of a determined effort has been made by police to prove or disprove my claims that identify some killers and others involved over these past nine years.

Let me run through as briefly as I can Mearle Whyte's story about meeting the murdered girls and what happened to her as a result and why she was too frightened to come forward with information to police. First, she and her mother meet the girls at the Pentland Hotel. Next day, three of the men who had left the hotel the previous day with the girls in the band member's car confront Mearle at Charters Towers and try to get her to go with them to Townsville, which she thankfully declined. Then when Mearle and her mother were returning to their home, these men tried to waylay them along the road. A night or two later, a man is described hiding outside their home, which indicates to me that it is very likely these men were there to silence Mearle and her mother.

Then when the body of Robin Bartram is discovered, Mearle

fully realises what happened to the girls. She does not go to Charters Towers for two years because of her fears for her safety. Then she runs into one of them at a rodeo in Charters Towers – this was most likely Wally Barry. Then at some time, she is on the veranda of her house in Charters Towers when a car pulls up outside her house and two shots are fired at her from the car which is dismissed as a rock. How anyone could throw a rock at her seated in a car outside the house is not possible to my way of thinking.

Then at some time over the years, she goes to the courthouse in Charters Towers about a government rental house and recognises the clerk as a man who sang in the band at the Pentland Hotel the day the girls were murdered.

Then she refuses to pick up their car left for service at a place in Charters Towers because, as she tells her husband, John, the man running the place is one of the killers.

Then when she gets the courage to go to police in 2003, she is humiliated by the officer in his dealings with her, which causes her to tell him some untruths to try and make a fool out of him. This only plays into the officer's hand in that he disbelieves her story unfortunately.

Now, put all this together and tell me that the police position that Mearle is mistaken in her belief she met the murdered girls at the Pentland Hotel could possibly be correct.

It is in your power to bring out all the truthful facts in this case by ordering a Commission of Inquiry not withstanding your previous denials to this inquiry stating there was no reliable evidence etc.

I believe your argument no longer has the same weight in view of David Cunningham's challenge to police about their cover-up of the true facts.

How long must the Australian public be denied justice in these cases? These rapes and murders have in the past created Australia-wide publicity, which has decreased somewhat in later years because of the successful campaign to stifle any publicity by police by denying the results of my investigations, which can be tested in an inquiry by questioning the still alive witnesses and hopefully before it is even too late for that to happen.

Yours sincerely,

M.J. Gurn

On 7th February 2023, Isabella Shoshani emailed me as follows:

A meeting would provide me with an opportunity to discuss this matter with you in person and to discuss possible options moving forward.

I will see if we can facilitate a meeting in Toowoomba and get back to you.

I replied, 'That would be good, thank you.'

I will see where this goes but I cannot think of any possible options.

On Tuesday 21st February 2023, I sent the underneath email to Isabella Shoshani.

Dear Isabella,

In response to your latest advice that you are arranging a meeting with me at Toowoomba. Have you established a date, time and place for this meeting please? I cannot stress enough that the timeframe for action by the government to take positive steps in this case is vital due to the aging of persons involved.

I understand that with everything taking place around the prevalence of crime that the government is very busy trying to sort out the problems, but we do need to have the matters I have raised with the government acted on a soon as possible. You would have received more recent information from David Cunningham setting out the lack of proper investigations into his sister's brutal killing, which supports my call for some urgency in this matter.

I await your advice please.

Best regards,

Mick Gurn

On 8th March 2023, Isabella Shoshani advised me that she could meet with me in Toowoomba on Tuesday 21st March 2023 or the morning of Wednesday 5th April 2023.

I advised David Cunningham and Bob Atkinson (former Commissioner of Police who agreed to accompany me to this meeting) of the dates of this meeting and I subsequently advised Isabella Shoshani that the 5th of April 2023 was suitable for us.

Bob Atkinson had been in touch with Isbella Shoshani, and she would advise us of the place of the meeting, which would be from 11am to 12pm. On Wednesday 5th April 2023, David Cunningham, Bob Atkinson and I met with Isabella Shoshani at the Picnic Point Cafe, Toowoomba. The meeting went from 11am to 12.10pm, during which time David and I set out various arguments why a Commission of Inquiry was necessary.

Miss Shoshani explained that the attorney general could not order a Commission of Inquiry in the hope that the persons I allege are presently lying as to their involvement would break down and admit their involvement or knowledge of these crimes.

We left the meeting feeling that there had a been a frank and open discussion and our opportunity to express ourselves openly. We all decided that our only avenue open now was to have my book *Hear Our Cry* published requesting the public to support us for a Commission of Inquiry.

Following this meeting with the attorney general's representative Isabella Shoshani on 5th April 2023, I wrote to the attorney general on 9th April 2023 by email enclosing a letter to Ms Fentiman pointing out various features of my previous letters to her such as why did she not obtain the facts I asked her to ask police before she made a decision on whether to order the Commission of Inquiry from the Minister for Police if she could not directly ask her questions of the police commissioner.

I went into other matters concerning whether there was much communication between departments in the government and questioned whether she had listened to the recorded interviews I had conducted on 2nd and 4th October 2014 with John Whyte and Paula Whyte. I offered to resupply these recordings if required.

The complete letter can be read as Appendix Number Seventeen.

On the $17^{th\ of}$ April 2023, I wrote to the minister for police Mark Ryan, which detailed the circumstances under which I claim that Inspector Peter Smith's actions and words when he went to Charters Towers in April 2018 amounted to perverting the course of justice.

Honourable Mark Ryan MLA
Minister for Police
Dated 17th April 2023
Dear Sir,
Regarding the unsolved rapes and murders of Robin Jeanne Hoinville-Bartram, eighteen years and Anita Cunningham, eighteen years, at Pentland Queensland in 1972, you would probably be aware by now that I along with David Cunningham (brother of Anita Cunningham), who had travelled from Victoria, along with ex Commissioner of Police, Bob Atkinson (as observer), met with Isabella Shoshani, Chief Political Adviser to Attorney General Shannon Fentiman at Toowoomba on Wednesday 5th instant to discuss these cases from the perspective of a Commission of Inquiry into these cases. We had a meaningful discussion, which I followed up with an email to the attorney general questioning whether you are fully acquainted with all aspects of these cases and

really wondering why no action has been taken into a perversion of the course of justice by you.

It has been well recorded that I have acquainted you and the attorney general through correspondence, directly and indirectly through letters etc to the attorney general, over a number of years that a cover-up by Queensland Police has occurred in relation to the mishandling of investigations into these crimes since 2003 when Mearle Elizabeth Whyte came forward to Charters Towers Police with information that she had met the two murdered girls at the Pentland Hotel in the winter of 1972 before being murdered but was not believed to cut a very long story short.

Those claims have been substantiated in letters to you from David Cunningham recently.

This cover-up has the potential to corrupt the justice system and has prevented, it seems, the press and media being honestly given particulars of these cases by the Police Media Section resulting in David Cunningham and I not being able to inform the public of the true facts of these cases.

I have, in correspondence over the years fully acquainted your government including the premier with sufficient evidence of this mishandling of the cases by Queensland Police, which unfortunately involves prior Commissioner of Police Ian Stewart and Commissioner Katerina Carroll not ordering an investigation into the words and conduct of this Detective Inspector in April 2015 when he travelled to Charters Towers supposedly to investigate the truthfulness of two recorded telephone interviews I had conducted with Mearle Whye's husband and her daughter on 2nd and 4th October 2014. This detailed vast differences to the police stance that the girls were never at the Pentland Hotel before being murdered.

There is also the failure of this inspector to carry out instructions of Assistant Commissioner Hogan to interview certain persons I asked to be interviewed, which in the normal order of things should have been done when he travelled to the area where these people resided, namely Charters Towers.

This inspector's conduct led me to state categorically that it is or was perverting the course of justice. When evidence of this crime was placed before ex-Commissioner Ian Stewart, he announced his early retirement twelve days later after he received my letter, which, to any sane person, would indicate that his retirement is allied with my letter to Stewart dated 13th February 2019. This will be attached to this letter to you in the form of a copy of a chapter of my book Hear Our Cry, which is presently being considered by a publisher.

Unfortunately, the replacement Commissioner Katerina Carroll similarly did not order an investigation about this same perversion of the course of justice despite her being fully acquainted with the circumstances in a letter from me reaching her on the day she commenced duties as Commissioner of Police in July 2019. When no action was taken by her about this perversion of justice, I further questioned her failure in a letter dated 9th May 2021, a copy of which will also be attached to this letter to you from me. Again, she took no action.

The public are entitled to ask why would two police commissioners not delve into allegations made by Paula Whyte when she revealed the true nature of the detective inspector's conduct and spoken words in April 2015 when she revealed the truth about these matters to David Cunningham during a phone call he made to her in April 2018 and which she revealed to me in emails under her own hand as a result of David's call to her.

To David Cunningham, she said that she was afraid of being identified in relation to giving evidence in investigations into these murders as she has been threatened and warned off on several occasions. She said that the inspector said to her that her mother must have a mental problem, that the family's story was fiddlesticks, 'to give it up' and 'don't try to go there' as the young men implicated have now become magistrates, lawyers and bailiffs. That they are people of influence who don't want this sordid story to come to light.

She also said that her mother had been treated badly by interviewing police years ago and that it seemed obvious to her that they were not interested in receiving information but instead were just trying to discredit the witness as a way to discount their testimonial evidence.

When Inspector Smith went to Charters Towers to investigate my recorded phone interviews with John and Paula Whyte as a result of his requesting a month's grace from Channel Seven TV before they did anything about a TV program on these murders, he had emailed me from Charters Towers in April 2015 virtually telling me Paula did not want me to contact her again, which was extraordinary in view of her attitude in contacts with me.

When Paula emailed me after David had spoken to her, she said in the first email that she did say she did not want to be involved with me or the case anymore but it was because he made it clear even before she was seated that her mother did not know what she was talking about and that the men involved that night are upholding citizens and that they could never do a thing like that and that her mother's accusations could get good people in trouble. She said he raised his voice and overpowered her, so she did nothing as she was pregnant at the time.

In a later email to me, Paula said, 'If okay with you, can you please forward me your number as I have decided from reading all the information that I am not going to back down from Mr Smith and his standover threats and if that puts me in danger in any way helping you to solve this case, so be it, at the end of the day I know my mother was telling the truth and I will not let these murderous bastards intimidate me and threaten me. I am here if you need talk to me. But I would also advise you to meet in person and make sure that if something was to happen to me that my family is safe cause I get the feeling that they don't want this case solved for some reason.'

Now, the full circumstances and emails in all this will be given to you to digest when you can read chapter 19 of my book, which I will attach to the letter.

All of this information has been placed before the attorney general over time and despite her reluctance to order a Commission of Inquiry, I have to wonder why it is that what Paula has alleged about threats to keep her mouth shut, the words of Inspector Smith about the good citizens who he obviously knows were part of the band, which had played for patrons at the Pentland Hotel the day the girls were murdered, then why wasn't any of this pursued to establish the truth of what she alleges.

I told Paula that she could expect to be interviewed by other detectives as I was confident that Commissioner Stewart would act on my information to him. Sadly, that did not happen.

I told her that I would report these facts to the Commissioner of Police Ian Stewart, which I did but he did not order an investigation of these matters and then the same inaction happened with Commissioner Carroll despite me explaining the whole circumstances to her in a detailed letter and a further complaint by me to her by letter on 9th May 2021.

Irrespective of whether the other persons I have identified as being involved would fail to admit their involvement in a Commission of Inquiry, which is the concern of the attorney general, there is absolutely enough other disturbing information I have put forth over the past nine years to warrant a Commission of Inquiry, which I hope will be the result of the public reading the true facts in my book.

There are circumstances of aggravation resulting from Inspector Smith's failed visit to Charters Towers in April 2015 and one is that he successfully deterred Channel Seven from doing a TV program about these cases and the other is that my investigations were virtually stalled and any possible police action also effected.

Of course, there is the possibility of the recidivist murderer Ivan Milat was one of the killers who had told the murdered girls to call him 'Cowboy'.

I wrote to you about these cases on the 11th of October 2021 wherein I requested you to obtain answers to a number of questions I asked you to ask police which I had also asked the attorney general to ask of police so she could make an informed decision on whether she would accede to my requests for a Commission of Inquiry.

Your Chief of Staff, Ellen McIntyre, replied to me on your behalf by letter dated 12th November 2021 advising me that as the case was an open case no information would be forthcoming. She said I could discuss the case with Detective Senior Sergeant Tara Kentwell of the Cold Case Unit.

Later, I had a conversation with Detective Senior Sergeant Tara Kentwell by phone and I asked her to tell me one thing and that was 'Is the police position still that the murdered girls were never at the Pentland Hotel?' She replied, 'I cannot tell you that.'

I asked that question because I had received a letter from Detective Inspector Smith in September 2014 to the effect that Mearle Whyte was mistaken in her belief that she had met the murdered girls at the Pentland Hotel.

I gave her further information for police to investigate concerning why the person who used the tracks under the bridges at Sensible Creek regularly did not report the unmistakable smell of the decaying body of Robin Bartram to the police. This person has a lot to answer adequately for.

My contradictory, to police, telephone recorded interviews from October 2014 clearly established in any reasonable person's mind that this statement that the girls were not at the Pentland Hotel was wrong and my stance that the girls were at the Pentland Hotel before they accepted a lift to Charters Towers with men who raped and killed them is correct and is further corroborated by a recorded telephone interview I had with another daughter of Mearle Whyte in March 2020.

Of course, the questions as to why these police commissioners have not taken any action in regard to this obvious perverting of the course of justice leaves them in the precarious position of aiding and abetting a crime if the interpretation of the law is extended to its extreme degree.

The substance of the facts of this perversion of the course of justice is clearly outlined when David Cunningham contacted Paula Whyte in April 2018 and further with subsequent emails back and forth with this woman by me. I was able to obtain from this woman sufficient information in her own hand, which proves the allegation I make about perverting the course of justice if read in conjunction with many other factors that I have uncovered concerning who was involved in these crimes.

These include information about band members who played in a band at the Pentland Hotel the day the crimes were committed. At least one of the band members was the deceased killer Walter Barry and at least one other band member singing in the band went on in life to become a magistrate but has not come forward with information about these crimes to police. Other members of his family have been named as members of this band and one band member has been named as a man who owns and runs a business in Charters Towers.

These emails contain statements from Paula Whyte to David Cunningham that she has been threatened. In the ordinary course of events, wouldn't the police spring to attention on such grave allegations? But _nothing_ happened, except, of course, to deny me any aid at all.

It is high time that the police stop this charade altogether and analyse the true facts I have outlined and pursue justice for these murdered girls.

You are the minister for police, and you have largely, it seems, been kept in the dark, but not by me, as I naively believed all my information would naturally be forwarded on to you as part of normal business of government between departments.

The attachments I believe will be sufficient to inform you my stance based on nine years of effort to get to the truth to have killers arrested, persons involved properly brought to account and hopefully locate the remains of Anita Cunningham.

It is up to you now to get to the bottom of this fiasco. You can do this by recommending to the attorney general that you after considering all aspects of these cases now more clearly outlined to you, a Commission of Inquiry.

Yours faithfully,

M.J. Gurn

I wrote again to the minister for police as under.

Mark Ryan MLA
Minister for Police
State Parliament
4th July 2023
Relative to the murders of Robin Jeanne Hoinville-Bartram and Anita Cunningham at Pentland in 1972

Dear Sir,

Having had no replies to my letters to you of 18th April 2023 and 12th June 2023, I again write asking questions as to what you have done to deal with the corruption exposed by me of the Queensland justice system as it relates to the incompetent and mishandled investigations by Queensland Police into the rapes and murders of Robin Jeanne Hoinville-Bartram and Anita Cunningham, both eighteen years, at Pentland Queensland in 1972.

I appreciate that the evidence supplied by me on this coverup strikes at the very heart of the Queensland police service and possibly involves two police commissioners. However, corruption is corruption wherever it falls and no matter who is involved and deserves thorough investigation and exposure into the public arena no matter how distasteful or embarrassing it becomes.

This battle by me to uncover the truth of this matter has been going on for nine years since I first exposed that the person with firsthand knowledge of these crimes who had knowledge of the identities of the offenders had died in Townsville Hospital not interviewed by police despite them having had advice from me allowing police from the 9th May 2014 to 27th June 2014 to learn the truth from this woman and solve these crimes resulting without any doubt in the arrest of these criminal sadists.

Since then, every possible obstacle has been put in my way to bring this corruption of the justice system to the public's attention with a coverup of police mishandling of investigations seeming to be the first priority of some, but not all, police.

The longer this situation is allowed to continue the worse will be the outcome for the government and the police so I would urge you to have the strength to tackle and correct this corruption because the truth will come out in the not-too-distant future not only Australia wide but also worldwide.

I am also inquiring whether the newly appointed NACC would have state crime within its ambit as corruption is corruption no matter where it appears in any Australian justice system.

Yours sincerely,
M.J. Gurn

CHAPTER THIRTY-ONE

I have said that responsibility for covering up these crimes' rests on the shoulders of the commissioner downwards or that the buck stops with the commissioner. Well, in this case, that is not quite correct because in Queensland, the commissioner is employed by the government of the day. However, the police personnel under the commissioner are employed by the commissioner.

An old saying for governments who want to stay in power is TO NEVER FALL OUT WITH YOUR POLICE FORCE. Whoever was responsible for changing legislation for the engagement of the commissioner in Queensland must have taken this saying to heart and then devised a very cunning way of ensuring the government of the day does not fall out with its police force by changing that legislation to that which presently exists.

However, this arrangement is such that the commissioner can be sacked by the government if the commissioner does not do what the government wants when they give a nod and a wink for something, and it is not followed up by the commissioner. This sacking must be approved by the Crime and Corruption Commission. It is probable that this subject is never mentioned or discussed by either party, but it is the genie in the room.

A police force should always be at arms-length and completely independent of the government of the day and autonomous in its actions. It is there to enforce the laws of the land by the citizens and for the protection of its citizens.

My view is that weakening the title of the police force to the police service undermined the importance of the police in the minds of the public especially the youth. They are not there for service but are there to enforce the law.

It is not too far down the track before we will see gun fights between police and criminals now that criminal's minds are blown apart with their drug taking. It could well be like the Tommy Gun wars of the Al Capone era in America which will test the fortitude of the government of the day to back their police forces without question. Unfortunately, my words have already started to come true with two unprepared police ambushed and killed near Tara.

It is imperative that a Commission of Inquiry into the covering up of these crimes by police be instigated, to investigate why this has occurred having in mind that I have said there must be a powerful force behind this situation for this to have happened.

It will be necessary for this inquiry to delve into what was meant by Inspector Smith at Charters Towers in April 2018 when he says that the young men implicated are now good people with friends in the police force. **That the young men implicated have now become magistrates, lawyers and bailiffs. That they are people of influence who don't want this sordid story to come to light.**

To my mind, those words of Inspector Smith conjure up very disturbing images of the law being circumvented to avoid solving these awful crimes.

What has happened here is not just that the justice system has been corrupted within the police force, but it also extends to stopping the press and media from properly and rightfully investigating and bringing to light this cover up.

I have mentioned a genie in the room previously in this

work but there is what could also be called another genie in the room and that is the reward money of $250,000 offered by the government for information leading to the arrest and conviction of the murderers of these girls.

I have previously said that I took part in a Channel Nine television program about these cases on 20th February 2020 and that in the television preambles promoting the program, it was mentioned a number of times during the day and night before about a cover up by the police but when the program was shown, no mention was made of any police cover up, which seems strange to my way of thinking. So I have to ask, have the police suggested to Channel Nine that the Whyte's' information is concocted to gain access to the reward money?

What prompted me to ask this question is because a Channel Nine representative did ask me if the Whytes knew about the reward money for the case and I replied that they did know about the reward money. In fact, Paula said that she would show the police where the car was sideways across the Flinders Highway after her mother and grandmother left the Pentland Hotel, but she would not show her father or her uncle Vince as she did not want them to be able to make any claim on the reward money. She claimed to have heard that her father and uncle had been discussing the reward money.

I advised Commissioner Stewart of this development in a letter. I questioned Vince Whyte about this matter. He denied any such conversation had ever taken place and said there was no way he had any claim on the reward as the information was from his brother and he was only passing it on to me.

So, Paula had her sights on the reward money without doubt, but I fail to see how that affects her or her father's or her sister's information. I mentioned this to David Cunningham and his reply was, 'Well, what is wrong with that? Isn't that what the money is there for?'

I do not believe any of the information from any of the Whytes is false. Their prime position is carrying out Mearle Whyte's dying wishes which includes a bedside promise by John Whyte to his dying wife to find someone to carry on the battle for justice for the murdered girls.

Further, Joan Whyte is so moved by the terrible treatment handed out to her mother by the police that she is studying law and is pursuing a career where she hopes to be able to make a difference, so this type of thing does not happen to anyone else's mother.

After you have digested the content of this work, I think you will realise that I am coming to the end of the road of doing everything I can think of to get this police cover up into the public arena to try and get some justice for these murdered girls. That is why I decided to write this work, which is a stressful exercise for me as the last thing I would ever want to do is criticise the Queensland police service. I wrote this work because I have no other options left. It is even worse for me because I know what to do, how to do it, to solve these crimes and I have some thoughts on others who could assist police who are not obvious to everyone at this time. They could have very useful information and in one case another possible suspect living in the area, but the police do not want to confide in me or ask me to assist which is not helping to bring the rapist murderers to justice.

I have believed for some time that the position where the Ford Falcon wagon was side on across the Flinders Highway was the place where these killers recaptured Anita after she had escaped from them under the railway bridge over Sensible Creek and that there was someone jumping up and down on something, which was likely to be someone assaulting Anita. The medium mentioned by Joan Whyte in her interview says that Anita died of blunt trauma and that she was probably raped by at least four men.

When Mearle and her mother first saw a campfire under the

Sensible Creek railway bridge, the mother said it was probably people having a party so she must have seen more than one person in the distance and if others chased Anita when she escaped **there would have to have been more killers involved than previously thought** because where the car was sideways across the road there was one man in the car and others towards the railway line including the person jumping up and down.

In chapter nine, I mentioned that I told the police that every aspect of Wally Barry's life should be examined. It is possible that his firearm, if he had one, was used in these crimes. It has been suggested to me that Barry should be looked at as a suspect in the many murders and disappearances that occurred along the Flinders Highway in those years. A Ford vehicle like the one described as being used to transport the murdered girls was used when occupants of that vehicle fired on Mearle Whyte when she was on the veranda of a house in Charters Towers whilst cuddling her daughter Paula. That vehicle is fairly well established as being owned by Wally Barry.

Having upset the establishment by writing this book, I expect there will be an attempt to discredit me in some manner and I wonder how long before the inevitable false anonymous charge will appear. Well, they will have a hard time with that because although I have my failings, dishonesty in respect to graft or the like is not one of them. I can confidently say that I never took a dishonest quid in my life.

I hope that by telling you a little of my history and investigative experiences convinces you that I am qualified to judge the worth of the police investigations into these murders.

What I need from the public now is support calling on the government to constitute a Commission of Inquiry to investigate the police handling of these murders since 1972 and more particularly since 2003 when Mearle Whyte first came forward to police with information.

The reason I favour a Commission of Inquiry rather than an inquest is that with the proper terms of reference given to such an inquiry, the commissioner(s) would be able to compel witnesses to give evidence with the prospect of serving jail time for failure to truthfully answer questions.

An inquiry would summon persons to the witness stand without having to first obtain statements from them as has been shown on television of several occasions recently during inquiries into child sex abuse and the banking industry. Hearsay evidence could be allowed by the commissioner(s).

These terms of reference would enable the commissioner(s) to inquire into all aspects of police investigations into these murders such as, what investigations did the Crime and Corruption Commission and the Ethical Standards Group of the police service make, along with who did they interview before coming to their decisions not to act in response to my complaints. (I doubt if the CCC could be forced to defend their position.)

Failure by police to properly investigate a complaint by not questioning witnesses to establish the truth of their recollections of events or failing to interview people who I had been advised by an assistant police commissioner would be interviewed is, to my mind, perverting the course of justice.

The inquiry would be tasked with uncovering who is the person or persons who have made threats to the safety of Paula Whyte to keep her mouth shut about what she knows of these crimes both before and since I became involved.

There are people who have stood silent when they could have come forward with information. The reasons for this lack of civic duty need explaining because there is the possibility that they stayed mute to disguise their involvement in these murders to the extent that their actions could be classed as accessories after the fact to these murders.

The commissioner(s) would need terms of reference to cover all foreseeable eventualities including the need to be able to extend their allotted inquiry time to conduct their hearings and handing down their findings. They must be able to refer some people to the chief crown prosecutor for possible charges to be laid against those persons if evidence comes to light of criminal conduct.

The inquiry should establish if the hierarchy of the police force from commissioners down are guilty of negligence of failing to see what was happening here right under their noses.

There is also the need for the commission of inquiry to establish from newspaper editors, crime reporters and Channel Seven why they refrained from getting involved and why they did not make sufficient inquiries themselves to see if my accusations against police were true or not. Who or what is the powerful force that has prevented David Cunningham and me from gaining traction and assistance from these press and media representatives in solving these crimes, despite the two of us writing and emailing them with credible evidence over a number of years?

The commissioner(s) should be able to find from the evidence presented throughout the inquiry that Anita Cunningham is deceased, which will probably make life easier for any children of Anita's parents when it comes to legal questions about whether she is alive or deceased.

In the end, I trust that the killers of these girls still alive are brought to justice through the hearing of an inquiry into the police handling of these murders.

Page 13 of the Brisbane Courier Mail on Thursday 21st May 2020 reports that the Queensland government has passed new laws which will allow coroners to compel witnesses to provide potentially self-incriminating evidence in inquests for cases that occurred prior to 2003. This power was previously only available to coroners for cases that occurred after 2003. This is good news, but I still think that a Commission of Inquiry is a much better option for these particular murders.

Despite the reluctance of the investigating police to confide in me or seek my help and with my objectives being to see finality of this case, I have provided information by email to Detective Senior Sergeant Tara Kentwell of the Homicide Unit to pass on to investigating police. There are several suggestions from me as to who might provide further valuable information and who may well be involved in these crimes who are not previously mentioned anywhere in this book. I have also given information about the possible location of the remains of Anita Cunningham and why that information should be considered seriously and not dismissed.

I wish to sincerely thank David Cunningham, who is Anita's brother for all the support he has given me in investigating these crimes since I first contacted him in August 2015. He has written supporting letters that I have asked him to write to the police, newspaper editors and the attorney general.

He has also written letters to various persons of his own volition.

I thank David for his foreword for this book.

The encouragement and support I have received from Peter Cameron, Trudy Brown and Morgan Oss is greatly appreciated and recognised here in this work.

I wish to thank Col Presnell for the many hours he has spent correcting my mistakes in grammar etc. and for suggesting alternative wording in some cases that I have adopted.

Finally, I say the public should not judge members of the Queensland police service on the behaviour of police involved in this case as they are not representative of the majority of police officers who are in the main dedicated, hard-working, honest, caring and work tirelessly to protect you.

Newspaper cuttings etc are attached after the appendix pages.

APPENDIX LIST

1 Application to Coroner for an Inquest
2 Application from Anita's brother for inquest to Attorney General
3 Letter from 14.1.2018 to Commissioner of Police
4 Letter from 12.10.2018 to Commissioner of Police
5 Proposition to Channel Nine by author
6 Anita's brother writes to Head of Homicide Unit
7 Letter of 2.3.2017 to Commissioner of Police New South Wales
8 Reply from New South Wales Police
9 Anita's brother writes to editor of Courier Mail for assistance
10 Application for a Commission of Inquiry to new Attorney General
11 Citation awarded
12 Letter to Attorney General dated 20.7.16
13 A case of attempted murder at Bundaberg
14 Letter dated 14.3.17 to Inspector Hansen
15 A genuine case of rape
16 A false complaint of rape
17 Letter to Attorney General dated 7th April 2023

APPENDIX NUMBER ONE

Application under Section 30 of the Coroner's Act 2003

In compliance with Section 30 of The Coroner's Act 2003, I, Michael John GURN, of [redacted], Queensland, an ex-Detective Sergeant of Police, hereby apply to the state coroner requesting an inquest be held into the disappearance and murders of Robin Jeanne Hoinville-Bartram and Anita Cunningham in 1972 at Pentland, Queensland.

This inquest is necessary in the public interest as the identity of the murderers has not been established by the investigating police and inquiries by email at the office of the state coroner and the state archives show that **an inquest has never been held into these crimes.**

It is possible that clues to the identity of the murderers could be established, and their being brought to justice if an inquest was held, and evidence was received by persons who have a connection with investigations into these crimes and these persons being examined and cross-examined on oath as to their knowledge of these crimes. Due to the time factor of 43 years since the crimes were committed direct evidence would probably come from only a few witnesses.

The main witnesses Mearle Whyte and Betty Madigan are deceased in 2014. Most of the oral evidence that would be available to an inquest will be hearsay evidence which I would ask you to accept and allow due to the unusual circumstances of this case and there being an apparent conflict of opinions between the police and some of the witnesses who could be summoned to give evidence.

As the person making this application, I apply to participate in this inquest and I apply to be given permission to ask questions of witnesses and make submissions at the inquest.

The body of one of the missing girls, Anita Cunningham,

has never been discovered. The body of Robin Jeanne Hoinville-Bartram was discovered in a decomposed state on 15th November 1972 under Sensible Creek Bridge on the Flinders Highway a few miles from Pentland and towards Charters Towers. The body was unclothed from the waist down and two .22 calibre bullets were recovered from her head according to published information on the public record.

In support of my application, I intend to enclose copies of written communications and emails between members of the Queensland police service and myself, including two recorded telephone interviews I did with John Kingstone Whyte on 2nd October 2014 and Paula Whyte on 4th October 2014, which I will provide in the form of a flash drive. Each of these interviews is approximately 50 minutes in length. I do not have the necessary equipment to transcribe these recordings into the written word. However, listening to the witnesses gives one an insight into the sincerity of their words. I will also supply a copy of the DVD showing the Channel Seven programs they showed on TV dealing with these murders.

I became involved in solving these crimes because of casual conversations with a man named Vincent Joseph Whyte about March 2014 who is a friend who phones me regularly. Vincent Whyte resides at Homestead, which is west of Charters Towers and before Pentland.

Vince began telling me that his sister-in-law Mearle Whyte, who was dying of cancer in Townsville Hospital, had been telling her ex-husband John Whyte for years that she had met the two murdered girls at the Pentland Hotel in the wintertime of 1972. Over a period, Vince relayed to me bits and pieces of information that I asked him to find out by asking his brother John. In time, I became convinced that there may have been an injustice done to Mearle in that her story was not believed by the investigating police and consequently the offenders had not been arrested.

The principal investigator when Mearle Whyte told her story was an ex-Police Officer Bob Black of Charters Towers.

I first reported my concerns to Inspector Smith of the Cold Case Homicide Squad on 9th May 2014, who rang me because of a phone call to a contact by me. I told Smith what I knew at the time and that Mearle was dying of cancer in hospital. Smith said he would probably get someone to interview her. Smith rang Vince Whyte at my suggestion and Vince told him what he knew at the time.

When I received additional information from Vince, I tried on two occasions to contact Smith by phone but was unsuccessful and my calls were not returned by him.

I then wrote my first of a number of letters to the police commissioner or other members of the police force on 29th June 2014, because there seemed to be no positive action on the part of the police. Mearle Whyte died in the Townsville Hospital on 16th June 2014 (should be 27th June 2014) and was not interviewed by the police before she died despite calls to Crime Stoppers by her daughter Paula that her mother wanted to tell them what she knew of the murders before she passed away. Priceless information died with her about the murderers, which is especially disappointing.

The position is that Inspector Smith of the Cold Case Squad seems to be relying on reports of ex-Officer Black who investigated Mearle Whyte's report to Black about the murders about 30 years after 1972 and discounted her story.

On 23rd March 2015, I wrote to the commissioner of police advising that because a phone call to Inspector Smith had not been returned, I contacted Channel Seven Sunday Night program representatives with a view to contacting the relatives of the deceased girls as that programme had featured three episodes about the murders in 2014 on TV. Unfortunately, despite initial interest by Channel Seven, the media outlet is no longer interested as a result of their discussions with Inspector Smith. I have not been able to contact the deceased girl's relatives.

The missing girl Anita Cunningham was said to be in the habit of playing with bangles on her arms and I suggested to the police that this girl's relatives should be asked if Anita was in fact in the habit of playing with bangles on her arms. I do not know if this has been done or not. As at the time of making this application, I have not had contact with the relatives of the girls.

The circumstances of these murders are briefly condensed as follows:

The girls, both teenagers 18 years of age, left Melbourne, Victoria in July 1972 on a hitchhiking journey to Bowen, Queensland, where the mother of the girl Bartram lived. It is believed that they intended traveling via Darwin, Mount Isa and the Flinders Highway, up to Bowen.

According to the information conveyed to John and Paula Whyte by Mearle Whyte that on an unknown date in wintertime but presumably in July 1972, on either a Friday or Sunday, the girls arrived at the Pentland Hotel in the company of a man who had hitchhiked with them from Mount Isa to Hughenden and then in another truck to Pentland.

There they met two women Betty Madigan and her daughter, Mearle Madigan then 19 years of age and a teetotaller, who they spent some time with having drinks in the hotel. Betty Madigan cashed a cheque at the hotel, which her husband Brian Patrick Madigan had given her to buy groceries etc. in Charters Towers which if traced may give an on or about date of the meeting. I have not been advised if tracing this cheque has been done by the police. The mother, Betty Madigan, seems to have had a strong liking for alcohol.

In the late afternoon the girls left the Hotel with some men in a car who had agreed to take them to Charters Towers despite being offered an alternative lift to Charters Towers by Merle Madigan who later became Merle Whyte by marriage to John Whyte.

Later in the day, the two Madigan's left the hotel to travel to Charters Towers and a few kilometres down the road when it was then dark, they came across the car the girls had left the hotel in with the men sideways across the road in the vicinity of Sensible Creek with headlights and interior lights on. Only one man occupied the driving seat and there was activity in the open ground towards the railway line. There was no sign of the girls. Betty and Mearle did not stop but continued to Charters Towers with Mearle obeying her mother's directions not to stop.

The Madigan's spent the night at the Mexican Caravan Park in Charters Towers where they had booked accommodation. The next morning being a Saturday or possibly a Monday, Mearle went to a hairdresser to have her hair done. Outside the hairdresser's shop, she was accosted by the man who had travelled with the girls from Mount Isa who had what looked like a long fingernail scratch down the side of his face. He was accompanied by two other men, one of whom is believed to be Wally Barry, now deceased. These men requested that Mearle travel with them to Townsville, but she declined.

She then joined her mother at the White Horse Tavern, which I ascertained had reopened after renovations on 17th May 1972. They shopped during the day and left in the evening for their home on Wando Vale Station some hours' drive away.

A car attempted to intercept them when they left Charters Towers, which Mearle believed was the same car in which the men were in earlier in the day in front of the hairdressers. They eluded that car by accelerating away.

Some nights later, a man was discovered hiding in grass at night outside their home on Wando Vale Station by Mearle's brother Kenneth (should be Dennis) Madigan, then about 15 years of age, who was outside trying to shoot wild pigs. This person ran away, and his identity is not known but suspicion must lie with one of the men who had accosted Mearle outside the hairdresser's shop in Charters Towers. The only explanation would seem to be that he was there to do harm to the women who could identify the men who left the Pentland Hotel with the murdered girls.

On 15th November 1972, the badly decomposed body of Robin Bartram was discovered under Sensible Creek Bridge. She had been shot and two .22 calibre bullets were recovered from her head. She was undressed from the waist down.

It is believed the investigation was done by Townsville detectives and detectives from Brisbane. No persons were arrested as a result of that investigation.

On 24th April 2014, Inspector Smith advised me by email that he had been to Charters Towers investigating this matter and I replied by email to him. He also said that he had advised Alex Cullen of Channel Seven the result of his review of the case and that I would receive a formal reply from him. As of today, this formal reply has not been received by me. Copies of those emails are attached in my letter to the commissioner on 7th June 2015.

Since Smith interviewed Paula and John Whyte, Vince Whyte has told me that his brother John, who has suffered head injuries and his mental recalls are not as normal as most people, recalls that his ex-wife Mearle had told him about the murders not long after they were married about 1975.

He now apparently recalls that on the night Mearle and her mother Betty met the two murdered girls at the Pentland Hotel, Mearle had agreed to drive the girls to Townsville the next day and that they were going to spend the night with Mearle and Betty in their unit at the Mexican Caravan Park but when the car the girls had left the hotel in with the men arrived at the caravan park well past midnight the car only contained the men and no girls. He now recalls that the car the men left the hotel in was a Ford Falcon vehicle as he asserted in his original interview with me. This car was owned by the deceased Wally Barry and that he had seen this car parked at Pam List's place in Charters Towers when he took his future bride, Mearle, there about her wedding dress.

This additional recall to what John Whyte stated in his

interview with me has not been verified by me by interviewing him but has been relayed to me by Vince Whyte. I cannot give an opinion about this additional information other than to say that his brother Vince says that John is a very honest person and has never been known to lie to him about anything although he had some trouble with police when he was a juvenile.

Based on the information given to me, I asserted in my correspondence to the police that Pam List of Charters Towers had denied to Mr Black any knowledge of this Wally Barry being at her place when Mearle and Irene Roth called at her place about bridesmaid dresses. Paula in her interview with me said that her mother named this Wally who she saw at Pam List's house as one of the offenders and one of the men who accosted her outside the hairdresser's shop on a Saturday morning.

I interviewed Irene Roth on 20th March 2014 over the telephone she confirmed that Wally Barry had been at List's house but that about that time List broke off her relationship with Barry. I took this as positive confirmation of that part of Mearle's story and advised the police accordingly by letter.

In one of my letters to the police, I suggested that Mearle Whyte's mother Betty Madigan should have been interviewed to corroborate Mearle's story, this could have already been done by the then investigator Mr Black but having in mind the attitude of Betty Madigan, it is possible that she did not support her daughter as her attitude was 'It has nothing to do with us.' This was said when Mearle told her mother at the White Horse Tavern in Charters Towers, 'I think they have done something to the girls.' At their house later on Wando Vale Station, after the person was found hiding near the house at night, the mother told Mearle to 'shut up about it.'

The father Brian Madigan did not believe Mearle and her mother that the man hiding in the grass was there to do harm to them and it was probably just pig shooters. When the body of Robin was discovered, the father told Mearle, 'We don't get involved in anything like that.'

The parents were isolationists who rarely came to town and apparently wanted nothing to do with anything that could involve them with the police. It would not surprise if Betty Madigan did not support her daughter if she had been interviewed by Mr Black.

Setting out all the differences in information and suggestions I made to the police about the investigation could go on and on. But the real point here is that I believe that Mearle and Betty (also deceased in March 2014) did meet these girls and that contradictions here could not be accurate as person's memories differ after 43 years and do not detract from the basic substance of their stories. Picking holes in statements of witnesses are not sufficient to discount the basic points of their memory recalls.

After 43 years, the differences matter little if one informant remembers somethings differently about what they have been told by Mearle Whyte; whether one remembers her saying one of the offenders had a scratch on the right side of his face and the other the left side of his face. One saying a Valiant car was involved and the other a Falcon. One saying the car was stopped near Sensible Creek Bridge and the other further along the road. It hardly matters if John Whyte, who has had head injuries affecting his brain, recalls his wife telling him about the events soon after their marriage or twenty years later. If these contradictions were not there, the whole story might take on the look of a conspiracy by the informants. I am personally glad these contradictions exist as it lends credence to their stories.

Could any reasonable person believe that two people separately interviewed could be lying in recalling two mostly consistent stories about Mearle Whyte and Betty Madigan meeting the girls at the Pentland Hotel in the wintertime, their leaving there with men in a car getting a lift from the hotel to Charters Towers. Mearle being accosted outside the hairdresser's shop in Charters Towers with one of the offenders having his face badly scratched with what appeared to be a fingernail scratch; about the man hiding in grass on the outside of the house on the outstation on Wando Vale Station at night and Mearle's brother Dennis nearly tripping over him.

One informant claiming Mearle was fired upon from a car on the road outside her house in Charters Towers. One has also to consider that one informant lives in Charters Towers and the other in Townsville and the interviews were conducted on different days over the telephone.

You will see from this application, the enclosed documentation and flash drive containing the recorded interviews that there seems to be conflict between what I assert and the position of Inspector Smith, but my whole and only focus in all this is bringing the offenders still alive to justice and an inquest might achieve this when persons are called to give evidence on oath. The relatives are also entitled to hear these disclosures, which may bring them some comfort in their grief.

It needs to be pointed out that Mearle Whyte was dying in Townsville hospital when she conveyed additional information to her daughter Paula and was therefore unlikely to be lying. The daughter took written notes of what her mother told her which should now be in the possession of the police. Merle's story is not dissimilar to a dying declaration except that it does not refer to her own death, but additional weight should be given to her claims due to her knowledge that she knew she was dying of cancer at the time.

I can assure you that I have no hidden agenda in making this application and at 82 years of age, it is unfortunate that I have to be involved to this extent but I believe that an inquest is necessary to bring closure to these crimes for the community and for the relatives, which has the very real possibility that additional information would be revealed from an inquest leading to the arrest of these rapists and murderers.

Having in mind the battle I have had to make the police take *my information seriously since May 2014, it will be no surprise if the police are dismissive of my application for an inquest. I do have an opinion about who should be summonsed as witnesses, which I will submit if asked.*

Yours faithfully,
M.J. Gurn
Commissioner for Declarations
Dated 29th June 2015.

I attached documents to this application. The list of these attachments appears below.

LIST OF ATTACHMENTS FOR CORONER

DVD of Hitchhiker Murders from Channel Seven
Flash drive containing interviews with John and Paula Whyte and Irene Roth
Letter to Inspector [redacted] dated 29th June 2014
Letter Commissioner of Police 4th July 2014
Letter from Inspector [redacted] dated 15th September 2014
Letter to Commissioner of Police dated 5th October 2014. Includes email to Inspector Smith
Letter to Commissioner of Police dated 6th October 2014
Letter from Inspector [redacted] dated 18th October 2014
Letter to Commissioner of Police dated 20th October 2014
Letter to Deputy Commissioner Barnett dated 4th November 2014
Letter from Deputy Comm. Barnett dated 18th November 2014
Letter to Dep. Comm. Barnett dated 6th January 2015
Letter from Assistant Comm. Hogan dated 8th January 2015
Letter to Assistant Comm. Hogan dated 5th February 2015
Letter to Comm. Of Police dated 21st March 2015
Letter to Comm. Of Police dated 7th June 2015

APPENDIX NUMBER TWO

In a letter dated 3rd June 2016, David Cunningham, brother of Anita Cunningham wrote to the attorney general as follows:
From PO Box VIC, 3451

To: *The Queensland Attorney-General, Yvette D'Ath GPO Box 149, Brisbane, QLD, 4001*
Dear Attorney, General,
I am writing to request the help of the office of the attorney general, and to draw her attention to the urgent necessity for an inquest into the disappearance and murder of my sister Anita Cunningham, and her companion Robyn Hoinville-Bartram.

There is also the question of why the case was neglected for 40 years and why, now, when evidence has been presented, is the case still being deliberately neglected or covered up?

It appears ironic and hypocritical for the police to judge the case important enough to offer a $250,000 reward for information leading to a conviction, while at the same time failing to follow up on information that is brought forward.

Example 1: Forty years ago, after police finally acceded to our requests to have Anita and Robin registered as missing persons, a family friend, Keith Galloway, was certain he had seen Anita, and observed her as she was working behind a bar in Melbourne. She disappeared into a back room as he was about to approach her, and then re-appeared at the exit with a disreputable fellow who gave Keith a dark look before the pair left.

Keith contacted police saying he had seen Anita working in a bar, gave the time and date, the location of the bar, gave details of her movements in the bar, and a description of her associate.

2: Whether in fact it was Anita or not is immaterial now, we may never know, but that is not the point.

The point is this:

Why is a highly credible, positive sighting of a known missing person, who can give vital information to a murder investigation into death of her traveling partner, totally ignored by both missing persons AND the homicide squad?

Keith was no ordinary witness. He knew very well what Anita looked like; he had known Anita for many years. Being the father of Anita's best friend, Ronelle, he had watched Anita growing up.

Keith was also a very highly regarded airline pilot with excellent eyesight and, if he claimed to have seen her, the information was definitely worth checking up on, even if only just a police visit to the bar with a photo of Anita to verify if it was her working at the bar or not.

Keith was never contacted again by police, either to

a. elicit further information, or

b. out of courtesy to say that they had investigated,

or c. to tell him the outcome of any investigation into his alleged sighting.

The reason, of course, is that there was no investigation.

Inspector Smith, of the Cold Case Squad, recently informed us there is nothing anywhere in police files to indicate the reported sighting and information was ever acted upon by the police!

A policeman was sent from Queensland to Melbourne at the time, and he turned in a report about another matter, but Anita's case was not mentioned. Why the police silence? Why the police failure to follow up on strong evidence?

They say fact is stranger than fiction, and certainly no work of fiction would expect a reader to believe that two departments of police (Missing Persons and Homicide), working independently, could BOTH deem this very strong lead totally worthless.

I can see only three alternative explanations. Either it is abysmally shameful, criminal negligence, or it is incompetence at a level which is too profound to be believed, or it was deliberate.

The first two alternatives strain credibility too far.

3: That leaves only the third alternative, which begs the question:

Who, or what, were the police covering up?

And why?

Whatever the explanation was for the failure to act on evidence brought forward, it continued until the present day.

What is the police interest in letting this case lie forgotten?

For 40 years, the police response to my sister's disappearance had achieved virtually nothing precisely because it had amounted to virtually nothing.

There was no police investigation into my sister's disappearance, and the investigation into Robin's murder seems to have been very scant.

Recently we learned that, for some reason, the case had been reopened some years ago, and the paperwork was surveyed, but no further leads seem to have been followed up.

Witnesses have come forward in recent years but seem to have all been dismissed out of hand. Can they all have been so transparently fake?

Example 2: My sister and I were very close, and I had also been on intimate terms with her murdered traveling companion, Robin, yet, AT NO TIME did police ever seek to contact me either by telephone, by letter, or in person, to enquire about the girls' traveling intentions or plans, their frame of mind when they left, their propensities or habits, or anything else that one would have reasonably expected an investigation to want to know!

When I expressed my amazement and profound disappointment about that particular part of the historical lack of police attention to these crimes to Inspector Smith, he said that often times family members are not questioned because family members can be suspects in these cases, to which I replied that I would have thought that is all the more reason why I should have been interviewed!

4: Recently it emerged during my conversations with police, the reason I was not interviewed is that my sister's disappearance was not being investigated, despite the discovery of her traveling companion's murdered remains!

It was only after Robin's body was discovered that the police were forced to take the parents' phone calls and requests to the police about the girls' disappearance seriously, and Anita was listed on the Missing Person's Register.

Even then, it seems very little, or nothing was done to investigate Anita's disappearance. We were recently told that Homicide had been doing some investigation into Robin's murder, but we were not kept informed because it was a matter for Robin's family, and even though the girls were together, the tragedy was treated as two separate cases which were handled separately, with apparently little or no communication between Homicide and Missing Persons.

Further examples:

There are furthermore recent examples, but I will not go into any details here about recent discoveries, which may become subject to court proceedings if an inquest is granted. Suffice it to say, it has recently emerged that, over time, credible eyewitnesses had come forward and contacted police to give information about the girls' disappearance and murder, but were dismissed by the police, and their testimony and evidence not followed up.

I realise the police have a difficult job and a big area to cover, and I have absolutely no criticism of the way my mother and I were received and treated by both Peter Smith and Bob Black recently, who were very polite, gracious and helpful to us when Channel Seven invited us up to Queensland to make the TV show about their disappearance.

But having said that, it's too little, too late when contrasted against 40 years of what I can only see as inaction and neglect or something worse.

It is comforting and appreciated and very nice of Mr Smith and Mr Black to go to the trouble of explaining to us the past investigations (and lack thereof), and the reasons for the lack of police attention to these matters in the past, but it seems all we're effectively doing is putting it to bed, and packing it away neatly with a whole lot of big, permanent question marks, which is actually just a continuance of the deliberate inaction of the past. A deliberate inaction in which I am now being asked to become complicit.

5: Over the past 40+ years, witnesses have taken their stories to their grave but there are still witnesses alive today who could shed a great deal of light on what happened to the girls, and some might know enough to solve this case, if only they could be brought before an inquest and be legally required to tell what they know. If their story is not told soon, they too, will take the truth to their graves and the truth will never be told, and justice will never have been served.

The 2 examples detailed above (which I have direct personal knowledge of) are from the past, but it seems the same treatment is being given to other witnesses who have come forward in recent years – no investigation, just dismiss it, ignore it, or cover it up.

I know of two ex-senior detectives, neither of whom know each other, both have been investigating this matter for different reasons, and both have their own separate lines of enquiry and different evidence which, in both cases implies that police have something to hide.

It's hard to bury your sister when she is only 19 and full of life and beauty and promise, but it's harder to live for more than 40 years in a silent void, never knowing what happened to her, whether she is alive or dead, whether she is prisoner somewhere, or in hiding, or in a rough and lonely grave, either close to where Robin was found, or some desolate place far from our reach, or whether to try to hold on to the faintest receding hope she'll one day appear on the front doorstep.

I don't have contact details for Robin's remaining family. Robin's mother and my mother were brought close by the tragic circumstances, but she died a long time ago and I believe there is only a sister still alive. The sister has apparently been active trying to find out what happened to Robin by consulting psychic investigators and spirit mediums, so I feel sure she would enthusiastically welcome an inquest if she was aware of the possibility.

In view of:

a. the sad lack of attention given to these matters historically, and

b. the fact of the recent discoveries that there are still strong lines of investigation to pursue, and

c. the pressing urgency of time due to the ages of the remaining witnesses,

d. also to quell public suspicion and show that justice has been adequately served in this matter,

I think now is the crucial time to finally give this case the attention it has been silently crying out for, for a long, lonely time.

I therefore humbly request that you please give the assent to commence an inquest urgently, so we can gather the evidence of the last remaining witnesses before they die, and learn the truth about what happened, and who was responsible.

Yours sincerely,
David Cunningham

APPENDIX NUMBER THREE

Commissioner of Police
Dated 14th January 2018
Dear Sir
Re: Pentland Murders

With reference to my recent letter of 18th December 2017, I forgot to send you a copy of an advertisement which appeared in the Northern Miner newspaper on 7th April 2017, inserted by David Cunningham, brother of the missing Anita Cunningham. Same is now attached.

A week ago, I forwarded copies of my letter to you of 18th ultimo, together with a copy of a letter to Inspector Hansen on 14th March 2017 and the advertisement seeking information from the public to the Premier Annastacia Palaszczuk, the attorney general Yvette D'Ath and the leader of the LNP Deb Frecklington seeking assistance in gaining justice for the murdered girls. Mr Bruce Morcombe, father of the murdered Daniel Morcombe, has also been contacted and asked to assist.

I have pointed out that the people of North Queensland around Townsville and Charters Towers do not understand how it is possible that so much knowledge of the movements of the murdered girls is known and yet there is no action on the part of the police.

I have made special reference to this disturbing interference with the informant witness Paula Whyte, which is obvious by the inferred change of heart of this person when interviewed by Inspector Smith in April 2015 to the frank, detailed and sincere information she gave me on 4th October 2014 in my recorded interview with her, even breaking down telling me what her mother Mearle Whyte told her in the Townsville Hospital waiting to die.

This situation could not have occurred without pressure having been applied to her by someone fearful of what she had revealed to me which would amount to criminal conduct and needs an *investigation of the circumstances. This situation has already been brought under your notice by the attorney general, as advised to me by her, by letter to you.*

The extraordinary email from Inspector Smith in April 2015 to me telling me in so many words I am not allowed to contact Paula Whyte again needs explaining. Why was this necessary in his view when all l am doing is trying to get some justice for the deceased girls, unless more would be revealed if I spoke to her again.

Then there is the incorrect statement from Inspector Smith about the possible involvement of Ivan Milat in this email to compound the necessity to send me this email in the first place and the unfulfilled statement that I would receive his review shortly, which has not happened.

Yours faithfully,
M.J. Gurn

APPENDIX NUMBER FOUR

Dated 12th October 2018
Commissioner of Police
Brisbane. 4001
Dear Sir,
Another to add to the list of my letters concerning the murders of Robin Jeanne Hoinville-Bartram and Anita Cuningham at Pentland in 1972. Also, now the suspected assault, robbery and death of Frederick James Whyte, 68 years at Charters Towers on Sunday 30th September 2007.

The police are largely relying on the investigations of ex-Police Officer Bob Black of Charters Towers Police in respect to the murders of Bartram and Cunnningham and disregarding my investigations wherein I maintain that I have informed you the identity of some of the murderers of these girls but such information has not been acted on by your detectives despite the high probability that I am correct in my identifications subsequent to the information I obtained in my recorded interviews with John Whyte and Paula Whyte on 2nd and 4th October 2014.

I have gone to some length to criticise the investigations of your ex-member Bob Black on whose policing abilities you are relying. With that in mind, I wish to bring under your notice the following information which should give you some concern in placing so much reliance on his work as he was also the investigating officer in the death of Frederick Whyte.

My criticisms surround the way the informant woman Mearle Whyte was treated by Black when she went to the police with information that she and her mother Betty Madigan had met the two murdered girls at the Pentland Hotel before they were murdered on that fateful day in 1972.

Your officers have failed to act on my information despite me giving you a means to test the credibility of my information by tracing a cheque cashed at the Pentland Hotel when the women were there and when they met the murdered girls.

There may be a train of thought that even if the date on the cheque was relevant to July 1972 when the girls could reasonably have been at the Pentland Hotel. This would not prove anything but in this case, it is relevant as Brian Madigan, the father, would not let his wife or family go to Charters Towers from Wando Vale Station more than once every six months and maybe every four months if you were lucky according to Paula Whyte. So, the cheque is very relevant to establishing when Mearle met the two murdered girls by opportunity.

I also advised you that five people had some knowledge of Mearle Whyte's story that she had met the girls. If I was to go further with finding others who had heard from Meryl Whyte that she had met the girls, I believe I could find at least three or four more people as she had six children and her daughter Paula who is principally involved is but one of these children and therefore others of her children must also know the story.

Plus, she was friendly with her sisters-in-law so there are probably others in that group who could also corroborate her, and no doubt will be called to do so in time as I will continue to chip away with investigations into these murders with a view to getting justice for the murdered girls.

[The next two paragraphs of this letter have been deleted as the wording identifies some police.]

When the body was found, the investigators had to borrow gas masks to handle the body due to the smell of the decaying body. I have previously suggested that the top clothing from the body should be tested for DNA matching. Whether this is possible due to the condition of the clothing from the rotting body, I do not know.

When the body was discovered, the head of the Homicide Squad in Brisbane, Det. Sen Sgt. Brian Hayes, went to North Queensland as part of investigations. He brought back body parts and placed them in the morgue suitably labelled. Another detective of the Homicide Squad attended the autopsy performed by Dr Tonge. There was not much left, just bones mainly. Dr Tonge recovered fragments of bullets from the head and even x-rayed the skull to make sure he got all the fragments. He placed them in a jar.

The jar with fragments of the bullets from the skull were delivered to Inspector Bardwell of the Firearms Section of the C. I. Branch in Brisbane. He identified the bullet fragments as to type etc. but it seems the condition of the bullets would make comparisons with other bullets difficult if not impossible.

Now, I will move on to another piece of policework on the part of Black, which is not entirely convincing but may be correct but there are unanswered questions. Vincent Whyte of Homestead said he received a phone call early on 1st October 2007 from ex-Officer Bob Black informing him that his brother Frederick had died in an unfortunate accident.

On the afternoon of Sunday 30th September 2007, Frederick James Whyte, a single man, born 8.6.39 (68 years) of Homestead caught a bus to Charters Towers, withdrew his pension money from the Commonwealth Bank ATM machine, of some $600. John Whyte took charge of the deceased bank account as next of kin and closed the account with the bank, verifying that the deceased did withdraw $600 by the ATM machine. John cannot remember if he was given the debit card for this transaction from the deceased property returned to him by the police.

The deceased arrived at the Commercial Hotel in Charters Towers about five p.m. and booked into room 11, upstairs in the hotel. He purchased a 375ml bottle of rum from the bottle shop. He bought two XXXX gold stubbies and then ordered a half nip of rum and water and then consumed a meal.

He was served some more rum and water in the bar. He was seen speaking to other people in the bar. He was observed by a Mr

Lawrence Peter McCrae, a patron and hotel guest, drinking at the hotel sitting on the front veranda from a rum bottle.

McCrae said Whyte was not sober. Between 9 p.m. and 9.30 p.m., McCrae went upstairs to his room. He saw Whyte passed out on the floor at the head of the stairs. McCrae gave Whyte no assistance. No one else was located who saw Whyte passed out on the floor. McCrae went to the TV room. Not long after that, McCrae said he saw Whyte walk past the TV room and back again. Shortly after, McCrae claims he heard a loud thump and thought Whyte must have walked into a wall or tripped over.

One guest stated that he went to bed about 8.30 p.m. and did not see anything suspicious or unusual. Another guest stated that he came back to the hotll about 9.30 p.m. and did not see anyone on the stairs. Another guest recalled using the stairs about 9.30 p.m. from the bar. He said he saw McCrae sitting in the television room but did not see the deceased anywhere. He did not hear anything unusual or suspicious. He then went to bed.

At about 10.30 p.m., McCrae went to bed. (Apparently, he did not then look down the stairwell.) About 11 p.m., McCrae got up and went to the toilet. McCrae looked down the stairs and saw Whyte lying face down on the middle landing which was seven stairs from the top of the first floor to the middle landing. He also saw a half full bottle of rum lying near Whyte. If this thump heard by McCrae a lot earlier was Whyte toppling down the stairwell, he was lying in the stairwell well for about an hour unseen by anyone else. Not likely as there were guests staying at the hotel.

McCrae drove to the police station and ambulance, but both were shut. He rang 000. Police arrived about 11.20 p.m., but Whyte was deceased. It is said that police located blood on the walls of the stairwell consistent with Whyte coming into contact with the wall.

An autopsy revealed abrasions around the right side of the nose, just below the right side of the lower lip and also scattered on the neck and upper chest. The abrasions were less than 2cm long, extending upwards at the right side of the forehead. His lungs showed severe emphysema. His 6th and 7th ribs were fractured on the left side of his chest and appeared recent.

The strap muscles of his neck are mentioned so there must have been something about the position of his head and neck for that to be mentioned. There is no mention of an internal examination to see the condition of the spinal cord at the neck to see if the neck was broken.

He was found to be heavily intoxicated, and cause of death was shown as emphysema. He had chest trauma and head trauma consistent with a fall on stairs according to the coroner's report, which contributed to his death from respiratory insufficiency. The brothers were told that the deceased head when found was at a peculiar angle to his body and lying on his left shoulder, suggesting a broken neck but no mention of that is made in the autopsy report, which does appear to be otherwise thorough.

The deceased brothers are Vincent Whyte of Homestead and John Whyte of Charters Towers. These men believe that their brother was robbed and was murdered in the attack, perhaps not intentionally. They think the attack began in his room, with him awakening to being robbed and fighting off his attacker, which led to blood being found in his room, on the door of the room across the corridor opposite room 11 and on the wall of the stairwell.

There does not appear to be any mention of blood in the room or on the opposite room door of the corridor in the coroner's report and this information comes from the brothers who made other inquiries at the hotel.

Constable Shead reported to his superior officer on 24th May 2008 that Officer Bob Black had attended and could find no evidence that Whyte's death was anything other than accidental.

Constable Shead's report is so brief it tells little of substance. He suggests the blood found on the walls (plural) could be from the deceased's mouth as he had emphysema? (Not likely as the *deceased never showed any signs of having emphysema according to his brother Vincent). He suggests he may have had some other injury from the fall. (This is apparently referring to the alleged thump heard by McCrae.)*

There is mention of photographs being taken but whether they clear up the possibility of the deceased's head being at a peculiar angle to his body is not known. Vince Whyte says that his brother smoked but never ever showed any shortness of breath or any cough to suggest he had emphysema.

John Whyte says that cleaners were employed to remove blood from the deceased's room, the door of the room opposite the deceased's room and the stairwell. He received this information from the then manager of the hotel. The police apparently put the blood on the stairwell down to Whyte coming into contact with the wall of the stairway.

The police apparently make no mention of the blood in the deceased's room or the hallway, which is even stranger. Any such mention by the police is not in the coroner's report or the brief report of Constable Stead.

Shead suggests the blood found on the walls (plural) could be from the deceased's mouth as he had emphysema?

For there to be blood on the wall of the stairwell, if Whyte toppled down the stairs he must have been bleeding profusely before he fell down the stairway. If he contacted the wall toppling down the stairs, he would not bleed that fast to put blood on the wall. The brothers attribute this bleeding to Frederick being struck on the nose, causing a nose bleed out in his room.

Vince Whyte claims that he received a letter from a doctor at the Charters Towers hospital, which verified that the deceased apparently had a broken neck among other comments on the deceased's medical condition, but he has misplaced this letter and has spent hours trying to find it in his house

John Whyte met a policewoman and another male constable

at the morgue by arrangement and identified his brother's body, which was in a body bag and draped on a chair and not on a table due to a shortage of room in the morgue there as there had been deaths of elderly people in the hospital. John said that his brother's head was lying on his left shoulder and the policewoman said to disregard this as it was a result of having to leave the body on the chair and not on a table.

As the body was in a body bag, John could not see if the deceased was dressed or not. Who undressed the body and took possession of his property is not shown and not listed in the coroner's report or the brief police report.

John Whyte was handed back under $30 of Frederick's money, the rum bottle but none of his clothing so we do not know how much blood was on his clothing. How the rum bottle was found near the body leads one to suspect that Whyte was carrying the bottle when he was near the stairs. Or someone smart enough to put the bottle near the body.

The abrasions and other injuries including broken ribs are more in keeping with those incurred in a fight and struggle and no mention is made anywhere about the money missing from his person in the coroner's report, which would have been in the area of $500. Whyte was known to always keep his money in his pockets and did not believe in having a wallet. His theory was that if you had money in a wallet, you lost everything.

I am, from my own experiences, concerned that no mention is made of what happened to the missing money in the coroner's report and that the injuries are consistent with those received in some sort of fight, rather than just toppling down a staircase. Also why is there no mention in the coroner's report of blood in room 11 or on the door opposite room 11. This blood trail would indicate to me the trail of a struggle.

In an article being prepared by reporters from the Northern Miner newspaper in Charters Towers for publishing at some time about the death of Frederick Whyte, the reporter says that the police attribute the blood on the walls above the stairs to Frederick hitting his head as he fell. The detailed autopsy report says nothing about a cut sufficient in size to cause this bleeding from his head. In fact, only abrasions are noted which one would not expect to be caused by falling down a stairwell but very likely in a physical struggle.

The coroner's report does not mention any problem with the deceased's neck. Now, back again to the murders of Bartram and Cunningham. As a result of Inspector Smith going to Charters Towers in April 2015, Paula Whyte would not communicate with me again until David Cunningham contacted her, and she then requested me to contact her.

I have previously advised you of what transpired and the explanations she gave for not wanting any further involvement at that time, which are plausible.

I put it to Paula that she must have been contacted by Black and threatened in some way before she spoke to Inspector Smith at Charters Towers Police Station. She does not deny this happened but nor will she say it did not happen. She is a frightened woman and said threats have been made to her about her part in my investigations but because of her fears she will not elaborate.

However, it seems an appropriate time to again remind you of what Paula said Inspector Smith said to her. She said that Smith told her that her mother must have a mental problem, that the family's story was 'fiddlesticks' and to 'give it up' and 'don't even try to go there' as the young men implicated have now become magistrates, lawyers and bailiffs. They are people of influence who don't want this sordid story to come to light and are friends of the police.'

Paula says she got the impression that Smith was doing all he could to protect Black. I have previously enlarged on all that so I will not go over it again but suffice to say these unanswered questions, I hope, will sooner or later be answered. I have advised Paula that she and her sister Joan, who can corroborate some of Smith's behaviour, to make written notes so that they can refresh their memories when they are called to the witness box at some time.

She said that when Black was shown the bullet holes at the house in Charters Towers (about 1984/5) where Mearle was fired on from a car on the street outside which broke louvres and narrowly missed Paula, then a five- or seven-yea- old girl, Black dismissed the complaint of bullets being fired at Mearle as 'probably from a sling shot'. In either case, what was done to find the shooter or locate the bullets in the wall that Paula believes could still be in the wall?

It is to be hoped that the police adopt a new approach and properly investigate both the murders of Robin Bartram and Anita Cunningham and the suspicious death of Frederick Whyte and do not wait until media pressure builds.

Your faithfully,
M.J. Gurn

There was no response to this letter about the death of Frederick Whyte.

APPENDIX NUMBER FIVE

Proposition for Channel 9 put to Adam Hegarty

Adam,
I have a proposition for Channel 9 in which I am prepared to go with a representative of Channel 9 to pursue this investigation to North Queensland but first let me state the position here against what appears to be the police position.

The police position is, as far as I can make out, 'THE MURDERED GIRLS WERE NEVER AT THE PENTLAND HOTEL.'

This is laughable. The body of Robin Hoinville-Bartram was located just a few miles from Pentland.

My informants have given their account of Mearle and Betty meeting the girls at the Pentland Hotel in recorded conversations with me, which I am prepared to let you listen to, which clearly puts paid to any suggestion that the girls were never at the Pentland Hotel.

After letters and frustration with inaction by police, I got a letter from Assistant Commissioner Hogan that three people I have asked to be questioned would be questioned but it may take six months for finality on that score.

This was not satisfactory, so I contacted Channel 7. Alex Cullen interviewed me. He listened to the tapes. He said Inspector Peter Smith of the Cold Case Squad had requested a month's grace before Channel 7 did anything on the story.

Smith goes to Charters Towers to investigate my recorded interviews and their allegations and to interview the three persons mentioned from Assistant Commissioner Hogan.

Smith does not interview the three persons as far as I can see. He does interview the daughter of Mearle, but he does not ask her if what she said in the recorded interview was true or not. He does not ask her if she wished to add or delete anything from the interview.

Instead, he berates the woman, telling her that her mother was delusional or words to that effect and tells her to forget the story and let it die with her mother.

Further, he tells her that others involved in this sordid mess are outstanding people and would never do anything like that and that they are people of influence, who are friends of the police who do not want the real story to come out. He said they became a magistrate, solicitor and bailiff. Plus, a lot more.

Smith emails me from Charters Towers (April 2015), telling me that the woman does not want any further contact with me. The tone of the email was threatening.

He said that neither the woman nor her mother had ever mentioned Ivan Milat being responsible. (Ivan Milat, however, is named in the interview). Smith says he will forward me the result of his review.

He interviews the husband of Mearle and tries the same stand over tactic with John Whyte who stands up to him and tells him that he does not know why he is wasting time with his daughter or him or me when he should be going after Ted West who holds the key to the whole thing.

Smith tells Cullen something and Channel 7 drop off.

I repeatedly ask the commissioner for Smith's review, but I never receive it.

It is not until three years later in April 2018 that the truth of Smith's behaviour at Charters Towers in April 2015 comes out when David Cunningham talks to the woman who gave me the interview and the true account of Smith's so-called investigations at Charters Towers in 2015 comes out.

I write to Commissioner Ian Stewart, pointing out these matters and expect him to order an investigation into Smith's actions at Charters Towers in 2015 telling him that Smith's actions amount to perverting the course of justice.

Nothing happens that I am aware of. Later, I write to Stewart again and tell him that I hold him personally responsible for this situation. A few weeks later Stewart takes early retirement.

New Commissioner Katerina Carroll takes over and on her opening day, my letter to her dated 8th July 2019 lands on her doorstep with new information that one of the murderers is still living in Charters Towers. Nothing seems to change. No action taken I am aware of.

The murdered girls have no voice but mine and I want closure of the whole investigation so I can put to bed this last five and half years of trying to get action from the police, newspaper editors, news commentators and others without result. Except from Trudy Brown, editor of the Norther Miner in Charters Towers and Peter Cameron in his traps column in the Sunday Mail over four years.

There must be something sinister involved here that I not aware of. I do not know why I have been blackballed and prevented from getting the true story out.

I had over 23 years in the police force with 18 years a detective. I have handled hundreds of investigations with commendations awarded for some successful closures. I do know the difference between truth and fabrications.

My proposition is that I am prepared to go with you to North Queensland to further investigate these murders if Channel 9 backs me with proper separate single motel accommodation at night, three meals a day and some spending money, a modern four-wheel drive vehicle and driver. I will not go with a heavy drinker or a joint smoker. I do not drink or smoke. You would need a special assignment and equipment to take statements and print them out for signing and probably video equipment. I would have a fair bit of my own luggage etc so it would be best to start at [redacted] by car.

The investigation would have to be done in the order I say, and the persons interviewed when I say. I do have a plan in my head. I know who I want to interview and some addresses. I anticipate the inquiry would take at least a week of intense traveling to Townsville, Charters Towers, Mount Isa, Maxwelton, Winton and Longreach. I expect it would take some 5000 to 7000 kms of travel due to the vast distances to cover which take a day to get to from one place to another.

However, if I got some admissions with the early inquiries that confirm Mearle and Betty meeting the murdered girls then the police would be forced to act and there would be no need for us to pursue inquiries in Mount Isa, Maxwelton, Winton and Longreach; we would only need to concentrate around Townsville, Charters Towers and Pentland at that stage.

Signed,
M.J. (Mick) Gurn
27th November 2019

APPENDIX NUMBER SIX

17/01/2020

To: Homicide Group Detective Inspector Damien Hansen

cc. Queensland Police Commissioner Katerina Carroll, Queensland Attorney General Yvette D'Ath

Dear Mr Hansen,

I am the brother of Anita Cunningham, who disappeared from Victoria in April 1972 along with her best friend Robin Hoinville-Bartram, whose partially decomposed body was discovered beneath Sensible Creek Bridge west of Charters Towers in August 1972.

I am writing to you, as the head of the Homicide Investigation Unit, about a troubling, weird and strangely suspicious story involving members of the Queensland police, but mainly for your advice on how best to proceed from here.

Victoria Police have been helpful with a positive professional attitude but since it's a Queensland case, most of the files are in Queensland. The Vic Pol FOO request was no problem.

Since the girls first disappeared, some of my experiences with Queensland Police have been less pleasant and professional, and the contrast seems remarkable. I won't go into all the details here, but I could if required.

Here's one notable exception. Things were suddenly different when Channel Seven flew my mother and I to Brisbane and Townsville for a TV story about the case; suddenly, police were exceedingly helpful. The charming and friendly head of the Cold Case Squad, Peter Smith, personally picked us up from our hotel in the morning. He was very kind and patient with my elderly mother, which we greatly appreciated, and looked after us very well. We had several meetings with him and another meeting arranged with one of the psychic detectives' police had been working with. The other one refused to meet us.

On one of the days, Mr Smith took us to an upstairs room in a police station where there was a map set up showing us the presumed route the girls had taken. He explained that after all these years and whatever leads and investigations were and were not pursued, nothing was known except two facts.

1. The date/place where the girls set off from, and

2. the date/place where Robin's body was found a few months later.

The take home message as we understood it was:

1. Nothing is known.

2. Although credible leads have been ignored in the past, we can dismiss new leads with existing knowledge (except for the 'psychic detectives' – police sprang into action on the strength of their 'evidence' and made themselves look incompetent).

3. Nothing will ever be known so let it rest.

Peter Smith introduced us to Bob Black, an ex-officer who had conducted a fruitless review of the case decades ago. I will not include our impressions of Mr Black.

Since then, it's been back to the old uncommunicative, unhelpful, withholding, almost antagonistic ways. I know it's not just a Queensland trait, because I have many friends in Queensland, and they don't have that attitude at all.

Also since that date, I became acquainted with ex-Senior Detective Mick Gurn who, through his extensive local knowledge, vast network of contacts built up over the years (he's 87) and impeccable reputation, had been approached by relatives of witnesses who had previously come forward with eye-witness accounts and a deathbed confession, which the QLD police had rejected out-of-hand, refused to hear and neglected to pursue.

During these witnesses' attempts to bring their knowledge to the appropriate authorities, they claim to have been humiliated warned and threatened by police.

As far as I can tell, the police position is that the girls were never at the Pentland Hotel, even though Robin's body was found only a few kilometres from Pentland.

Since meeting ex-Senior Detective Mick Gurn and knowing him over recent years, I have come to know him as a thorough, astute, intelligent and fearlessly honest man of integrity and dogged tenacity.

I also began personal correspondence with a witness who claimed that she and her mother had been warned-off and threatened by Peter Smith (behaviour totally at odds with my own experience with Mr Smith).

The witness believed that Peter Smith was trying to protect his mate, Bob Black. According to witnesses, Black had mistreated and verballed Mearle Whyte who had been with the missing girls at the Pentland Hotel earlier in the evening on the night of Robin's murder.

I put in an FOI request to VicPol who were polite and professional, and I got the information in good time.

However, my RTI request to QLD Police unfortunately was treated quite differently from my Victorian experience. My initial telephone interaction was pleasant and helpful and then I submitted my written request. Subsequent phone calls were not so friendly, and I encountered delays, resistance, lack of helpful information and an attitude that seemed like resentment or hostility. When the request-fulfillment time frame had blown out and I phoned and emailed to see when I might expect a response, I was told that they didn't have time to reply to further emails and please don't ring, and that I just had to continue waiting.

They asked me what in particular I was looking for. I said I would like to have the whole file but if I can't I would at least like a copy of the review.

After another excessively lengthy wait, I phoned up again and I was told the file had been sent to me, but they couldn't say whether it had been posted or emailed. I knew full well it hadn't been emailed, as I hadn't received any emails from RTI for months (even in my spam folder), and the post office confirmed it had never arrived or they would have put it, or a notice-to-collect, in my PO box.

I insisted it be re-sent and to please confirm with me once it was sent, and they said OK.

Again, it never arrived.

I asked again for it to be re-sent both by email and mail.

I was then told that my request had been refused.

Reason? Because, they said, it was no longer a cold case but was now an active investigation.

I asked how I could know when the 'active' status had ceased, and I could re-apply under RTI.

I was told that I cannot be informed when the 'active' status is removed.

Questions:

1. Is it true that I must keep putting in fresh RTI requests to QLD Police in the hope that one day the case will no longer be 'active' and my RTI request might be re-considered?

2. If the status of the case is in fact no longer 'cold' but is now 'active', why would QLD Police not be interested in talking with me? Or at least be helpful in their attitude to my efforts to investigate?

3. Why has there not been an investigation into the mishandling of this case in the past?

4. Why there is now a refusal to look at all the evidence ex-Senior Detective Gurn has amassed?

5. Can an independent review of the case be made (keeping an open mind about the veracity of Mr Black's reporting on the case), then investigate it from the point of view of the witnesses, including what is contained in the 4 voice recordings of interviews which ex-Senior Detective Gurn made with Paula and John Whyte, and the later information he has given Queensland Police over five and a half years?

Mr Gurn's information could be easily verified by verifying the cheque transaction by Betty Madigan at the Pentland Hotel with Ted West, and by speaking with the persons Mr Gurn has named, such as Paula Whyte, John Whyte, Merle Whyte's brothers and Ted West (or [redacted]), and the band members, who if they are now such solid citizens (as Smith claims) must know at least that Merle and Betty were there in the hotel that day they played in the band at the hotel even if they were not involved and only their band members Wally Barry and Pam Barry – aka Rogers or List – were involved.

Thank you for attending to this letter and for your consideration of this puzzling and grievous matter, which seems to have been cloaked in official silence for almost 48 years.

Sincerely,
David Cunningham

APPENDIX NUMBER SEVEN

Commissioner of Police
Police Headquarters
Sydney NSW
Dated 2nd March 2017
Relative to: Ivan MILAT as a suspect in the murders of Robin Jeanne Hoinville-Bartram and Anita Cunningham at Pentland, Queensland in 1972.

Dear Sir,

I am writing this letter to you because I do not know what branch of your service to post it to and you will no doubt forward it correctly.

I am a retired detective sergeant of police in Queensland resigning in 1975 after 23 ½ years' service with over 18 years as a detective. Since early 2014, I have been investigating the murder of Robin Jeanne Hoinville-Bartram and the suspected murder of the missing Anita Cunningham. The body of Robin Bartram was discovered in a decomposed state in a shallow grave under Sensible Creek bridge just east of Pentland, Queensland in November 1972. She was undressed from the waist down and had two .22 bullet wounds to the back of her head. The body of Anita Cunningham has never been discovered but she is most assuredly deceased, suffering the same or similar fate to Bartram.

I accidently became involved through casual conversations with a friend who lives at Homestead on the Flinders Highway between Pentland and Charters Towers. This man said that his sister-in-law Mearle Whyte, who was dying of cancer in the Townsville Hospital, claimed that she had met these two girls at the Pentland Hotel in 1972.

After a number of conversations with my informant, I became convinced that there may be some truth in what he was telling me so I passed the information to a detective inspector of the Cold

Case Squad in a phone call on 10th May 2014, who said he would probably get someone to interview Mearle Whyte. I gave him further information in a letter dated 19th May 2014, saying that Mearle was not expected to live. Mearle Whyte died in hospital on 26th June 2014 but not interviewed by the police despite her daughter also ringing Crime Stoppers telling them that her mother wanted to tell the police all she knew of the murders before she passed away.

I do not intend on going into everything that has transpired since Mearle's death as it is a complete shamble. Me naming Queensland police officers for this debacle to police in New South Wales will not do anyone good so I will not do that.

I will broadly relate significant details to give NSW detectives a picture of what has happened and why I consider there is a possibility that the infamous Ivan Milat took part in the killing of these girls and I use the plural, believing that Anita is also deceased.

When I realised that the Queensland detectives were not following up my information and had not interviewed Mearle Whyte before she died, I interviewed Mearle's ex-husband John Whyte and her daughter Paula Whyte over the telephone on the 2nd and 4th October 2014. I recorded those conversations on a voice recorder. The information in those recordings leaves any sensible person with no doubt that Mearle Whyte did meet the two murdered girls at the Pentland Hotel in the wintertime of 1972.

These two girls left home in Melbourne in early July 1972 on a hitch-hiking trip to Bowen, north Qld, going via Mount Isa and then to Bowen (which would necessitate them coming down to the Flinders Highway). The story goes that Betty Madigan and her daughter Mearle Madigan, (later Whyte) then 19 years, travelled to the Pentland Hotel on a Friday or a Sunday afternoon from their home at the Twelve Mile Outstation on Wando Vale Station where Betty was the cook, and her husband Brian Patrick Madigan was in charge of the bullock paddocks.

When these women entered the hotel, Betty Madigan cashed a cheque in the hotel given to her by her husband to buy groceries etc for their home which is about a 100 kms from Charters Towers. The women were at the bar first then went and sat with two girls at a table. The girls' luggage was pushed up against a wall. The girls engaged in conversation with Betty and Mearle. The girls said that they had hitchhiked from Mount Isa in a truck with a male companion they had met. The truck only took them as far as Hughenden and they obtained another lift in a truck to Pentland, which was as far as that truck was going. They knew the man who accompanied them as 'Cowboy. He had very little luggage of his own. At the hotel, this man was known as Richard or John so he must have introduced himself to others at the hotel where there had been a band playing for customers enjoyment.

The girls were described as one dark-haired, girl which fits Robin, and a blond girl, which fits Anita. At their table, Robin or Anita told Mearle not to take any notice of Richard who was seated at the table as he was an idiot. The blond girl is said to have been playing with bangles on her arm, but no confirmation has been made that Anita wore bangles.

It transpires that the girls wanted a lift to Charters Towers, and they accepted a lift from men including this Richard going to Charters Towers. Mearle asked the girls if they were sure they wanted to go with the men as they could come with them to Charters Towers where they had accommodation booked at the Mexican Caravan Park. Apparently, Robin wanted to go with Mearle and Betty, but Anita decided they would go with the men, which was a fatal mistake.

A man who Mearle identified and who may have worked behind the bar in the Pentland Hotel helped load the girls' luggage onto the roof rack of a car of one of the band members. The girls left with an unknown number of men, including Richard.

Betty Madigan apparently liked her beer and eventually they left the Pentland Hotel with Mearle driving as she did not drink alcohol. It was then dark. They travelled about 8 or so kms towards Charters Towers and in the vicinity of Sensible Creek Bridge, they came across the car the girls had left the hotel in sideways across the road with one man at the steering wheel. All the doors were open and all lights on including high beam towards a railway line.

There was some activity near the railway line and someone called out 'stop them'. Betty told Mearle not to stop. They continued on to Charters Towers and stayed at the Mexican Caravan Park. Apparently, Mearle and Betty had arranged for the girls to stop with them in their unit at the caravan park and Mearle would drive them to Townsville the next day. The girls never arrived but the same car did arrive with only the men in it but no conversations took place with the men.

The next morning, either a Saturday or a Monday, Mearle went to Betty Noonan's hairdressing salon in Charters Towers and three of the men the girls had left the Pentland Hotel with were pacing up and down outside the salon. When Mearle emerged, she was confronted by the man who had travelled with the girls from Mount Isa.

This man had a long fingernail scratch down the side of his face and Mearle questioned him about this and he said something about a disagreement. Mearle asked him where the girls were, and he said they were with their family. They tried quite persuasively to get Mearle to go with them to Townsville, but she declined and walked down the footpath to the White Horse Tavern where her mother was. She told her mother that she thought the men had done something to the girls. Her mother told her it was nothing to do with them.

Later that day, Mearle and Betty were on their way back to the cattle station when a car flashed its lights at them and some sort of attempt was made to intercept them but Betty, who was then driving, accelerated away from this car and eluded them. Mearle said she thought it was the men who had accosted her in front of the hairdressing salon earlier in the day.

One or more nights later, Mearle's younger brother Dennis Madigan, then 15 years of age, was outside trying to shoot wild pigs when he stumbled across a man hiding in grass near the outstation. This man ran away. The father, Brian Madigan, was not at the station as he was away. The family turned all lights off and had an uneasy night tell dawn. Next day, there was evidence of people having been near the home of cigarette butts on the ground and some beer cans. (I have established that the owner of the car the girls left Pentland in worked at one time on Wando Vale Station and would know the way to the Twelve Mile Outstation at night over very rough country.)

When the body of Robin Bartram was discovered in November 1972, Mearle said her father told her, 'We don't get involved in anything like that.'

Paula Whyte said in her interview with me that she took notes of what her mother told her in hospital before she died. In relation to John Whyte's interview, he basically corroborated Paula with minor discrepancies; however, they both were very critical of the way Mearle had been treated by the police officer from Charters Towers in 2003 and 2005 claiming that he humiliated Mearle, asking her about [redacted] and why did she want to become involved, what did she hope to get out of it and was she involved.

It now transpires through my work that it seems Mearle was so upset with this officer that she deliberately told him incorrect parts of her story to make a fool out of him in revenge for his treatment of her. This has muddied the waters considerably. The officer who interviewed Mearle in 2003 and 2005 had personal knowledge of Mearle having dealt with Mearle's children who had come under the notice of police, especially her eldest son Colin.

This officer did not believe Mearle's story and effectively has convinced the Queensland Police Service that there is no truth *in what I have outlined herein, which is extraordinary having in mind the unlikelihood of two other girls being the ones Mearle spoke of when you consider rationally the entire circumstances. He submitted that Mearle said she met the girls three weeks after the White Horse Tavern was pulled down in 1971 and could not possibly be the same girls.*

However, I established that the White Horse Tavern in Charters Towers was reopened on 17th May 1972 by the local MP Mr Lonergan.

Considering Mearle is thinking back 31 years, she most probably meant three or so weeks after the White Horse Tavern reopened, which would put the time she met the girls close to July 1972. John Whyte specifically says that Mearle told him that it was in the wintertime of 1972 as her father was doing something with cattle that they did in the wintertime.

There is a lot more I could write about in this case but for the purposes of New South Wales detectives, the issue here is was Ivan Milat the man who travelled with the girls from Mount Isa and was he one of the killers and probably rapists? I am absolutely convinced as to the authenticity of Mearle meeting the murdered girls in the circumstances outlined. Persuading the Queensland Police to have the same construction of the case seems hopeless.

I have complained to the police directly, to the Crime and Corruption Commission and have personally applied for an inquest to the coroner under Section 30 of the Coroner's Act. It took the coroner three months to tell me he did not have power to order an inquest as the killings happened before 2000. The only person who could order an inquest is Attorney General Yvette D'ath and I have had correspondence from her that she will not order an inquest as I am relying on second-hand information from a deceased person.

However, notwithstanding all these setbacks, I have an assurance from the shadow attorney general in Queensland, Ian

Walker, that if the LNP win the next Queensland election he will order a review having in mind my investigations with a view to ordering an inquest.

There are numerous ways to prove Mearle Whyte was telling the truth on her death bed and I have given all those initiatives to the police without result.

In so far as the NSW detectives are concerned, I would like your detectives to further inspect the 400-odd trophies confiscated from Ivan Milat to see if there is anything that could be linked to the property of these girls, especially the backpacks.

Also, some clothing was recovered from the body of Robin Bartram, and I have asked that DNA comparisons be made, if any, from this clothing with Milat. Also, the bullets recovered from Robin Bartram's body be compared with bullets from the many firearms taken from Milat. Milat was known to use his brother Richard's name at times.

Overall, there is little point in me going into the numerous investigations I have conducted but suffice to say I would not be wasting my time and money on these investigations if I was not totally convinced about Mearle's story. I have identified the car the girls left the hotel in, its owner and the identity of the man who put the girl's luggage on its roof rack as it left the Pentland Hotel.

The man who accompanied the girls from Mount Isa had little possessions. Milat was on the run from NSW Police from 1971 till he returned from New Zealand in 1974. Isn't it extremely likely and logical that he was on the run in Queensland, then, having murdered the girls, got money from the girls' bodies, which enabled him to get to New Zealand. One of Milat's nicknames was 'Cowboy'.

This is the typical old story of police getting bogged down by people with tunnel vision who will not accept any version but the one they are convinced of, unfortunately.

The only people who have given me any assistance is David Cunningham, brother of Anita and Peter Cameron, journalist, with the Sunday Mail in Queensland who has written several articles in this paper about my investigations and is working at the sidelines to assist me.

Yours faithfully,
M.J. Gurn

APPENDIX NUMBER EIGHT

On 8th March 2017, New South Wales Police, under the hand of S. Wooster, Manager Secretariat, Office of the Commissioner, wrote,

> Dear Mr Gurn,
>
> I refer to your correspondence to the NSW Commissioner of Police, dated 2nd March 2017, regarding the murder of Robin Jeanne Hoinville-Bartram and the suspected murder of Anita Cunningham in 1972.
>
> I wish to acknowledge receipt of your correspondence under reference number D/2017/253756.
>
> The matter has been referred to the relevant command within the NSW Police Force for attention and direct response.
>
> On behalf of the Office of the Commissioner, I would like to thank you for bringing this matter to the attention of the NSW Police Force.
>
> This is an electronic acknowledgment of your correspondence. A response is not required.

APPENDIX NUMBER NINE

This letter is to Mr Weir, Editor of the Courier Mail, from David Cunningham.

Dear Sir,

I am David Cunningham, elder brother of the missing murder victim Anita Cunningham.

I write in support of the letter (13/9/2018) sent to you by ex-Senior Detective Mick Gurn drawing attention to the stonewall he is facing in seeking answers to the fate of my sister and her companion, Robyn Hoinville-Bartram, and asking your assistance to examine the recently uncovered evidence so as to understand the impenetrability of official resistance to resolving the truth behind these tragic events.

I am sure your readers would be fascinated by some of the incredible twists and turns this story has taken and by new revelations, more of which are sure to result from following the new leads which authorities continue to ignore.

Private individuals like us are limited in our powers to pursue investigations. That's why we need the authorities to pursue these leads. It would be very easy for police to follow up on even one of the leads Mr Gurn's discoveries have generated, and the result would be decisive. How easy would it be for police to request Westpac Bank to confirm where a cheque was cashed? Likewise, it would be simple to establish whether or not the girls were in fact at the Pentland Hotel that night as witnesses claim.

Public awareness of the developments in this neglected tragedy, and double murder might sway the attorney general to grant an inquest. Brisbane Courier Mail could be on top of the story as future revelations develop.

Mr Gurn requested you look at the material he provided to

Kate Kyriacou and Peter Hall, (26/9/19), as well as to you in his 13 September letter.

Since becoming acquainted with Mr Gurn over the last few years, I have been very impressed with the amount of evidence he has been able to gather in a comparatively short time, due partly to his knowledge of the territory and the people of north Queensland, but mainly to his skills honed by decades of experience as a senior detective, and despite the unwelcome reception his efforts have encountered from the police. I have spoken to one of his witnesses myself on a few occasions and I found her to be credible and sincere.

Mr Gurn's experience with police resistance to investigations in this matter is unfortunately not isolated. I will add here for you a couple of brief episodes from my own experience, illustrating the mystifying actions of police in relation to this murder.

Before I begin, I must stress that I state nothing against any particular police officer and that the individual police I have dealt with have all been polite, courteous and respectful. However, the way the case has been handled just beggars belief.

Bear in mind that although they were traveling together, Robin's body was discovered a few months after the girls went missing, so the case was split and Robin was handled by the Homicide Squad, while Anita, whose body has not yet been found, was handled by Missing Persons, and as Inspector Smith of the Cold Case Squad explained to me, there was not much teamwork or information sharing between the different departments back then.

Two brief illustrations follow:

1. Not long after Robin's body had been found, a family friend reported to the police he had seen Anita working in a bar in Melbourne.

At this time, Anita was a registered missing person and connected to a current murder investigation into the death of Robin Bartram, so one might naturally have assumed police would be very keen to find her (as a missing person) and talk to her (in connection with the murder of her traveling companion).

Especially since the witness seemed so rock solid.

Keith Galloway was an airline pilot with proven observational skills and he had known Anita very well for many years. His daughter Ronelle was best friends with Anita at school, and Anita was at their home a lot, so Keith knew her face very well. Our families used to have dinner at each other's homes. If he had reported seeing her, it was an extremely credible report.

The obvious thing to do then would be to interview Keith to get as much information about the sighting as possible, and then send a detective equipped with a photo of Anita to the bar and ask if she had worked there or if they had seen her.

Keith says he never heard back from the police after he reported the sighting. I was told by Inspector Smith that although a QLD policeman was sent to Melbourne at that same time to investigate another matter, there is no record of Keith's sighting ever being followed up by police.

I tell this story not to make any statement about the actual accuracy of Keith's presumed sighting, in fact I rather doubt it, but purely on the face of the report it was **highly credible**.

I tell it purely to show how resistant and completely uninterested police seem to have been in pursuing investigation into Robin and Anita's murders, even when evidence seems strong.

2. Even though police appear to have been reluctant to follow genuine credible leads, they have not been completely inactive.

In 2009, a self-styled psychic detective approached police with the news that she's solved the case by communicating with the spirit world.

A few minutes on Google would have easily, simply and conclusively resolved her story in the negative, but no, apparently this was the bulletproof evidence the police had been waiting for because they took the psychic seriously and backed their hunch with action!

Ann -----s theory was that my sister Anita had, for reasons unknown, murdered her best friend Robin with a rifle she never had, and single-highhandedly, without a vehicle, disposed of the body. She had then assumed a new identity (as Jody Borland, my ex), and incestuously given birth to a child with me, her brother, as the father.

What's more, I was currently a solo father in Melbourne (she got that bit right) and the child's mother (allegedly the real Anita Cunningham) was living in a flat in Ipswich masquerading as Jody Borland.

Now that whole concoction might sound unlikely, confusing and far-fetched to you as it does to me, but obviously the police, who had discounted much more promising evidence prior to this revelation, thought it was just what they'd been waiting for and to their credit, they decided to pursue it.

Jody woke to the police banging on her door at 6.30am and was quizzed about her real identity.

Half an hour later, the police must have realised they'd been duped so they left, but that was not the last psychic to have police attention.

These two examples from the past give some idea of why confidence in police ability to assess the value of evidential leads is lacking.

It seems the current police attitude towards the case can be summed up as 'case closed', wrapped up, waste no more time on it.

Inspector Smith of the Cold Case Squad told me only two things are known, the date the girls left, and the date and location of Robin's body was found. That may be true, but why the apparent determination to keep it that way?

Perhaps they feel they cannot justify spending any time following up on a 45-year-old case, but we read often in the news about such cases being re-opened in the light of new evidence and then solved.

Kindly consider publishing a story based on ex-Senior Detective Gurn's discoveries, informing the public that one particular eyewitness wanted police to hear her death bed confession but police refused. There are now five witnesses and police are refusing to cooperate by following leads.

Hopefully that will give us the publicity needed to galvanize some official help. I am willing to help with any inquiries.

Thanks for your time and attention reading this letter and considering its contents.

Regards,
David Cunningham

APPENDIX NUMBER TEN

Attorney General, Ms Shannon Fentiman
Parliament House
George Street,
Brisbane 4001
Dated 6th December 2020
Dear Ms Fentiman,

Congratulations on your appointment as Attorney General in the returned Labor Government of 2020. I have written previously on a number of occasions to your predecessor, Yvette D'Ath, about the unsolved murders of Robin Jeanne Hoinville-Bartram and Anita Cunningham at Pentland, Queensland in 1972. I would therefore assume that your present office staff and advisers are fully acquainted with all of the facts I have outlined to Ms D'Ath in letters and emails asking her to order an inquest. Your office would have volumes of correspondence on this subject or should have I would think.

M/s D'Ath did not accede to my requests or the requests of David Cunningham, who is a brother of the murdered Anita Cunningham, on the grounds that I am relying on second-hand information. I will try to convince you that my information is sound by referring you to three telephone recorded interviews I did with the husband of the woman, Mearle Whyte, who with her mother Betty Madigan gave graphic details of meeting these girls at the Pentland Hotel in 1972 to her husband and two of her daughters Paula and Joan Whyte. There are an additional seven related persons who have knowledge of Mearle Whyte telling her brothers and other children of this meeting of hers with the deceased girls Bartram and Cunningham over the years and after she married John Whyte and had six children with him.

In contrast, the police stance on this matter is that the murdered girls were never at the Pentland Hotel and is outlined in a letter to me from Inspector Peter Smith dated 15th September 2014 before they were murdered, which is totally ridiculous. This stance is being perpetuated by senior police to cover up serious incompetence by police in 2003 who disregarded everything Mearle Whyte told them and have virtually said her claim of meeting these murdered girls is false.

This stance of police has now gone to the utterly ridiculous stage of my reluctantly having to state that Inspector Peter Smith is guilty of perverting the course of justice by failing to properly investigate my recorded telephone interviews on 2nd and 4th October 2014 with John Whyte and Paula Whyte when he went to Charters Towers in April 2015 to investigate these recorded phone interviews of these people with me and his extraordinary remarks to Paula Whyte concerning other people involved, who, in his words, could not have been involved as they later in life became a magistrate, a solicitor and a bailiff. And further that he did not interview three other people in North Queensland who I was told in writing by Assistant Commissioner Hogan would be interviewed by police at my request. The third recorded telephone interview with Joan Whyte did not occur until 7th March, this year, 2020.

Two years and eight months have now elapsed since I made the accusation against the inspector but no action has been taken on my complaint that I am aware of as I have not been advised by police the result of any investigations that have been made into my complaint and to my knowledge the persons who could give information have not been interviewed further so it is reasonable to assume that no action has been taken in the matter.

In an email to me from Inspector Smith in April 2015 from Charters Towers, he told me that he would be giving me his review of his investigations in Charters Towers, but this review has never materialised despite my several requests for same from the commissioner of police.

Mearle Whyte died of cancer in Townsville Hospital on

27th June 2014, not interviewed by police despite my informing Inspector Peter Smith on 9th May 2014 that Mearle wished to give additional information to the police before she died despite her daughter Paula ringing Crime Stoppers, begging them to have someone interview her mother before she died. You might think that this occurrence is tragic itself, but it gets much worse over the years since 2014 when you read about how every endeavour I have made to bring the real story about these girls being raped and murdered has been thwarted by police and the press and media with some exceptions.

The situation now, however, is much more serious and requires a Commission of Inquiry, which I will deal with in this letter.

Such has been my frustration with the lack of police activity in solving these murders that I have been compelled to write a book, which I have titled Hear Our Cry, to ask the public to support my goal of obtaining justice for these murdered girls by requesting you to order a Commission of Inquiry as outlined previously. My book has not yet been published.

My quest for justice for these raped and murdered girls has been going on for the past six and a half years and just how much to write to you is hard to decide, as my file is inches thick. I suppose the start should be that the purpose of this letter is to ask you to order a Commission of Inquiry into the police handling of investigations into these murders, with emphasis on the mishandling of investigations since 2003, which I have touched on in page one.

I should now tell you that my complaint about police inactivity in solving these crimes is based on a number of factors. First, we must go back to the hitchhiking murdered girls from Melbourne, Victoria arriving at the Pentland Hotel in the winter of 1972 in the company of a man who they only knew as 'Cowboy' and who had joined them in Mount Isa. This man was most likely the infamous and recidivist murderer Ivan Milat. There, the girls met Mearle

Whyte and her mother Betty Madigan and had some drinks with them in the hotel. Later, the girls left the hotel in the company of at least one member of a band that had played for patrons that day at the hotel and other men.

A little later when darkness had set in, Mearle and her mother left the hotel and at a point on the Flinders Highway towards Charters Towers, they came across the car the girls had left the hotel in sideways across the road with all doors open, with all interior and exterior headlights lights on and shining towards the railway line. They saw activity towards the railway line of people and as Mearle, who was then driving, slowed down someone from the activity towards the railway line called out to stop Mearle and Betty. They did not stop and went to the Mexican Caravan Park and stayed the night.

Fortunately, they did not stop, or they would also have been murder victims without doubt.

The next morning (a Saturday), Mearle came out of a hairdresser's shop in Gill Street, Charters Towers and was confronted by three of the men the girls had left the hotel with the previous day who wanted Mearle to accompany them to Townsville, which she declined. Mearle saw that the man 'Cowboy' had a long scratch down the side of his face which she interpreted as a fingernail scratch. Mearle questioned 'Cowboy' about the scratch, and he said there had been a disagreement at the creek and that the girls were with their families.

It should not be necessary for me to once again rewrite all that has transpired as your office already has detailed correspondence from me on this subject. Robin Bartram's decomposed body was found in a shallow grave under Sensible Creek railway bridge about 8 kms from Pentland on 15th November 1972 with two point .22 bullet wounds to the back of the head. The body was undressed from the waist down. Anita Cunningham's body has never been located.

I should move on for the purposes of this letter to say Mearle did not come forward to police with information about meeting the murdered girls until 2003 and again in 2005. When she did come forward, it seems she was interviewed by former Police Officer Bob Black of Charters Towers Police.

Black's handling of his interviewing Mearle about her meeting the murdered girls according to what Mearle told her husband and her daughters over the years from 1972 to 2003/5 was unprofessional to say the least and appears to have been conducted in a flippant and insulting manner and with far too much familiarity with questions about her private life, etc. This line of questioning of Mearle by Black caused her to resent him to the point she gave him false information about aspects of her meeting the murdered girls to make a fool out of Black, but which only sought to build on Black's assessment of Mearle's story as false unfortunately.

The upshot was that Black has apparently reported to his superiors that Mearle's story is false, to put it bluntly, and this impression is gained from Inspector Smith's letter to me on 15th September 2014 wherein he says that Mearle was mistaken in her claims to have met the murdered girls. This is a shortened assessment of the whole story as I have said the whole story has already been outlined to the former attorney general in letters from me and also in an application for an inquest initially and in email correspondence to and from the former attorney general.

Once you have read my transcription of the telephone recorded interviews, I did with Mearle's husband John Whyte and her daughters Paula and Joan, you should not have any doubt that Mearle Whyte and her mother Betty Madigan did meet the murdered girls at the Pentland Hotel in the winter of 1972.

In addition, there are another seven people who have independent knowledge conveyed to them over the years by Mearle.

It is probably best if I paste here in this letter extracts from *my book, which I hope to give a clearer picture of why I ask for a Commission of Inquiry into the police handling of these cases.*

EXTRACTS *follow, indicated by quotation marks. Aliases for people named in my book have been used to hide their identity.*

'I have titled this book Hear Our Cry – meaning hear our cry for justice, which is written to try to obtain justice for these murdered girls. I am determined to uncover and reveal to the public this mishandling of terrible double murders of two innocent girls by the Queensland police service, which could have been the easiest case to solve in 2003 of any case I have known. I still believe that the offenders can be identified and arrested if investigations are sourced from the information I have provided to police in the last nine years.

My hope is that the public will demand a Commission of Inquiry into the police handling of this case with powers to force witnesses to answer questions and refer respective persons who are considered guilty of the crimes to prosecutors for charges to be laid and those responsible for the mismanagement of police work to be exposed.

Justice for the murdered girls has been denied to them till now. It is my contention that the police have been remiss in their inquiries initially caused through the inexperience and incompetence of some investigating police and that this false stance that the girls were never at the Pentland Hotel in July, 1972 is being perpetuated in an attempt to save face by other senior police due to misplaced loyalty and against the weight of evidence that I have uncovered in the last eight years.

The very sad part of all this is that an inquest has been denied by the attorney general Yvette D'Ath, who had the say in this instance. In an inquiry or inquest, those involved could be questioned on oath on the witness stand to get the real truth. The attorney general's position regarding her decision to order an inquest would normally be influenced to a degree by what the police tell her, I would think.'

'The reason I favour a Commission of Inquiry rather than an inquest is that with the proper terms of reference given to such an inquiry, the commissioner(s) would be able to compel witnesses to give evidence with the prospect of serving jail time for failure to truthfully answer questions.

An inquiry would summon persons to the witness stand without having to first obtain statements from them as has been shown on television of a number of occasions recently during inquiries into child sex abuse and the banking industry. Hearsay evidence could be allowed by the commissioner(s).

These terms of reference would enable the commissioner(s) to inquire into all aspects of police investigations into these murders such as, what investigations did the Crime and Corruption Commission and the Ethical Standards Group of the police service make, along with who did they interview before coming to their decisions not to act in response to my complaints. (I doubt if the CCC could be forced to defend their position.)

Failure by police to properly investigate a complaint by not questioning witnesses to establish the truth of their recollections of events or failing to interview people who I had been advised by an assistant police commissioner would be interviewed is, to my mind, perverting the course of justice.

The inquiry would be tasked with uncovering who is the person or persons who have made threats to the safety of Paula Whyte to keep her mouth shut about what she knows of these crimes both before and since I became involved.

There are people who have stood silent when they could have come forward with information. The reasons for this lack of civic duty need explaining because there is the possibility that they stayed mute to disguise their involvement in these murders to the extent that their actions could be classed as accessories after the fact to these murders.

The commissioner(s) would need terms of reference to cover

all foreseeable eventualities including the need to be able to extend their allotted inquiry time to conduct their hearings and handing down their findings. They must be able to refer some people to the chief crown prosecutor for possible charges to be laid against those persons if evidence comes to light of criminal conduct.

The inquiry should establish if the hierarchy of the police force from commissioners down are guilty of negligence of failing to see what was happening here right under their noses.

There is also the need for the commission of inquiry to establish from newspaper editors, crime reporters and Channel Seven why they refrained from getting involved and why they did not make sufficient inquiries themselves to see if my accusations against police were true or not. Who or what is the powerful force that has prevented David Cunningham and me from gaining traction and assistance from these press and media representatives in solving these crimes, despite the two of us writing and emailing them with credible evidence over a number of years?

The commissioner(s) should be able to find from the evidence presented throughout the inquiry that Anita Cunningham is deceased, which will probably make life easier for any children of Anita's parents when it comes to legal questions about whether she is alive or deceased.

In the end, I trust that the killers of these girls still alive are brought to justice through the hearing of an inquiry into the police handling of these murders.

Page 13 of the Brisbane Courier Mail on Thursday 21st May 2020 reports that the Queensland government has passed new laws which will allow coroners to compel witnesses to provide potentially self-incriminating evidence in inquests for cases that occurred prior to 2003. This power was previously only available to coroners for cases that occurred after 2003. This is good news, but I still think that a Commission of Inquiry is a much better option for these particular murders.

Despite the reluctance of the investigating police to confide in me or seek my help and with my objectives being to see finality of this case, I have provided information by email to Detective Senior Sergeant Tara Kentwell of the Homicide Unit to pass on to investigating police. There are several suggestions from me as to who might provide further valuable information and who may well be involved in these crimes who are not previously mentioned anywhere in this book. I have also given information about the possible location of the remains of Anita Cunningham and why that information should be considered seriously and not dismissed.

I wish to sincerely thank David Cunningham, who is Anita's brother for all the support he has given me in investigating these crimes since I first contacted him in August 2015. He has written supporting letters that I have asked him to write to the police, newspaper editors and the attorney general.

He has also written letters to various persons of his own volition.

I thank David for his prologue for this book.

The encouragement and support I have received from Peter Cameron, Trudy Brown and Morgan Oss is greatly appreciated and recognised here in this work.

I wish to thank Col Presnell for the many hours he has spent correcting my mistakes in grammar etc. and for suggesting alternative wording in some cases that I have adopted.

Finally, I say the public should not judge members of the Queensland police service on the behaviour of police involved in this case as they are not representative of the majority of police officers who are in the main dedicated, hard-working, honest, caring and work tirelessly to protect you.'

Once again, I have to say that I have received tremendous support for my investigations from Peter Cameron who mentioned my endeavours to gain justice for these murdered girls on at least 16 occasions in his traps column in the Sunday Mail newspaper over four years until he retired. Huge support of my efforts has come from Trudy Brown, Editor of the Northern Miner newspaper in Charters Towers, through her efforts by the Townsville Bulletin Newspaper. Channel Nine showed a segment about this case on Queensland television in a program on 20th February 2020 in which I was interviewed.

Despite all this, the Brisbane newspapers, the Courier Mail and Sunday Mail, have not supported me or David Cunningham and have not even had the decency to reply to correspondence from us. Why have the editors of these newspapers blackballed David Cunningham and me and stopped us from gaining traction in our efforts to see justice for these murdered girls? How they have been hoodwinked in this day and age is remarkable to say the least when their editors claim from time to time, they are all about truth and justice. I hope the people or entity behind this abuse of the justice system protecting certain individuals will be revealed to the general public with a Commission of Inquiry **because anything less than this official procedure is unlikely to uncover and expose their identities.**

This case is still solvable with at least one offender still alive, named by me to police. I have told the police how to go about solving this case. From other citizens, this may sound presumptuous on my part but I have the knowledge and experience to make this claim. I have named at least two other male offenders who are now deceased.

I implore you to correct this abuse of the justice system in this state.

I will attach to this presentation copies of the recorded interviews I speak of along with other relevant material including the prologue to my book from David Cunningham, which explains the pain and suffering of his mother and family of losing Anita and the frustration of the family with the lack of police activity in solving the case despite an extraordinary amount of sound evidence from me. I ask you to see reason for the sake of justice in this state and order a Commission of Inquiry in line with my suggestions.

'I think I can expect that you will follow custom and forward this application by me to police for comment. I urge you to disregard the anticipated comments from police which will be along the following lines.

'Extensive investigations have been made into the claims of Mr Gurn and evidence has not been uncovered to support his claims against the inactivity of police in solving these crimes.'

'All persons whose identities were made known to former Police Officer Bob Black have been questioned and deny all knowledge of involvement in these crimes. There is no evidence to connect any such person.'

'The claims by Mr Gurn regarding the perverting of the course of justice by Inspector Smith are being considered.'

For you to make a judgment on whether you will order a Commission of Inquiry, you would need answers from the police to a number of questions such as: is the police position still that the murdered girls were never at the Pentland Hotel before they were murdered?

Ask why Mr Gurn has not been forwarded the review of Inspector Smith's investigations at Charters Towers in April 2015 into the recorded interviews he did with John and Paula Whyte, which he said he would give Mr Gurn and which Mr Gurn has requested from the Commissioner of Police on a number of occasions since without result.

Ask the police why they have not supported Mr Gurn's attempts to trace particulars of the cheque cashed by Betty Madigan at the Pentland Hotel most likely in July 1972 when she met the murdered girls, which would support her and her daughters claims of meeting the murdered girls and establish the date of this transaction and meeting, which is the day the murders and rapes were committed.

Ask how the investigation into the letter sent on 23rd February 1973 from Chillagoe to a friend of Anita Cunningham was so bungled. This bungling has been pointed out to police by Mr Gurn and forms Chapter 26 of his book Hear Our Cry. *This bungling failed to identify the person who posted this letter to a friend of Anita Cunningham and who must have been in possession of some article from the possessions of Anita for him to get the address in Victoria. This mishandling may have solved the murders or obtained vital information about the killers eight months after the murders and rapes.*

Ask if the police have searched areas indicated by Mr Gurn in an attempt to locate the remains of the murdered Anita Cunningham and more recently in light of more recent information, he has given police and forms part of the recorded telephone interview he did with Joan Whyte in March 2020.

Ask who were the police present at any time Bob Black interviewed Mearle Whyte and if they support Black's opinion of Mearle meeting the murdered girls.

Ask if detailed signed statements were obtained by Black from Mearle Whyte and Betty Madigan when Mearle first approached the police in 2003 with information and if so, make these statements available to you as part of your deliberations. Obtaining these statements is fundamental practice in police investigations.

Ask what inquiries Queensland Police made of police in New Zealand in an attempt to discover if Ivan Milat was in New Zealand and the dates he was there. (Mr Gurn has done this.)

Ask if police contacted New South Wales Police to see if any of the 400-odd, recovered items in the arrest of Ivan Milat could be connected to the murdered girls Bartram and Cunningham. (Mr Gurn has done this.)

Ask if the murders of Bartram and Cunningham were advised to New South Wales police for consideration should Ivan Milat make any admissions in his final days of life. (Mr Gurn has done this.)

Ask if any DNA was found on the clothing of Robin Bartram's body, not consistent with her own DNA and if any such sample has been checked against the DNA of Ivan Milat.

Ask if inquiries have been made into whether Walter (Wally) Barry could be connected to these murders and what was the information from Mount Isa Police which caused Inspector Nicola in charge of Townsville District to order a search around Sensible Creek with machinery etc., to try and find the remains of Anita Cunningham.

Examination and cross examination of all police involved and a long list of witnesses I can provide details of who would be called to the witness stand in a Commission of Inquiry to get the truth of the many aspects of why these cases have not been solved and why this failure of police to act professionally has allowed murderers and rapists to enjoy years of freedom since 2003 when they should have been behind bars had the cases been handled by more competent police.'

Yours sincerely,
M.J. Gurn

APPENDIX NUMBER ELEVEN

CITATION

IT WAS REPORTED TO THE POLICE THAT A WOMAN HAD BEEN RAPED ON 9 MAY 1971. NO POSSIBLE SUSPECTS WERE KNOWN AND ONLY A VAGUE DESCRIPTION OF THE OFFENDER WAS AVAILABLE. A LONG AND PAINSTAKING INVESTIGATION WAS CARRIED OUT BY DETECTIVE SERGEANT 2/C M. J. GURN, DETECTIVE SENIOR CONSTABLE K. C. SCANLAN AND DETECTIVE CONSTABLE 1/C J. L. GRAHAM. P. C. CONSTABLE 1/C K. C. MORRIS RECEIVED AND PASSED ON CONFIDENTIAL INFORMATION WHICH WAS INSTRUMENTAL IN LOCATING THE OFFENDER WHO WAS ARRESTED AND SUBSEQUENTLY CONVICTED IN THE SUPREME COURT.

APPENDIX NUMBER TWELVE

Honourable Yvette D'Ath
Attorney General
GPO Box 149
Brisbane 4001
Dated 20th July 2016
Att. Gen ref. No 571194/1,3162253
Dear Ms D'Ath,

Following on from my letter to you of 18th May 2016 in which I asked you to reconsider your decision not to order an inquest be held into the murders of Robin Jeanne Hoinville-Bartram and Anita Cunningham at Pentland in 1972, I have to now inform you that I have been able to further corroborate the story of Mearle Elizabeth Whyte of meeting these two girls at the Pentland Hotel in 1972. Although this information is still classed as hearsay evidence, it is substantiated now and although no use in a criminal trial which would happen if arrests were made, there is no reason why a coroner cannot admit this real evidence into an inquest.

There is a very real need to get the police involved and other persons onto the witness stand in an inquest in an attempt to identify the offenders. **Such an inquest is likely to discover the identity of the offenders.** *I can contribute the names of persons who should supply more light in any such inquest.*

Dennis Madigan contacted me when the manager of Wando Vale Station told him that I was looking for him. The manager had been contacted by me to try and ascertain who worked on Wando Vale Station in or around 1972.

Without any shadow of a doubt, the version supplied to Mearle's daughter and husband about her meeting these girls has been corroborated by her brother Dennis Vincent Madigan, 58 years, born 13th September, 1957, who was 15 years of age at the time, in that he verifies that he nearly stumbled over a man hiding in grass at night at the Twelve Mile Outstation on Wando Vale Station whilst out pig shooting shortly after his mother Betty Madigan and his elder sister Mearle Madigan, then 19 years of age, returned from a trip to Charters Towers. Mearle and his mother told of the meeting with the girls. At the time, he said he did not take much notice of the story, but when the body was discovered, the family knew it was one of girls Mearle and his mother had met at the Pentland Hotel.

There is no doubt that this man hiding in grass and others with him who were waiting nearby with a car at a gateway were there to silence the women who could identify them as the killers, but their plan was flaunted by the intervention of Dennis Madigan. Dennis says that Mearle told the same story about meeting the girls all her life.

Dennis has been in touch with another brother Mick Madigan, a windmill expert, whose home is in Winton but is currently working at Bowen Downs. Mick has been difficult to contact by me as he is often not in areas where he can be reached by telephone but has also corroborated Mearle's story to Dennis and has further information to offer.

For these killers to travel at night into the bush over 100 kilometres northwest of Charters Towers and locate the Twelve Mile Outstation on Wando Vale Cattle Station over very rough country tracks, one of these men at least would have had to be familiar with the way to get there and wait near the outhouse in the dark, probably waiting for the women to walk outside presumably to the toilet.

It now transpires that Dennis Madigan recalls my chief suspect (person of interest as the police now like to call these people) worked on Wando Vale Station about that time. He states his brother Mick Madigan would be able to offer more information on a group of unsavoury characters who associated together about that time in the Charters Towers area.

Wally Barry came to Charters Towers with a woman, most probably Pam Rogers, and it is known that he was prone to assaulting her. She was most likely with him on Wando Vale Station. Pam was later known in Charters Towers as Mrs Barry. Just after the murders, Pam ditched Barry and took up with [redacted] in Charters Towers and is now known as Pam List. Both Barry and Pam were involved in country and Western music. She was the vocal member and Barry a guitarist.

Other names of men who could have been on the band have previously been given to police, one such person being [redacted] in Charters Towers. his involvement, if any, in the murders is not known. Despite his denials, a person named [redacted] put the girl's luggage on the roof rack of Barry's car and saw the murdered girls to the car. Whether he also left in the car with the man who had travelled with the girls from Mount Isa, (who the next day had his face badly fingernail scratched) and Wally Barry and an unknown number of other men but there were three men who accosted Mearle on the street in Charters Towers when she came out of the hairdressers and wanted her to go with them to Townsville, which would no doubt have been the end of Mearle.

There was an ex-jockey type, named Gary Patterson, who is a criminal, well known to police who was known as 'Cowboy', which is the name the murdered girls knew the man who travelled with them hitch-hiking from Mount Isa. I personally have grave doubts that Paterson would be connected because he does not fit the stature of the person. I am still of the opinion that the most likely person was Ivan Milat. The police have no idea where Milat was from 1971 to 1974 when he returned from New Zealand. Dennis also refers to a David Fielder, who was apparently charged in relation to shooting at some backpackers in the Charters Towers area, date unknown, when the backpackers gear was stolen. Again, I have no knowledge of this person either and has not been mentioned to me anywhere else.

I have no doubt that Dennis Madigan of Maxwelton (a six hour and 549-kilometre drive from Townsville) will give a signed, detailed and written statement if asked. Another brother, Pat Madigan, resides in Charters Towers. I have not yet interviewed him but there is little doubt he would corroborate Mearle's story also because Mearle is said to have given the same story all her life to her family.

I have tracked down Betty Noonan, the hairdresser in Charters Towers, to whom Mearle Madigan (as she then was in July/August 1972) went to have her hair done the next morning after meeting the girls at the Pentland Hotel when the three men were pacing up and down in front of the hairdresser's shop waiting for Mearle to come out. Knowing how women converse with their hairdressers, it is quite likely that Mearle told Betty Noonan something about the events and Betty may have also noticed that one of the men had a deep fingernail scratch down the side of his face.

However, I was forced to abandon my intention of speaking with Betty Noonan when I discovered she is suffering from dementia and is in Eventide Home in Charters Towers. I decided such an interview might cause her distress.

Again, this just goes to highlight the urgency for investigations that should be done by the police. We already have valuable witnesses passing away and not interviewed despite two representations to Inspector Peter Smith by me to interview Mearle Whyte (nee Madigan) before she died on 27th June 2014 and her daughter, almost crying, on the phone to Crime Stoppers, saying her mother wanted to tell the police everything she knew before he died, but again sadly passing away not interviewed by the police, mixed with the stalling tactics I have endured and deterring Channel Seven from being involved. I had asked Channel Seven for their assistance to go to Charters Towers and investigate myself. Plus, there has been some sort of interference by somebody with the witness Paula Whyte as previously addressed by me.

As previously stated, when Betty and Mearle Madigan entered the Pentland Hotel in 1972, Betty cashed a cheque at the bar. I have previously publicised the fact that obtaining details of this cheque will give an or about type date that the cheque was cashed and would add value to the credibility of Mearle's story about meeting the girls. Again, no such action has been taken by the police to investigate this angle.

I have spoken with the manager of the Westpac Bank in Charters Towers, a Samantha Williamson, who after apparently getting advice from her superiors, stated that the request for this information has to come from a written request by the police. She did indicate that it would take some delving into records to get this information, but it could be done.

I first believed that the cheque had been drawn on the Commonwealth Bank, but Dennis Madigan informed me that his father dealt with the bank of New South Wales in Charters Towers, situated near the White Horse Tavern. The bank of New South Wales is now Westpac Bank.

I have been in contact with Karenne Forster, who resides with her husband Geoff, on a cattle property on the outskirts of Pentland. Karenne is the daughter of Mr and Mrs Peut, who were the licensees of the Pentland Hotel in 1972, who have passed away. Karenne is unable to help with the depositing transactions of the hotel in 1972 with reference to the cheque in question.

I have also uncovered another aspect of this case which deals with the actual discovery of the body of Robin Bartram in November 1972 and which might be just too much of a coincidence in my mind, but that is something I will elaborate on to detectives when and if they actually begin investigating these crimes. I am not prepared to deal with Inspector Peter Smith of the Cold Case Squad who has indicated he wants no further contact with me in his email in April 2015 after his unsuccessful trip to Charters Towers. He refuses to give me his review of his investigation into the *case, after being reluctantly forced to do something when Channel Seven became involved and sought a month's grace from Channel Seven before they did anything or went public.*

Knowing how much time and distance will be involved by the police investigating these crimes the most likely and sensible body to progress this case would be the Townsville detective office. After two and half years investigating these crimes, I have a clear mental picture of what happened that fateful day in 1972.

David Cunningham has been in touch with the New South Wales police with a view to examining the 400-odd so-called trophies kept by the infamous Ivan Milat from his victims to see if anything is recognisable that belong to his sister or Robin Bartram.

There were trucks going to and from Hughenden from Pentland in 1972 and this needs further inquiry. I have some leads on these trucks from Dennis Madigan.

I will once again forward a copy of this letter to the commissioner of police and to the officer in charge of the Townsville C.I. Branch. Most of my correspondence to various persons has been sent express post as I understand the need for the urgency of these inquiries due to the length of time since the murders and persons ageing and dying.

In the interests of justice and in the public interest, I again ask you to urgently cause an inquest into these murders to happen. Many good things come out of inquests, and I am hoping for the same here.

I have kept a chronological record of my investigations into these murders which is fast approaching 100 pages. The full story about these crimes will eventually be told and judging by the past public interest in the case will generate a lot of press and TV coverage, which unfortunately will not be good for the police service I fear but I warned them two years ago of this possibility, but they still ignored my advice.

Responsibility rests with police a lot higher up than Inspector

Smith who I believe was caught between a rock and a hard place and is not totally responsible for the situation that has developed. However, he should now be in possession of the notes taken by Paula Whyte of what her mother told her about the murders.

Yours faithfully,
M.J. Gurn

The response from the attorney general was again negative.

APPENDIX NUMBER THIRTEEN

A CASE OF ATTEMPTED MURDER

As I said earlier, I will mention here and there some cases I have been involved with and one case I dealt with was the attempted murder of a man named Wondrock. He was involved in a dispute in a Bundaberg Hotel with another man named Eardley at night. Eardley left the hotel but later returned confronting Wondrock before shooting him in the stomach with a .45 revolver at point blank range.

Wondrock was taken to hospital by ambulance and I and other detectives were called to the hotel. The names of those at the hotel were taken and some told their stories and others claimed not to have seen anything which is what you tend to strike in these cases.

We established who the shooter was, and we went to his house on a property outside Bundaberg. The house was in darkness and despite repeated rapping on the door no one came to the door. We broke into the house and found Eardley in bed. There was no sign of the firearm, and he denied involvement.

He accompanied us to the C.I. Branch office at Bundaberg Police Station where Eardley had nothing to say.

I had several witnesses confront Eardley and repeat what they had seen including the shooting. I then charged Eardley with attempted murder. He was subsequently committed for trial in the Bundaberg Magistrates Court to the Supreme Court, Bundaberg. Word came through that Eardley was to be represented at his Trial by a very accomplished criminal barrister from Brisbane in the person of Bill Cuthbert, who I had encountered when I was working in Brisbane, and I knew he would try every trick in the book to get an acquittal for his client.

In preparation for the case, I had obtained signed statements from every person present at the hotel on the night of the shooting, which included a number who claimed they saw nothing and knew nothing. Doing this prevented Cuthbert from possibly producing one of them later to give a version favourable to his client when called to the witness stand. Defending criminal barristers, sometimes, are not shy of bending the rules a little here and there to get what they want in my experience.

Wondrock miraculously survived with the large bullet going right through his body and lodging just under the skin on his back missing his vital organs and leaving a lump in his back. I was present when a doctor lanced his back, after local anaesthetic, and removed the bullet. I took possession of the bullet from the doctor, which I later produced at the trial. During the trial, Cuthbert was successful in stopping the Crown from producing a replica .45 revolver for the jury to see what a formidable weapon a .45 revolver is. They are big and heavy to hold.

The trial proceeded and the weak country jury, as so often happens in country locations, returned a verdict that Eardley was only guilty of grievous bodily harm. The presiding judge demanded Cuthbert produce the firearm. Eardley was convicted and sentenced to two years imprisonment.

We took the accused to his home where he crawled under the house and recovered the firearm buried under his house. The firearm, if it had been available to the jury, would have convinced them as to the seriousness of the murder charge and of the size of the weapon and bullet from this firearm. They may have correctly returned a guilty verdict on the charge of attempted murder.

The Crown Prosecutor in this case was Jim Gibney. I strongly opposed Jim giving Cuthbert my statements from witnesses who had not given evidence in the committal proceedings in the Magistrate's Court.

Jim and I had some intense conversations about this matter. I explained that we work so hard to arrest offenders and put them before the courts and for the prosecutor to make it easy for the defence barrister to conduct his case did not sit well with me. Anyway, the prosecutor had the last say.

This sort of openness would be great if it worked both ways for the Crown and defence, but it doesn't. The odds are strongly with the accused, and I believe it has got worse over the years. I have had nothing to do with criminal courts since 1975 except for being recalled as a witness for the police in old cases, once in Brisbane and once in Sydney, so I don't really know the present-day position.

Crown Prosecutor Jim Gibney went on in his career and was appointed a judge of the District Court and I am pleased to say it was a deserved appointment for a very decent man. I knew a fair bit about Jim as he lived not far from me in Brisbane at one time. He never lost his common touch, still having a beer at the Alderley Alms Hotel.

Crime is rampant today especially amongst the youth, both boys and girls, because they have nothing to fear from being caught by the police. The punishments awarded by the courts are no deterrent to stop them committing crime. This situation comes down to poor parenting really. These kids are what their parents have made them in most cases.

In my day of dealing with these issues, a charge of burglary was a guaranteed five-to-ten-year sentence in jail. Today, it is a bond and promise to be a good boy or girl. Sentences today in Queensland of two or three years for a serious crime would incur a sentence of 20, 30 and 40 years in America.

It is obvious that some of our magistrates and judges are entirely unsuited to be enforcing the laws of the state. If you cannot live within the boundaries of the law, then you should be removed from society one way or another.

APPENDIX NUMBER FOURTEEN

The following letter to Inspector Hansen says a lot about what I was doing and should give readers a clearer insight into the investigations I was making and the responses I received at times.

> Detective Inspector Damien Hansen
> Homicide Investigation Unit
> State Crime Command
> Homicide Group
> 200 Roma Street
> Brisbane 4000
> Dated 14th March 2017
> Dear Inspector,
> I refer to your letter of 27th September 2016 to me and I wish to advise you of the results of some further investigations I have made in connection with the murder of Robin Jeanne Hoinville-Bartram and the missing and suspected murder of Anita Cunningham at Pentland in 1972.
> In my weakened position of no authority, now not being a police officer any longer, I can only go so far but for what it is worth, although I feel it is probably a futile exercise, I will be able to say when an inquest is held or other inquiry into the manner this case has been handled by the police, I will be in a position of being able to truthfully testify that I have given the police all the information I have gleaned. It will be up to the individual police officers to explain their positions.
> To start with, I have forwarded a dossier to the commissioner of police in New South Wales dealing with the suspect Ivan Milat as it relates to these murders at Pentland having mind that I have a strong suspicion that he was the man who accompanied the girls hitchhiking from Mount Isa and took part in their murders. The

names of no Qld police officers, past or present have been given to NSW Police.

The connecting fabric Is that the murdered girls knew this man as 'Cowboy', which was one Milat's nicknames. He used the name Richard at the Pentland Hotel, and he was known to use his brother's name at times. This man had little possessions of his own at the time. Milat was on the run from NSW Police from 1971 until he returned from New Zealand in 1974. Mearle Whyte said he had the same shaped face as Milat. She would have liked to have seen a photo of Milat clean shaved. Robin Bartram was shot in the back of the head with two .22 bullets, which is like some of Milat's victims in Balangalo Forrest. It is possible he got the money to go to New Zealand from the murdered girls.

There is another connecting aspect of New Zealand in all this, which I will go into later, which I hope will reveal a New Zealand connection to other suspects by anything Milat told NSW detectives about his stay in New Zealand.

Over 400 trophies, as Milat called them, were recovered from Milat during his arrest which included backpacks from his victims. I have asked that these trophies be examined to see if there is anything that could be linked to the girls Bartram and Cunningham. I have told the NSW police that I have asked Qld Police to have DNA tests done on the clothing worn by Bartram when her body was discovered in Sensible Creek, Pentland, for comparisons on a data base and particularly with the DNA of Milat. Also, that the bullets from her body be compared with bullets from the many firearms recovered in the arrest of Milat. From what I have read about Milat is that with his infatuation for firearms he was unlikely to go anywhere without a firearm even a concealable firearm.

There is also the possibility of a bullet being recovered from the front wall of a veranda of a house in Charters Towers when Mearle was shot at from a car on the street as mentioned by Paula to me in my interview with her. This bullet, if found, is more likely connected to Wally Barry as this occurrence happened some years after 1972. It is not known if Barry had any firearms. Of course it could have been Barry's firearm used in the murder.

If bullets were recovered from the bodies of the dead bush turkeys left near Robin Bartram's body, these could also have comparison tests done on them. If they were not recovered at the time, they might still be there and recoverable with a metal detector depending on high up the bank they lay as Sensible Creek runs very fiercely in flood time. If the birds were killed with a shotgun, that would rule this out. Luckily, no flood occurred in the creek before Robin Bartram's body was recovered.

There is no doubt in my mind that I have correctly identified Ted West as the man who saw the girls to the Falcon Station Wagon of a band member at the Pentland Hotel and who put their baggage on the roof rack of this car. I am confident that the man Walter (Wally) Barry owned and drove this car from the Pentland Hotel. Barry has since died of cancer in a Brisbane hospital. The police have a trump card to play here and that is the immunity from prosecution offered with the reward and I would be offering this to West to tell the truth now.

I have previously written about Barry to the Qld police and will not go into all that again. He was living with Pam Rogers who was known in Charters Towers as Pam Barry. I previously believed that she had only a peripheral connection to these murders but after talking to her on the 13th instant on the phone, I am now of the opinion that she was heavily involved. Both Wally and Pam were connected to bands and played country and Western music. Barry was said to be a guitarist and Pam the vocal part.

Because I was informed that she seemed to be slipping in health, I decided I could not wait any longer for the detectives to interview her in case she passed on. I had a conversation with her, and she is, despite any outward appearances of ill health, very switched on and a determined liar.

She immediately stated that she was not in Australia at the time of the murders and that she was in New Zealand. She stated that Wally Barry was also in New Zealand at the time, but she was not with him. (She jumped straight in to tell me Wally Barry was in New Zealand, but I had not even mentioned his name to her at that time.) She claimed that she was only with Barry after the time of the murders. (It is known that she came to Charters Towers with a man, believed to be Barry and ex-Sergeant [redacted] says that this man was known to 'touch her up' or assault her.)

She was well known for years before 1972 as Mrs Barry in the town. I know of one lady who knew her as Mrs Barry in the town. She denied that she had sung in a band at the Pentland Hotel at the time but that she did sing there later. She denied that Wally Barry ever had a Falcon Station Wagon. She said she did not know where I was getting my information from because to her it was very queer. She claimed she knows nothing about these murders. She said she was not with Wally Barry at the time of the murders but was with him later.

She denied that Barry ever worked on Wando Vale Station. (Dennis Madigan remembers Barry working on Wando Vale Station.) She said Barry would not know one end of a horse from the other. (John Whyte knows that Barry worked on other properties in the area.) She denied she ever received any letter or other communication from Barry admitting his part in the murders. (This is unfounded rumour but could be true.)

The interesting part of what she said relates to the fact that she claimed that she and Barry were in New Zealand at the time of the murders and surprise, surprise, that is where Milat returned from to NSW in 1974.

Now, isn't it reasonable to suspect that after the murder of these two girls these offenders decamped to New Zealand in the belief that a hunt would be on for them and normally it would have been if Mearle had come forward at the time and disregarded her father who told her, 'We don't get involved in anything like that.'

Also, when the body was discovered at Sensible Creek, there must have been an enormous amount talk in the town about it. How the investigating police missed out on this is astonishing. There was a local policeman stationed in Pentland but whether he was involved to assist or not, I do not know. There were a number of transports working out of Pentland at the time, which raises the possibility of one of them bringing the girls and their male companion to Pentland from Hughenden.

John Whyte says that when he worked at the Cape River Meatworks, Wally Barry worked there and Pam List, who was known then as Pam Barry. I have established that the list of names of employees who worked at the Cape River Meatworks at Pentland at the time is useless in so far as correct names are concerned but the names of Walter (Wally) Barry might just appear there. Pam List could have used the name Barry, or Rogers her maiden name, I believe. Whether they worked at the Meatworks or not is irrelevant really, but it does put them as being familiar with Pentland. This woman has been involved with Wally Barry, another man named Rogers (unrelated) and List, who she has been with many years now.

Pam List's brother David was married to Irene Whyte (John Whyte's sister) and had a number of children to him. She is now with a man named Roth in the Northern Territory, but she is not connected other than she accompanied Mearle to Pam's place when they visited about Pam making the bridesmaid dresses for Mearle's wedding and when Mearle said Wally Barry was there and she recognised him as one of the murderers. He is most likely the same man she ran into at a rodeo in Charters Towers. According to Paula, Pam denied all knowledge of Wally Barry being at her place when questioned by Bob Black, but Mearle was adamant Barry was at her place then.

Because I did not want to jeopardise any questioning that may take place of Pam List by detectives, I gave her little or no information to prevent her having a reply ready when questioned or when she takes the stand in an inquest when it is held if no arrest takes place in the meantime. I never mentioned anything about Betty and Mearle Madigan meeting the girls at the Pentland Hotel. I never told her anything at all about my recorded conversations with John and Paula Whyte. I did not mention anything about her making bridesmaid dresses for Mearle Whyte (Madigan at the time) in 1975. I did not tell her that I knew she was with Wally Barry long before she claimed to. I never mentioned the name Ivan Milat to her at all.

There are people who could give evidence about her being with Barry from about 1967. She had some sort of split up with Barry about 1976 and he went to Mount Isa. He most probably took up with some woman in Mount Isa and that is probably where his Falcon Station Wagon ended up. Inquiries about any such woman could prove useful.

On the 13th of March 2017, I also interviewed John Fox of [redacted] in Charters Towers who I was told may have been part of the band that played at Pentland on the day the girls left the hotel with their murderers. I am satisfied he had nothing to do with these murders and was not part of this band. He had no useful information to offer. Contrary to other information, he said he did not discover the body of the girl Bartram at Sensible Creek. **(My opinion about Fox has changed in light of additional information I uncovered.)**

However, the names of men named [redacted] or similar spelling keep cropping up as being part of the band at Pentland on the fateful day. The names of Stan, Laurie and Matt [redacted] are mentioned but which one was in this band, I do not know. It is said one of these men is or was a magistrate. I have not followed up anything about these men at this time but if one of them was a member of the band and if he was not directly involved, he may be in a position of give vital information about who the girls left the hotel with and what part Ted West played. Again, the immunity from prosecution could be used here.

Any reasonable person listening to the recorded telephone conversations I had with John and Paula Whyte could only deduce that Mearle and Betty Madigan did meet these girls at the Pentland Hotel and that what unfolded afterwards is a truthful account of what happened.

Unfortunately, I have not been able to uncover anything about the third man Mearle named as ARTHUR (however, I suspect he was a meat worker or a ringer from a station in the area) who was outside Betty Noonan's hairdressing salon in Charters Towers the next morning when Merle appeared and was confronted by the man who accompanied the girls from Mount Isa and the man with the car who I believe was Wally Barry who had shoulder length hair with nothing at the front of his forehead. At this time, the man from Mount Isa had a deep fingernail scratch down the side of his face and when asked about this by Mearle said there had been a disagreement. When asked where the girls were, he said they were with their families. These men tried very persuasively to get Mearle to go with them to Townsville and thankfully she refused, which would have been the end of Mearle.

When Mearle and her mother Betty Madigan left Charters Towers the day after being at the Pentland Hotel, there was an attempt to intercept their car by a car which Mearle said was the same car the men had been in in front of the hairdressing salon earlier in the day.

I have previously urged the police to disregard the reports of ex-Officer Bob Black on this case as he was told some correct and some incorrect statements by Mearle Whyte to make a fool out of him as revenge for the way he treated her. Black will not be the only police officer who would be called at an inquest but also any officer who was with him when he interviewed Mearle Whyte.

There is also the obvious interference with the witness Paula Whyte after my interviewing her that needs a lot of explanation. Presently, Paula does not want anything further to do with these investigations but that will not prevent her being called to the witness stand and her interview with me gone into at length where records from Crime Stoppers will play a part including the notes taken by Paula which she took of what her mother told her when she was in hospital in Townsville dying and which should now be in the hands of the police.

In one communication from Inspector Smith, he said that Bob Black had reported that when he interviewed Mearle Whyte, she said that she had met these murdered girls three weeks after the White Horse Tavern in Charters Towers had been pulled down in 1971 and consequently these could not be the same girls as the body of Bartram was discovered in November 1972 and that she had been dead about three months. However, I established that the White Horse Tavern was reopened on 17th May 1972 by Mr Lonergon, the local member of Parliament.

Considering that Mearle was thinking back 31 years, she most probably meant about three weeks after the White Horse Tavern was reopened, which would put the time of her meeting the girls close to July 1972. Further, we know that John Whyte specifically said it was in the wintertime of 1972 as Mearle's father was doing something with the cattle which he did in the wintertime. In any case, to be realistic how many pairs of girls would be on the Flinders Highway hitchhiking around this time. To discount Mearle here that she must have been talking about another pair of girl hitchhikers is ridiculous. And then there is the fire under the Sensible Creek Bridge, which would have been built for warmth in winter and seen by Mearle. One can only conjecture on this but it must be relevant in some way.

I ask your assistance in writing to the manager of the Westpac Bank in Charters Towers to locate particulars of the Bank of New South Wales cheque cashed by Betty Madigan at the Pentland Hotel this fateful day, which is what she requires to perform this task. Samantha Williamson, manager of the bank in Charters Towers has all the information that I asked her to obtain. I have asked the managing director of Westpac Bank in Brisbane to intervene also but without response to date.

Shadow Attorney General Ian Walker has my complete file on this case and has been kept up date with copies of all correspondence in connection with the case.

I can only once again ask you to begin investigations with the starting point being my recorded conversations with John and Paula Whyte. If this is done, I am confident you will achieve a favourable result.

Yours faithfully
M.J. Gurn

APPENDIX NUMBER FIFTEEN

This would seem to be an appropriate time to tell you about the rape case I have referred to earlier, which occurred during my police career. This was a very interesting case with the result the least expected from my superior inspectors who in the main did not believe the complainant woman. There were some unflattering comments circulating in the office about me pursuing the case, but I found the result fulfilling for the effort put into arresting and convicting the offender and particularly for recognising that the complainant woman was telling the truth.

After I was promoted to detective sergeant 2i/c at the Criminal Investigation branch, Brisbane I was directed to work at the South Brisbane area office or the Woolloongabba C.I. branch office even though I was living on the north side of Brisbane at Aspley, which involved crossing Brisbane and having to change buses to get there.

I reported for duty on the morning of 11th May 1970 for the 8.45 am shift. The detective sub-inspector in charge of the office for that shift was Don Buchanan. He gave me a rather unenviable job to follow up of an alleged rape of a woman at night on 9th May 1970 in her own bed in her own home whilst asleep by a complete stranger whilst her husband, who was a gun dealer, was on the phone downstairs talking to overseas clients due to the time difference between countries. The detectives who had been called to investigate the case during the night had indicated that the complaint was very unlikely in the circumstances, which it was on the face of it.

In company with Detective Senior Constable KC Scanlan, I interviewed the woman complainant and her husband at their home in Old Cleveland Road, Coorparoo. This lady had had a miscarriage and was home from hospital after treatment. That night she had taken some sedation tablets and was affected by them and drowsy. She awakened from sleep to find she was being raped. At first, she thought it was her husband until she realised it was not him and that he must be dead downstairs for this to be happening. She remained calm and did not fight the man off.

The complainant, a professional woman, was 37 years of age and of good character. She accompanied me to the Woolloongabba C.I. Branch where I talked to her for some hours and obtained a written and signed statement from her describing in detail this assault on her. I told Detective Sub-Inspector Don Buchanan that I believed the complaint was genuine. He replied, 'If you think this is fair dinkum, get out and catch the bastard.' The general feeling in the office was that the complaint was false.

I took possession of her nightgown, a singlet and two bed sheets and a blanket. Scientific tests revealed spermatozoa on the blanket and one sheet when examined at the Laboratory of Microbiology and Pathology.

When the attacker was leaving the house after raping the woman, he stole a miniature television set. One black sock was found on the bed, which he had obviously worn to hide any fingerprints he may have left whilst in the house. I began the search for the offender. As the black sock was new and branded PMG (issued by Postmaster General to staff), I started making inquiries at and around post offices in various parts of Brisbane for information. One place I visited was the Broadway Post Office in Fortitude Valley and found no useful information but unknown to me, the man who had accompanied the offender and waited outside the complainant's house in his car while the offender went inside was working at the post office. When this man heard I had been to his workplace, he resigned and went to the Gulf of Carpentaria and worked on a cattle station outside Burketown in North Queensland.

Information came in because of publicity about the television set. I had circulated posters and photos of the stolen television set to pawn brokers and other places in Brisbane where the set could be sold for money. I recovered the TV set on 28th June 1970 from a man at the Arcadia Hotel, Elizabeth Street, Brisbane who had bought it from a man named Colin Mervyn Giffin after information was received at the CI branch. I arrested Giffin on 12th June 1970, accompanied by Det. Const 1st c JL Graham. The other offender who had remained in their car on the street outside the complainant's home whilst Giffin entered the home was a man named Leslie George Meecham.

I obtained a typed and signed record of interview from Giffin over several hours with breaks in between whilst I left the office and made other inquiries concerning the case. I arrested Giffin.

The next day, Giffin appeared in the Magistrates' Court on a charge of rape and was remanded in custody for committal proceedings to a later date.

I flew to Mount Isa with Detective Constable 1i/c JL Graham and then we went by police car to Burketown where Meecham was being held by Burketown Police on a charge of possession of a concealable firearm. I arrested Meecham at Burketown on warrant. He appeared before two Justices of Peace and was remanded to the Brisbane Magistrates' Court. With Mount Isa detectives we escorted Meecham back to Mount Isa from Burketown and then back to Brisbane by plane.

Interestingly, the police car we travelled in from Burketown to Mount Isa had no brakes for most of the journey as 'bulldust' had filled the wheel drums with dust, causing the brake pedal to be inactive.

Word got around the Woolloongabba CIB office that a senior detective inspector told other police that my case would be thrown out in the committal proceedings in the Magistrates' Court because my recorded interview with Giffin was faulty. You may remember my mention of me giving a lecture on records of interview to the class in my time at the Chelmer College in chapter eleven.

Giffin was committed for trial from the Magistrates' Court in Brisbane on 6th July 1970 after evidence was heard on the charge of rape to the August 1970 sittings of the Supreme Court, Brisbane.

On 11th August 1970, Leslie George Meecham pleaded guilty in the District Court, Brisbane before Judge Nicholson to entering the dwelling house of the complainant's husband in the night-time with intent on 9th May 1970. He was represented by Mr McLaughlin, Barrister. He was admitted to probation for two years and disqualified from holding a driver's license for two years.

Meecham was entirely ignorant of Giffin raping the woman until he returned to Meecham's car parked outside the complainant's house after the offence. In law, however, he is deemed to be just as guilty as the principal offender in these circumstances. The offenders had gone to the complainant's house to steal a firearm originally, but Giffin took advantage of the sleeping woman in her bed when the opportunity arose.

As was normal practice, I went to the crown prosecutor's office to discuss the case with the prosecutor just before the trial. Rape charges were usually presented by the chief crown prosecutor, who was Mr. ---------- said to me, 'How much did you have to belt him to get him to sign that record of interview?'

I just looked at Mr --------- and made no reply whatsoever. This man obviously did not believe such an unlikely rape had occurred or that a conviction could be achieved. He would not present the case for trial and gave the task of conducting the trial to one of his junior prosecutors in Mr Ken McKenzie who did a very admirable job. No allegation of me assaulting the accused was ever made in the trial.

The trial proceeded in the Supreme Court Brisbane on

20th August 1970 before Judge Stable. Giffin was represented by Barrister Frank Gardiner, charged with the rape of the complainant woman. The complainant gave her evidence confidently and Gardiner was unable to find any chink in her evidence. (I had prepared her for every likely question she would be asked. I told her to always tell the absolute truth and not to guess at anything. As an example, I told her if you are asked did, he place his hand on your breast and you answer truthfully, 'Yes.' The next question would be which hand. I told her if you are unsure, say you do not know because if you say which of his hands it was then the next question would be, 'How do you know that if it was dark?')

This did happen at the trial and Gardiner swung around to look at me in the back of the court to see if I was signalling the complainant with her answers, which I wasn't. The jury noted this by the look on their faces.

The trial continued over three days with a break for a weekend in between. The jury returned a verdict of guilty on 25th August 1970. He was sentenced to twelve years imprisonment. I immediately rang the complainant woman and informed her the result of the jury's verdict and the length of Giffin's imprisonment.

Giffin's barrister Gardiner appealed the verdict to the Court of Criminal Appeal, which dismissed the appeal. He then appealed the case to the High Court of Australia where the appeal was again dismissed and Giffin served his jail time.

A few days later, Buchanan said to me, 'You got that bloke, eh?'

I replied, 'Yeah I did.'

That was all that was said. That was as near as Buchanan could bring himself to say, 'I was wrong, and you were right,' but I understood what he meant. Along with other police, I received a commendation and a citation in a scroll for my work on this case.

The citation can be viewed as Appendix Number Eleven.

This photo of the stolen TV set was circulated to pawnshops etc.

SPECIAL CIRCULAR

TV 5-202E

BRAND: Sony T. V.

MODEL: 5/202

COLOUR: MM Grey

PICTURE TUBE: *unable to transcribe*

DIMENSION: $7\frac{7}{8} \times 4\frac{1}{4} \times 7\frac{1}{4}$

WEIGHT: 8 lbs

APPENDIX NUMBER SIXTEEN

Now that you have read how a genuine case of rape was handled, I will tell you about another reported case of rape, which, on the surface, seemed genuine but there were some things about the woman's story that I found puzzling. She was a 44-year-old woman who lived in Brighton, a suburb of Sandgate.

The story begins in June 1972 when I was on rest days and not in my office at Sandgate CIB when this complaint was received. One of my senior detectives, a detective senior constable, received the complaint of rape by a woman who said that she and her husband had been out in their boat fishing since 5 am that day. They had taken a good haul of fish and returned home about 3.20 pm.

She had been wearing slacks and a long-sleeved blouse whilst fishing but after she and her husband had placed their fish haul into tubs under the house to soak, she changed into a striped dress and a pink petticoat but did not change her underclothing. Then she washed her hair and set it in some plastic rollers. After that, she prepared scaling knives and boards to clean the fish. She commenced cleaning the fish while her husband watered the garden.

The underneath of the house is enclosed and is on high stumps about eight feet off the ground with a tilt-a-door at the front to gain entrance to the underneath section. The underneath section is a cemented floor. About 4.30 pm, she and her husband had some beer. About 7.30 pm, her husband decided he would go to the hotel and buy some bottles of beer. She decided to stay home as she was too tired to go with him. Just prior to that, she told her husband she was cold, so he shut the tilt-a-door and two other doors under the house.

Her husband went upstairs and got her purse. There were two ten-dollar notes in the purse and she gave her husband one ten dollar note to buy some beer. Her husband left by one of the two doors under the house, but the door did not shut very well and was about an inch or two ajar. She heard her husband drive away in their car. She remembered that she heard a car outside her house about five minutes later. She thought it sounded like their car, and she heard a car door slam. She thought her husband had forgotten something and had returned. She heard a door open under the house as it scrapes the concrete, but she did not look up from cleaning the fish.

Near this door under the house, she said there were two pairs of panty hose, one dark and one light in a basket. She said she then felt a pair of hands around her throat, and she was pulled backwards and fell off the chair, landing on her back. She said that the person released his grip around her throat. From her position on the ground, she was slashing at the man with the fish knife. He grabbed her right wrist, and the knife flew out of her hand.

She said that he pulled on the front of her dress, which opened. He then started grabbing at her underclothing. She heard her petticoat tearing at the front. She said the man had hold of her wrist and pulled her across the floor while she was trying to break his hold. She thought she was successful in kicking him between the legs on one occasion. He then kicked her about the legs.

She thought she called out something and he told her to shut up. He dragged her to some old carpet on the floor. She was on her back with her head near a concrete house stump. By this time, her dress was open at the front and her petticoat was torn. As far as she remembered, she was still wearing her pink panties.

She said that her attacker was standing over her but had a throat hold on her. She remembered his fingernails biting into her throat. Then he knelt between her legs and put his knees across the top part of her legs and was pushing them apart.

At this time, her dog was jumping up at him and he said, 'You bastard.'

At that time, she remembered what she thought there was a stocking in one of his hands. She said she thought he was going to strangle her with the stocking, and she called out, 'Please, God, help me.'

The man then said, 'Do you believe in the Jesus club too?'

She said she was a severe asthmatic and by this time she was getting breathless. She said she had a heart condition with angina, which causes her to black out at times. She said she was feeling faint from the pressure exerted on her throat. He was still pulling at her underclothes.

She said that at that time she passed out and could not remember anything else that happened to her. The next thing she remembered was her husband sitting on their double bed on which she was then lying. She broke down and started crying hysterically. A short time later, police came into the room, one of whom was one of my senior detectives.

She said that she had never seen her attacker in her life before and had no knowledge of who he was. She described him as about eighteen to twenty years old, about 5'5" with a thin face and thin build. He had long black hair, thick and down to his shoulders. He also had a full black beard about a half inch to an inch in length. He was of dark complexion wearing a suede jacket. She described the jacket as a Davy Crockett jacket and fawn in colour. He was wearing faded light blue jeans and cowboy boots.

The complainant was taken to a doctor and examined. She said that the ten-dollar note was missing from her purse. She went on to describe various tears to her clothing. The doctor could not detect any injury to the woman's vagina but was reasonable sure she had had sexual intercourse in the twenty-four hours before he examined her, which was no help and normal for this woman.

The woman's husband said he came home from the hotel

and found his wife unconscious under the house with a stocking around her mouth and around a house stump.

Of course, this complaint attracted wide media and newspaper coverage. Police were checking out several persons who could be the attacker and pursuing information from the public. A lot of police time and energy was expended on this complaint in the following days not only in Brisbane but in other centres also as a general alarm had been sounded.

I resumed duty in my office at Sandgate two days after the reported rape. I studied the report of one of my senior detectives about this rape. This detective and I made some inquiries, and we spoke to the complainant woman and her husband. The complainant woman accompanied us to the Sandgate CIB office where my detective senior constable took a very detailed written and signed statement from this woman, which is a standard police procedure in dealing with this type of case or any serious case, for that matter.

Three days later, we took the complainant woman to the photo section of the CI Branch in Brisbane where she was shown composite photographs of criminals, but she did not identify anyone as her attacker.

These inquiries went on almost daily, chasing down leads in this rape case. Seven days later, I even interviewed the person who had previously lived in the house before the complainant and her husband resided there in case she could throw any light on the offender's identity without success. The same day, the complainant viewed more photographs of possible suspects without identifying anyone.

Nineteen days later, I looked up police records and learned that the complainant had made a similar complaint three years previously when she was living further along the coastline to Sandgate to the effect that whilst under her house, she was attacked, with the offender decamping after grabbing her around the throat. There were marked similarities in the descriptions she had given except for the man's beard.

I interviewed the ex-husband of the complainant woman as I wanted to know more about her. Something just was not right about this complaint. Her recall of the event was just too detailed for a woman undergoing such a traumatic assault.

Accompanied by Detective Constable First Class Barry Carpenter, I went to this woman's house. I brought this woman to my office where I obtained a statement from her retracting her complaint and explaining her actions after I had talked quietly to her for quite some time.

She stated that on the day of the attack, she had gone fishing with her then husband and had forgotten to take her cortisone tablets. When she got home, she took a double dose of her cortisone tablets to make up for the dose she had missed. Unbeknown to her, she accidently took Valium tablets by mistake. She said that these tablets made her feel depressed, which caused her to take three other tablets that she took for depression.

Under her house, she was not feeling well and her husband said he would go and get two bottles of beer. Even before her husband left her, she could feel herself going numb and dizzy and the beginning of a feeling of wanting to claw at herself mainly around the neck.

When her husband left her, she began to claw at her clothes and body. She said she went 'mad'. She remembered rolling around on the cement floor and began chewing on old pantyhose on the floor probably left there by her dog after playing with them. She said she did not remember tearing her pants off or tying them around her mouth and the post under the house but was sure she had done that herself.

She said she awoke on the bed in the house and was hysterical and hardly knew what she was doing even then. She said that her husband asked her if she had been attacked by anyone and this put the idea in her head that she had been attacked by a man. She said she told the police what she could see in her mind.

By then, she said she had to continue with her story to save face with her husband. She said she had hardly slept with worry about making a false complaint and on one occasion was tempted to ring police and confess. She denied that the complaint of being attacked three years earlier was also false, but she would not admit that this was the case.

I furnished a report to the Inspector in Charge of the Criminal Investigation Branch along these lines that he may be pleased to instruct if any action was to be taken against the complainant for making a false complaint to police. I pointed out that at the time of making the complaint her judgment was affected by the drugs she had taken and that it would be an impossibility for any medical person to say what result the drugs would have on a particular individual.

That was the end of that case. The media and press were advised that the police were taking no further action on the complaint.

I went into some detail with this complaint to point out to the public how difficult it is for police to know if very convincing people making a complaint are genuine or not. This sort of thing happens in other complaints and not necessarily in alleged rape cases. It takes years of experience in dealing with people for an investigator to see flaws in what people allege sometimes.

There was a rather nasty reaction by the detective inspector I told you about in the last genuine rape case I detailed where he said to other police that my record of interview was faulty. He was not pleased apparently with the trial outcome and subsequent appeals being thrown out because when I reported on the complaint of the woman in this case that was false, he issued me with an order to submit the conversation I had had with this woman before she retracted her false complaint of rape.

This was a very petty, stupid and obviously vexatious order which was quickly countermanded by Inspector Merv Hopgood.

I never found out what this inspector had against me. I had worked with him for the first six months of my going to the CI Branch in 1957. As far as I knew, we got on quite well. He was a strange man but a very good investigator. He was, however, very sarcastic at times, sly and very cunning.

APPENDIX NUMBER SEVENTEEN

Ms Shannon Fentiman
Attorney General
7th April 2023
Dear Fentiman,
With reference to the Pentland Murders.

David Cunningham, Bob Atkinson and I had an interesting and informative meeting with your representative Isabella Shoshani on the 5th instant who outlined your position clearly that you could not order a Commission of Inquiry into the murders of Robin Jeanne Hoinville-Bartram and Anita Cunningham in the hope that those involved or have knowledge of these crimes who are at present obviously lying about their involvement or knowledge would tell the truth when called to the witness box when confronted with the evidence I have gathered over the past nine years.

Miss Shoshani admitted that she has not listened to the recorded telephone interviews I did with John and Paula Whyte, which I asked you also to listen to when deliberating on whether you could order a Commission of Inquiry or not. It follows to my way of thinking that you or your advisers also have not listened to those recordings, which were originally forwarded to Yvette D'ath years ago. I have asked Miss Shoshani to locate and listen to these recordings and if she cannot locate the USB memory stick with these records on them, I will post her the recordings so she and you can listen.

It is all very well to read my transcription of the recordings, but it is an entirely different matter to actually listen and be impressed with the obvious truth and sincerity of these Whyte's in describing what Mearle told them over the years supported by about ten adults. It then follows that an inquiry would be similarly impressed on hearing these recordings along with the one I did with Paula Whyte, another daughter on the same subject. In my mind, these recordings absolutely destroy the police stance.

What I am trying to convey to you and to your advisers is that the lying witnesses would have great difficulty denying various propositions put to them to maintain their lying stance and the impossible position Inspector Smith would face when confronted with the various failures on his part in his investigations, which I have pointed out to you amount to perverting the course of justice. These failures led to the police successfully convincing the press and media there is nothing to see here, which led to isolating David Cunningham and me and our efforts to bring to the notice of the public the true facts about police investigations and why the cases were not solved in 2003. I maintain that the cases would probably have been the most easily solved double murders and rapes of any murder case in the history of the state if handled professionally by police in 2003.

There is another confronting aspect of all this, which I find hard to understand. You, as the all-powerful face of justice in this state, cannot obtain from the police any information on their stance on these crimes where I asked you to ask several questions to the police so you could be better informed in making your decision on whether you can make an order for a Commission of Inquiry or not.

Surely you could seek the information from the minister for police if you could not directly request information from the commissioner of police. In my time in the police force, we had to treat ministerial files from the minister for police with urgency to answer his questions about our work.

There was an occasion I had communication with the minister for police by letter from me on 11th October 2021 who advised I should seek my answers from Detective Senior Sergeant Tara Kentwell of the Cold Case Division. I did that and when I asked her for the answer to the one question that I was able to ask – 'Is the police position still that the murdered girls were never at the Pentland Hotel?' – she replied, 'I cannot tell you that.'

I still supplied her with information, which was new or a line of thought as to why the person using the tracks under the Sensible Creek bridges did not report the decaying body to police, which obviously makes him a suspect in these crimes. The smell of the decaying body was impossible to miss. This line of thought would also make him the chief suspect in placing the decaying bodies of bush turkeys in a position where anyone trying to trace the cause of the decaying smell of the body would not look further on seeing the bush turkeys. This person could also have directed the murderers to this quiet spot on the Flinders Highway, which would have been almost unknown to the public and an ideal place to attack the murdered girls. A lonely 20-odd kilometres from Pentland.

I had asked the minister for police, Mark Ryan, to ask the police the same questions I asked you to ask of the police so you could make an informed decision on granting the Commission of Inquiry. This query was ignored by the minister for police.

I am coming to the belief that I should have been directing **all** my correspondence to the minister for police, to you and the commissioner of police and not solely to you even though the government is one unit. It looks like the departments operate in their own bubble and correspondence is not forwarded on to departments in which they would obviously are involved.

At present, it looks like they are isolated entities. One is like France and the other is Germany. Side by side but not operating as one unit of government.

We left the meeting with Ms Shoshani appreciative of your stance but with a firm belief that the only way forward for David Cunningham and me now is to get my book published and let the public know the real truth about these crimes and hopefully there will be a demand from the public for a Commission of Inquiry into the whole episode.

I ask does the minister for police even know that my investigations reveal that Inspector Smith's actions and words to witnesses in April 2015 constitute perverting the cause of justice. Does the minister for police even know that I confronted former commissioner of police, Ian Stewart, by letter dated 13th February 2019, advising him that I held him totally responsible for no investigations being ordered by him in?

Is the minister for police aware that on the day she commenced duty as the new commissioner of police in Queensland, Katerina Carroll received a letter from me dated 9th July 2019 setting out the matters contained in the previous paragraph asking her to address these issues and clean up this mess in layman's speech.

Is the minister for police similarly aware that Commissioner Katerina Carroll took no action in these matters despite a further letter to her from me dated 9th May 2021 wherein I said to her, 'When you took office, I wrote to you officially and personally concerning the inadequate investigations into the rapes and murders of Robin Jeanne Hoinville-Bartram and Anita Cunningham at Pentland in 1972 wherein I asked and expected that you would take action to see that justice for the murder of these girls would be carried out but unfortunately nothing changed. At least one of the killers remains at large, living in Charters Towers despite the information I have given you over these years and more recently, information from another recorded interview with a credible witness corroborating previous information.

That letter went on with further details naming a man who left the Pentland Hotel with the murdered girls in the band members car and who went on in life to become a magistrate. (This man sang in the band and did not leave with girls as far as I know.) I also supplied the identity of another man who was one of three men who confronted the original informant Mearle Whyte outside Betty Noonan's hairdressing salon in Gill Street, Charters Towers the morning after the murders (possibly on the 7th July 1972) who attempted to get her to go with them to Townsville no doubt to silence her as well.

Do the failures of these two police commissioners to have extensive investigations carried out into the inspector's action at Charters Towers in April 2015 amount to aiding and abetting a crime if taken to the ultimate understanding of the law?

I cannot see why it is necessary for me to again formulate a case for the minister for police when all this information has already been given to you, which I had hoped would in the normal case of business have been conveyed to him and possibly why no action has been taken by the minister for police.

As I said to Isabella Shoshani, I am not interested in bringing down the government. All I want is justice for the murdered girls by arresting the murderers and identifying all involved, dead and alive and of course, locating the remains of Anita Cunningham.

Yours faithfully,
MJ Gurn

Inquest needed Milat is dead:

CRIME | **Trudy Brown**

A RETIRED police detective remains determined to find out who killed two girls near Pentland in 1972, following the death of serial killer Ivan Milat this week.

Milat was sentenced in 1996 to seven consecutive life sentences for murdering seven backpackers, whose bodies were found in makeshift graves in the Belanglo State Forest in the 1990s.

Retired detective sergeant Mick Gurn said he feels that with Milat now dead, other people involved in the case may talk. "They could justifiably have been frightened to come forward before now," Mr Gurn said.

Mr Gurn remains convinced Milat was involved in the deaths of Anita Cunningham and Robin Hoinville-Bartram.

The two girls disappeared in July of 1972 and were last seen together at the Pentland Hotel.

The body of Robin was discovered in November 1972 in a decomposed state at Sensible Creek, between Pentland and Charters Towers.

"My five years of investigations into the murders of Robin and Anita at Pentland in July 1972 has led me to more confidently state that the infamous Ivan Milat was involved in these murders," Mr Gurn said.

Mr Gurn said the evidence he has gathered in the case of the Pentland murders suggested Anita and Robin had hitchhiked from Melbourne to Mount Isa before heading east.

He believes that in Mount Isa they met a man they only knew as "Cowboy", a nickname Milat is known to have gone by.

"Former NSW police assistant commissioner Clive Small,

now
ex-cop

in his book Milat, says that when Milat returned from New Zealand in 1974 he had been in New Zealand for about two years, which would be from 1972 to 1974," Mr Gurn said.

"He was on the run from NSW Police and in my opinion in Queensland as well.

"I believe he went to New Zealand with two others believing the hunt would be on for them, as it normally would have been in 99 out of 100 cases."

Mr Gurn said a Crime and Corruption Commission coercive hearing would be the best way to get all of the witnesses involved to testify.

Alternatively an inquest would at least provide the opportunity for all of the witnesses to be questioned under oath. Mr Gurn said he would continue to press the State Government and the Queensland Police Service for one of these outcomes.

"I have taken this battle to get justice for the murdered girls." Mr Gurn said.

Anyone with information can go to the Facebook page dedicated to the case: facebook.com/anita-cunningham-2183571365226465

COMMENT

Opinion

TRUDY BROWN
MANAGING EDITOR, THE NORTHERN MINER
trudy.brown@news.com.au

Complaints vs. evidence

DID you know that Charters Towers has to be the worst place to live on earth?

There's nothing to do in town, ever.

No one does anything interesting.

It's boring and you have to be a millionaire to have enough money to make your own fun.

Yes, it's true, I've heard all of these statements made and more since I moved to town in 1998.

The problem I have with them is that I simply can't and will never agree.

You see as a journalist in Charters Towers I have never had a week where it has been a struggle to find news to fill the paper because there is so much that goes on in town.

In fact today's paper is a perfect example of that point.

Take for example that the council has put together not one, but two Australia Day activities for the community to enjoy.

Not only that, but those activities are free for the public to attend. I know some places where people are charged a fee to attend Australia Day Award ceremonies and parties in the park.

Then there is the Goldfield Ashes. Sure, it is one of the bigger events on the local calendar, but it's a reflection of the cricket played on weekends at clubs by junior and senior players in town.

Speaking of clubs, have a flick to page 19 where you'll find the first of nine pages filled with information about various clubs, groups organisations in the community that invite you to get involved.

Whether you're interested in social welfare issues, enjoy the arts and theatre, or are a passionate sports lover there has to be something there that will pique your interest.

We live in a wonderful community that provides so many opportunities to have a fabulous work-life balance.

Rarely a day goes by that I am not grateful to live in a place like the Towers. How lucky can you get?

SERVICES DOES A GREAT JOB

I AM writing to express my appreciation for the Prospect Community Services support workers that visit Eventide.

As a resident of Eventide, I see the excellent service these workers provide, and the dedication they have to their clients.

They are an invaluable part of the community, and their service provides much-needed support to each and every one of their clients -- they all return from outings with a big smile on their face.

I myself do not receive support, but as a resident I see the benefit and the cheer that it brings my fellow tenants.

I wish to let Prospect Community Services know just how much they help the community and I hope they can continue to do so well into the future.
KEN SELLARS, Eventide.

FAMILIES DESERVE TO KNOW THE TRUTH

CONCERNING the murders of Robin Hoinville-Bartram and Anita Cunningham at Pentland in the winter of 1972; I have been informed that when the woman who met the girls at the Pentland Hotel with her mother was on her deathbed in hospital she begged her husband to try and find someone to get justice for these murdered girls as the Police would not listen to her.

This was despite pleas from her daughter to Crime Stoppers to interview her mother before she died and my own advice to the Police that the woman was dying. It is only for the courage and tenacity of her husband, and a daughter who has withstood threats and intimidation to keep her mouth shut about these murders that I, a retired Detective Sergeant, have been able to piece together what really happened to these girls after four and half years of delving into the circumstances.

All of my information has been reported by me to the Commissioner of Police in detail.

Queensland Police refuse to admit that their investigations in 2003 and 2005 were seriously flawed. They are relying on a Police Officer's reports into the deceased woman's story which lack credibility because basic investigative procedures could not have been followed for this serious situation to develop in the first place.

The press in Brisbane, in contrast to your local *Northern Miner* newspaper, which has particulars of the detailed

Letters must be signed and contain either street address or PO Box number.

MAIL PO Box 178, Charters Towers, Qld, 4820 or 73 Gill Street, Charters Towers	**FAX** 07 4787 3037	**TWITTER** twitter.com/northern-miner
EMAIL miner@news.com.au	**SMS** 0416 905 586 Include name, suburb	**FACEBOOK** facebook.com/thenorthernminer

One letter writer wants to see justice for the families of Anita Cunningham and Robin Hoinville-Bartram (pictured above) who went missing near Charters Towers in 1972. Picture: SUPPLIED

investigations I have made, refuse to give me any assistance or traction to get the story out into the public arena with a view to having the Attorney-General order an Inquest into the murder of Robin Bartram, which would also involve Anita Cunningham.

The Attorney-General has to date denied this inquest to me where those involved would be subjected to cross-examination of their testimony which would likely unveil the true story.

There are persons who are involved directly and indirectly still living who could provide vital information but they do not have the courage or decency to come forward.

Their actions are only half a step away from being accessories after the fact or even perverting the course of justice and I would urge them to contact me through *The Northern Miner*.

Immunity from prosecution has been offered to persons who did not commit the actual crimes, so there is no reasonable excuse for their silence other than trying to save their reputations.

One has to wonder just who is really behind keeping the truth from the public and obtaining justice for these naive, trusting and innocent girls who were murdered in the most degrading and terrifying manner with complete lack of any compassion for the gratification of persons who could only be described as animals.

MICK GURN, Pittsworth.

ACTION SPEAKS LOUDER THAN WORDS DO

I CALL upon the Member for Kennedy to get the funding secured for the Charters Towers hospital upgrade.

When Mr Katter had the balance of power in the Julia Gillard government Charters Towers and Kennedy missed out. Then his party had the balance of power in the last State Labor Government and still Charters Towers and the region missed out.

Now he must deliver for Charters Towers.

We have a promise for the Big Rocks Weir, but this will evaporate if the Morrison Government does not get back into power.

People are sick of our hospital being used as a political football and of the constant media stories in which our local MPs call on someone to do something.

At my stand at the Charters Towers Show this year this was a constant topic of conversation. It is time for our local member to deliver.

In 2005 the Ingham hospital started a $44 million upgrade, in 2007 Ayr hospital received $9.6 million and in 2014 Townsville started a $340 million upgrade, while in Charters Towers our hospital been "downgraded" to a regional health centre.

We deserve better!

FRANK BEVERIDGE, LNP candidate for the seat of Kennedy.

TAX SCAMMERS HAVE PLENTY OF HANG UPS

WHEN these clowns called me last month telling me 'I owed the tax office thousands and faced two years in jail' we'll I told him "I'm behind on my rent, can't afford electricity or my medication and I have a bad knee and toothache. Go ahead and lock me up, I'll get free room and board, no bills, free medication — plus they'll fix my knee and teeth up, when will the police be around to pick me up or should I just go down to the station?"

The bugger hung up on me.

So much for making promises you can't keep.

RICHARD BINGLEY, Aitkenvale.

www.ingramcontent.com/pod-product-compliance
Lightning Source LLC
Chambersburg PA
CBHW051417290426
44109CB00016B/1329